Rhetoric & Composition
PhD Program

PROGRAM
Pioneering program honoring the rhetorical tradition through scholarly innovation, excellent job placement record, well-endowed library, state-of-the-art New Media Writing Studio, and graduate certificates in new media and women's studies.

TEACHING
1-1 teaching loads, small classes, extensive pedagogy and technology training, and administrative fellowships in writing program administration and new media.

FACULTY
Nationally recognized teacher-scholars in history of rhetoric, modern rhetoric, women's rhetoric, digital rhetoric, composition studies, and writing program administration.

FUNDING
Generous four-year graduate instructorships, competitive stipends, travel support, and several prestigious fellowship opportunities.

EXPERIENCE
Mid-sized liberal arts university setting nestled in the vibrant, culturally-rich Dallas-Fort Worth metroplex.

English
DEPARTMENT

Contact Dr. Mona Narain
m.narain@tcu.edu
eng.tcu.edu

composition STUDIES

Volume 47, Number 2
Fall 2019

Editors
Matthew Davis
Kara Taczak

Editorial Consultant
Bob Mayberry
Aja Y. Martinez

Book Review Editor
Bryna Siegel Finer

Editorial Assistants
Wafaa Razeq
Yana Polikarpov

Former Editors
Gary Tate
Robert Mayberry
Christina Murphy
Peter Vandenberg
Ann George
Carrie Leverenz
Brad E. Lucas
Jennifer Clary-Lemon
Laura R. Micciche

Advisory Board
Sheila Carter-Tod
Virginia Tech University

Elías Dominguez Barajas
University of Arkansas

Qwo-Li Driskill
Oregon State University

Susan Martens
Missouri Western State University

Aja Y. Martinez
Syracuse University

Michael McCamley
University of Delaware

Jessica Nastal-Dema
Prairie State College

Annette Harris Powell
Bellarmine University

Melissa Berry Pearson
Northeastern University

Margaret Price
The Ohio State University

Jessica Restaino
Montclair State University

Donnie Sackey
The University of Texas at Austin

Christopher Schroeder
Northeastern Illinois University

Darci Thoune
University of Wisconsin-La Crosse

SUBSCRIPTIONS

Composition Studies is published twice each year (May and November). Annual subscription rates: Individuals $25 (Domestic), $30 (International), and $15 (Students). To subscribe online, please visit https://compstudiesjournal.com/subscriptions/.

BACK ISSUES

Back issues, five years prior to the present, are freely accessible on our website at https://compstudiesjournal.com/archive/. If you don't see what you're looking for, contact us. Also, recent back issues are now available through Amazon.com. To find issues, use the advanced search feature and search on "Composition Studies" (title) and "Parlor Press" (publisher).

BOOK REVIEWS

Assignments are made from a file of potential book reviewers. If you are interested in writing a review, please contact our Book Review editor at brynasf@iup.edu.

JOURNAL SCOPE

The oldest independent periodical in the field, *Composition Studies* publishes original articles relevant to rhetoric and composition, including those that address teaching college writing; theorizing rhetoric and composing; administering writing programs; and, among other topics, preparing the field's future teacher-scholars. All perspectives and topics of general interest to the profession are welcome. We also publish Course Designs, which contextualize, theorize, and reflect on the content and pedagogy of a course. CFPs, announcements, and letters to the editor are most welcome. *Composition Studies* does not consider previously published manuscripts, unrevised conference papers, or unrevised dissertation chapters.

SUBMISSIONS

For submission information and guidelines, see https://compstudiesjournal.com/submissions/..

Direct all correspondence to:

> Matthew Davis, Co-Editor
> Department of English
> UMass Boston
> 100 Morrissey Blvd
> Boston MA 02125–3393
> compstudiesjournal@gmail.com

Composition Studies is grateful for the support of the University of Massachusetts Boston and the University of Denver.

© 2019 by Matthew Davis and Kara Taczak, Co-Editors

Production and printing is managed by Parlor Press, www.parlorpress.com.

ISSN 1534–9322.

Cover art by Stephen J. McElroy.

https://compstudiesjournal.com/

composition STUDIES

Volume 47, Number 2
Fall 2019

Contents

From the Editors: A New Journey 9

Articles

Layered Feminist Historiography: Composing Multivocal Stories
Through Material Annotation Practices 14
   Grace Wetzel

Unspeakable Failures 48
   Kelly Myers

"I Can't Do Cartwheels, So I Write": Students' Writing Affect 68
   Amy D. Williams

Writing Workshops in the Public Turn 87
   Charles N. Lesh

Literacy as Threshold Concept: Building Multiliterate Awareness
in First-Year Writing 108
   Amanda Sladek

Emerging Public Literacies: A Micro-Case Study of
Public Writing Pedagogy 127
   Tyler S. Branson

Improving Instructor Ethos through Document Design 146
   Joanna Wolfe, Ryan Roderick, and Andrea Francioni Rooney

Course Design

English 3374: Writing, Rhetoric, and Multimedia Authoring 167
   Estee Beck

English 382: Special Topics in Multimodal Composition 181
   Jaclyn Fiscus-Cannaday and Sophia Watson

Engl 101: Writing in Wikipedia 193
   Matthew A. Vetter and Oksana Moroz

Where We Are 203
Dialogue and Disciplinary Space
 WPA-L Working Group and nextGEN

Book Reviews

Teaching Readers in Post-Truth America, by Ellen Carillo 211

What Is College Reading?, edited by Alice S. Horning, Deborah-Lee Gollnitz, and Cynthia R. Haller
 Reviewed by Meghan A. Sweeney

Cross-Border Networks in Writing Studies, by Derek Mueller, Andrea Willliams, Louise Wetherbee Phelps, and Jennifer Clary-Lemon 220
 Reviewed by Christopher Eaton

The Internationalization of US Writing Programs, edited by Shirley K Rose and Irwin Weiser 224
 Reviewed by Megan J. Busch

Sustainable WAC: A Whole Systems Approach to Launching and Developing Writing Across the Curriculum Programs, by Michelle Cox, Jeffrey R. Galin, and Dan Melzer 227
 Reviewed by Mandy Olejnik

Translanguaging Outside of the Academy: Negotiating Rhetoric and Healthcare in the Spanish Caribbean, by Rachel Bloom-Pojar 231
 Reviewed by Rachel Griffo

Thinking Globally, Composing Locally: Re-thinking Online Writing in the Age of the Global Internet, edited by Rich Rice and Kirk St. Amant 234
 Reviewed by Jeffrey G. Howard

Contributors 237

From the Editors: A New Journey

Successful journeys ... require good company.

—Marcia B. Baxter Magolda

Greetings and Welcome!

It's our pleasure to welcome you to our first issue of *Composition Studies* as editors. We are excited, honored, and humbled to be at the helm of *CS* for the next couple of years.

With Gratitude

We open this issue with gratitude. First, to outgoing editor Laura Micciche, whose steadfast guidance and careful stewardship kept both the journal and the editorial transition in safe hands. Laura's tenure at the journal saw not only the publication of exceptional research, reviews, and designs, but many changes and accolades—among them the introduction of the Where We Are section, the 2017 Outstanding Composition and Rhetoric Journal Award for Inclusive Editorial Practices, and the innovative and creative cover art. She ensured our editorship began smoothly, and she shepherded the articles in this issue through the review process. We are grateful for her service to the journal and to us throughout the transition.

We would also like to take a moment to thank the Advisory Board members for welcoming us on board—in person and electronically—and for remaining willing to devote their attention and labor to the success of the journal. Bryna Siegel Finer, the book editor during Laura's editorship, remains the book editor in ours; thanks to Bryna for agreeing to stay on and for the excellent slate of reviews in this issue.

Finally, we would like to thank the editorial assistants who have worked on this issue. Wafaa Razeq has helped set up and get organized as we prepared for this first issue. Her work ethic is unparalleled and her organizational strategies have helped us transition editors. Additionally, Yana Polikarpov was integral in the editorial transition and helped forward our digital vision. Yana has now transitioned off the editorial team, and we look forward to welcoming Emmy Boes to the team in the next issue.

Last, to the staff at UMass Boston who provided a tremendous amount of assistance with the arduous effort involved in relocating the journal from University of Cincinnati to UMass Boston: we are in your debt.

Our Journey

In 2022, *Composition Studies* will celebrate 50 years of existence–quite a milestone for a journal in a field which is itself not much older than that. We want to continue to celebrate and uphold the rich history of the journal and also continue to move it towards the future. We will continue to publish articles, book reviews, course designs, and Where We Are sections. In the spring 2020 issue, we will unveil a new section to the journal, much like each of the editors before us.

In looking toward the future, we see three changes that align with our aims for the journal in our editorship:

1. We will celebrate and promote collaboration within the pages of the journal. This obviously begins with co-editorship. As long time collaborators through research and writing, we bring different experiences, knowledges, and histories to all of our projects. And we see difference as a guiding concept for exploring what we know and what we don't know. A collaborative spirit has long animated the field, and by encouraging it here we hope to celebrate the difference that collaboration requires.

    Therefore, we encourage and will seek out various types of collaboration beginning with the following: each of the next three years, the journal will feature a summer special issue guest edited by collaborative teams from the field. The first one, which will be guest edited by Heidi Estrem, Dawn Shepherd, and Samantha Sturman, will focus on corequisite writing courses specifically addressing equity, access, and institutional change.

2. The topics addressed in upcoming issues will continue to focus on researching in teaching, theorizing, and administering writing, and we encourage authors to take up this work in a variety of genres, modes, and/or media. Research into 21st century literacies has shown that a writer's identity – both our own and our students'—branch out in varied directions and include multiple modes of communication. And while the identities, environments, modes, media and genres may be new, the motives undergirding the study and research into them are not. Through attention to text technologies, then, we invite authors to question and explore our field's changing sense of identity—what it is or could become—whether they identify as scholars, instructors, administrators, writers, or all four.

    Additionally, we want to acknowledge and celebrate the range of artistic abilities people in the field bring with them by showcasing some of them on the covers, so we will be seeking out composers, artists, photographers, doodlers, and the like to create issue covers based on their interpretation of the topics covered in that issue. Stephen McElroy, who is an Assistant Professor of Arts and Humanities and Director of First Year Writing at Babson College, created this issue's cover.

3. Part of moving forward means change, and for us, one of the biggest changes comes in developing the online and social media presence of the journal. We know that how information is circulated, disseminated, retrieved, mediated (or remediated), and managed depends increasingly on the ever-proliferating modes, media, and genres in which reading and composing happens. We also know this means a shift in how knowledge is produced and accessed. Of course, *CS* already provides access to some of the pieces of each issue online; we will continue this practice. We also hope to create a bigger and more accessible online presence by being active on social media, by maintaining and updating a blog on our website, and by hosting the aforementioned digital, open-access special issues. We will start small: in this issue, we are making all of the Course Design syllabi accessible online so that the wonderfully developed courses can be easily shared.

Our goal as editors, then, is to look towards the future by building on the past.

This Issue

As you will see, this is a packed issue! We have seven fantastic articles, a cluster of Course Designs, five reviews, a review essay, and a Where We Are dialogue. All of the pieces in this issue, in some way or another, present provocative ways forward in the teaching and research within Rhetoric and Composition.

The Articles

First up is Grace Wetzel's article, which argues for a unique pedagogical approach to creating multivocal stories—a layered feminist historiography, in her words—by focusing on annotation practices of an archival text from the late/early 20th century. Next, Kelly Myers addresses public failure stories as a way to better understand unspeakable failures—that is, failures that do not end in "success." Amy Williams' article focuses on an ethnographic case study of high school writers as they prepare for college. Her study adds depth and dimension to the understanding and study of affect in the teaching of writing. Charles Lesh then shows how writing workshops, when designed with a sensitivity to the locations and identities students bring into the classroom, can open deliberative, "protopublic" spaces for students. In addition, he shares a model for writing workshops grounded in collaborative design, multiplicity, and attention to space and location. Amanda Sladek presents research from a mixed methods study of 111 first year writing students' literacy narratives in response to a multiliteracies focused prompt. Her results suggest that the ways in which students understand literacy depends upon the topics about which they write, the definitions of literacy within their narratives, and their ability to reject the "literacy myth." Next, Tyler Branson presents a micro-case study of public writing pedagogy and argues that in-class public writing activities can encourage *emergent* public literacy skills. His piece provides not only new methodological insights—further developing microhistory with respect to case study methods—but also interesting parallels with the protopublic spaces highlighted in Lesh's writing workshops. And finally, Joanna Wolfe, Ryan Roderick, and Andrea Francioni Rooney, report from a comparative study of student perceptions about course document designs. Drawing on individual and collective responses to the design of two writing prompts, they argue that document design is a relatively "low-cost/high-payoff" strategy that can help with students' perceptions of both the instructor and the assignments.

The Course Designs

The course designs in this issue cluster around various forms and definitions of digitality, including multimedia authoring, feminist multimodal composition, and Wikipedia-based education.

Estee Beck provides a critical and personal reflection on the design of an upper-level Writing, Rhetoric, and Multimedia Authoring course, one that fits uneasily among the Literature courses of the department's curriculum. Beck's rumination is helpful for learning what it is like to try—and then try again—to integrate multimodal composing into a culture and curriculum that is heavily invested in print. Beck finds, among other insights, that *tactility*—as both a physical sensation and as a concept—creates bridges for students among their other coursework, multimodal composing and—potentially—their work in other disciplines.

Jaclyn Fiscus-Cannaday and Sophie Watson's Feminist Multimodal Composition course design includes a dialogue between teacher and student as a way to meaningfully reflect on the course experience. The course, a multimodal design, focuses on the intersection between feminism and multimodality. Students produced texts that centered social justice issues as a means to discuss the issues of ethics and accessibility in product design. Together, Fiscus-Cannaday and Watson were able to conclude that this type of course can provide opportunities for students to practice activism and to figure out who they are inside of the system of higher education.

Matthew Vetter and Oksana Moroz detail the creation of a first-year writing course that familiarizes students with the processes of knowledge production and curation by framing engagement with Wikipedia through the lens of Anne Beaufort's five knowledge domains. Doing so allows Vetter and Moroz a multifaceted view of how a course's design, content goals, and assignments can examine and develop students' discourse community, subject, genre, rhetorical, and process knowledge.

The Where We Are Section

The Where We Are sections have previously taken up various issues in the field—#MeToo in the academy, Latinx rhetoric and composition, and HBCU writing programs to name but three. In this issue, we have a variation on a theme: the Where We Are stages a dialogue between two recently-formed groups—the WPA-L Working Group and the nextGen Listserv Team—both of which have been integral in (re)forming disciplinary spaces over the past year. We invited these groups to dialogue, not to rehash recent events of our (electronic) disciplinary spaces, but to share their thinking about *how* and *why* we make decisions about which disciplinary spaces to inhabit, reform, create, or leave. Borrowing somewhat glibly from The Clash, we were thinking of this as the "should I stay or should I go" question, though you will see that the groups have productively blurred the boundaries between those dichotomous choices.

The Book Reviews

The issue concludes with five reviews and a review essay on works that urge educators to think more broadly in terms of what and how they attend to language, networks, and communities. These topics include teaching reading in post-truth America, cross-border networks, the internationalization of US writing programs, sustainable WAC programs, translanguaging outside of the academy, and thinking globally.

As the quote that opened our editorial suggests, we know that successful journeys require good company. We are glad to be in your company on this journey.

MD and KT
Boston, MA and Denver, CO
October 2019

Articles

Layered Feminist Historiography: Composing Multivocal Stories Through Material Annotation Practices

Grace Wetzel

This article shows how the annotation practices in an archival text entitled *Progress and Achievement: A History of the Massachusetts State Federation of Women's Clubs: 1893-1931* anticipate key feminist rhetorical research commitments and in doing so present a unique pedagogical approach to creating multivocal stories in the writing classroom: layered feminist historiography. I define layered feminist historiography as a research and composing practice that utilizes aggregated layers to construct a multivocal narrative about the past. Such an approach invites students to (re)construct a history through material engagement and exciting DIY annotation practices. This article shares outcomes of a layered historiography assignment in a writing-intensive women's rhetorical history course. Through a qualitative analysis of projects and written reflections, I show that DIY material annotation yields valuable skills for students.

In her keynote address at the 2018 Conference of the Rhetoric Society of America, Andrea A. Lunsford—referencing Chimamanda Ngozi Adichie—underscored the dangers of monolithic stories about people, cultures, and history. Lunsford encouraged listeners to thus pursue "narrative justice" by striving "to create and sustain just narratives that are invitational, inclusive, expansive, and playful" ("RSA at 50: (Re)Inventing Stories").[1] This article shares one pedagogical approach to creating such multitudinous stories in the writing classroom: layered feminist historiography. I define layered feminist historiography as a research and composing practice that utilizes aggregated layers to construct a multivocal narrative about the past. Such an approach invites students to (re)construct a history through material engagement and exciting DIY (Do-It-Yourself) annotation practices. Importantly, this pedagogical approach has been inspired by a dynamic archival text entitled *Progress and Achievement: A History of the Massachusetts State Federation of Women's Clubs: 1893-1931* that adopted similar practices many decades ago.

Published in 1932, *Progress and Achievement: A History of the Massachusetts State Federation of Women's Clubs* narrates the formation and growth of this influential constellation of women's clubs. The specific copy I analyze—housed in the rare books collection at The Huntington Library—contains abundant layers of clippings, photographs, and other materials that are pasted and otherwise inserted into the original text. In total, there are approximately fifty such annotations layered across the volume (some pages feature one layer; other pages feature several layers while still others remain unannotated). Such layers and their arrangement enrich, expand, unsettle, and otherwise complicate the original text, adding intricate new dimensions to the story of the Massachusetts Federation. Put differently, the volume's trove of historical complexities and various angles of vision reflect how layered annotation can work to resist "a single story" in favor of more "multivocal, multifocal, multimedia, multiethnic"[2] understandings (Adichie "Single Story"; Lunsford "RSA at 50"). This resonates strongly with Lunsford's affirmation of "multiple rhetorics" in her pioneering *Reclaiming Rhetorica* and also with important feminist rhetorical research practices and values as more recently outlined by Jacqueline Jones Royster and Gesa E. Kirsch (Lunsford "Reclaiming" 6).

In this article, I show how the layered annotation in *Progress and Achievement* anticipates key feminist rhetorical research commitments and in doing so presents a unique pedagogical application with valuable benefits for writing students. I first examine how the layers in *Progress and Achievement* enable a polyphonic narrative about the past: one that diversifies the original story in ways that resemble the commitments of feminist rhetorical research. I contextualize this exploration in relation to nineteenth- and early twentieth-century scrapbooks as well as modern feminist zines, both of which point to the volume's place in a long-standing tradition of material engagement for the purposes of active historical participation and (re)construction. Second, I discuss how *Progress and Achievement* inspired my implementation of a layered historiography assignment in a women's rhetorical history course. Through a qualitative analysis of student projects and written reflection papers, I show that material annotation yields dynamic multimodal composing skills, rhetorical facility, and archival/research capacities. These outcomes result from a DIY application of feminist rhetorical research values such as embracing complexity and "multiplicities," illuminating excluded histories and voices, and resisting closure (Royster and Kirsch 90). Such skills are significant in preparing our students not only to compose flexibly and innovatively, but to tell stories with openness, attentiveness, and nuance in a world where this is greatly needed. Finally, this article concludes by asserting the value of opportunities to see archival research subjects as both scholarly forerunners and pedagogical mentors.

Layered Feminist Historiography: Embracing "Multiplicities" through Material Engagement

Progress and Achievement: A History of the Massachusetts State Federation of Women's Clubs: 1893-1931 was published during a period in which clubwomen's federations were prevalent at both a state and national level—as were histories about them.[3] This particular volume charts the Federation's "early history," founding ideals, growth, achievements, and various administrations (viii-ix). Authored by a History Committee comprised of Mrs. Walter A. Hall, Mrs. Joseph S. Leach, and Mrs. Frederick G. Smith, it draws from club scrapbooks, oral testimony, record books and manuals, and a prior written account to tell this story. The authors express "hope [that] this small volume will find a place in the libraries of clubs and individual club women, and give each reader inspiration to carry on the ideals of our founders" (ix).

Notably, one copy of this volume found a unique "place" in the hands of someone—likely a future Massachusetts clubwoman[4]—who (probably during the 1950s[5] or over the years leading up to this time) extends, unsettles, and enriches the original record composed by Hall, Leach, and Smith. In doing so, this rhetor performs what I term layered feminist historiography.[6] Figures 1, 2, and 3 (from the opening of the first section, "Organization") illustrate this polyphonic approach to history.

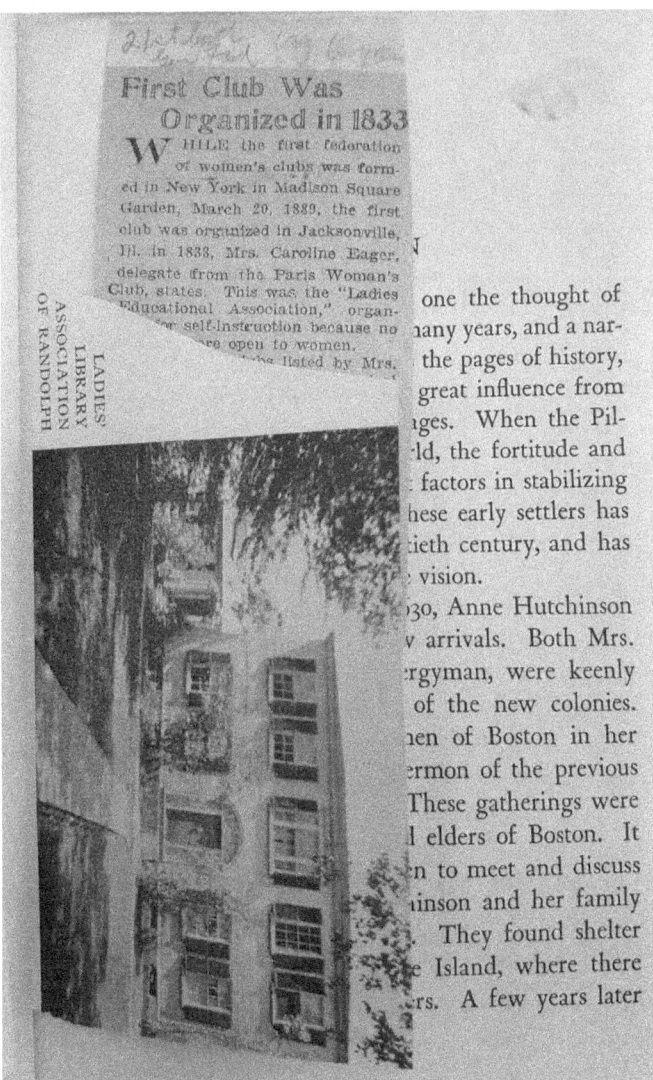

Figure 1. 637450, The Huntington Library, San Marino, California.

Readers encounter the annotated opening page of the "Organization" section featuring a newspaper clipping and photographic reprint (figure 1), the original text (figure 2), and additional prefatory clippings on the adjacent page (figure 3). The immediate effect of such an arrangement signals that history is not neatly available for our access and processing. Indeed, this layout disrupts the tidy printed paragraphs and professional document design of the published book: history instead appears as a polyphonic layering of parts.

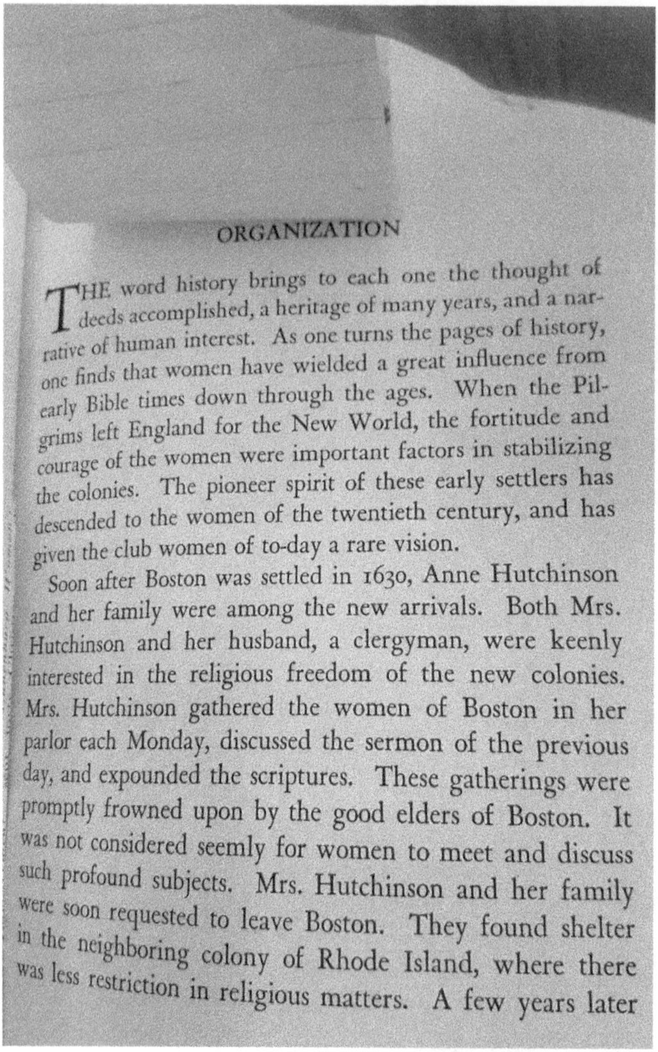

> ORGANIZATION
>
> THE word history brings to each one the thought of deeds accomplished, a heritage of many years, and a narrative of human interest. As one turns the pages of history, one finds that women have wielded a great influence from early Bible times down through the ages. When the Pilgrims left England for the New World, the fortitude and courage of the women were important factors in stabilizing the colonies. The pioneer spirit of these early settlers has descended to the women of the twentieth century, and has given the club women of to-day a rare vision.
>
> Soon after Boston was settled in 1630, Anne Hutchinson and her family were among the new arrivals. Both Mrs. Hutchinson and her husband, a clergyman, were keenly interested in the religious freedom of the new colonies. Mrs. Hutchinson gathered the women of Boston in her parlor each Monday, discussed the sermon of the previous day, and expounded the scriptures. These gatherings were promptly frowned upon by the good elders of Boston. It was not considered seemly for women to meet and discuss such profound subjects. Mrs. Hutchinson and her family were soon requested to leave Boston. They found shelter in the neighboring colony of Rhode Island, where there was less restriction in religious matters. A few years later

Figure 2. 637450, The Huntington Library, San Marino, California.

These layering practices may be classified amongst dynamic forms of material engagement such as scrapbooks, collage, zines, and other "'maker' activities" that involve a DIY "emphasis on 'doing'" (Ratto and Boler 5, 18). Of these, layered annotation most clearly resembles scrapbooks. Exceedingly popular in the nineteenth- and early twentieth-centuries, particularly, scrapbooks enabled people "from all classes and backgrounds, and with surprisingly diverse educations" to purposefully compile newspaper clippings and other materials in order to "'write' a book with scissors" (Garvey 10, 27). Clubwomen actively participated in such practices. As Amy Mecklenburg-Faenger observes, for instance, "[s]crapbooks were one of the primary ways in which women's organizations in the Progressive Era could perpetuate and preserve a history of their own making" (142).

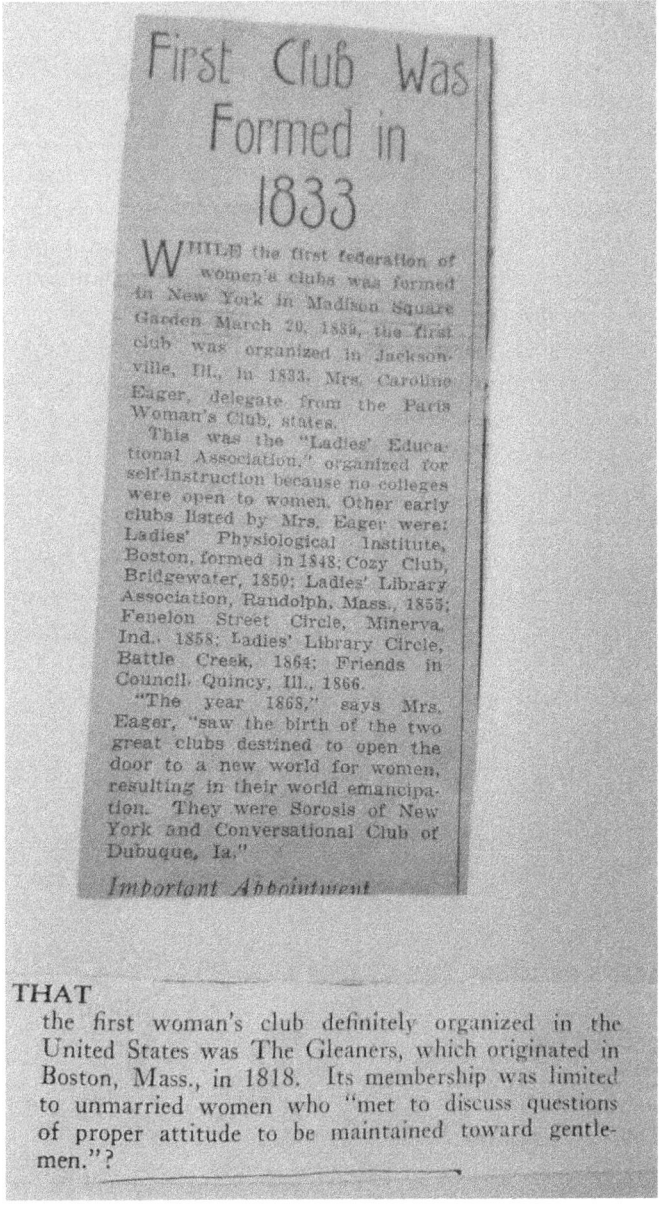

Figure 3. 637450, The Huntington Library, San Marino, California.

The scrapbooks assembled by such clubwomen and their contemporaries constructed "meaning out of disparate materials" and thus strongly resemble the richly layered *Progress and Achievement* (Garvey 131). An important differentiating feature, however, involves the relationship between the layers and the book onto which they are mapped. According to Ellen Gruber Garvey in *Writing with Scissors: American Scrapbooks from the Civil War to the Harlem Renaissance*, scrapbook makers used blank books or more often "reused and pasted over books": "[t]he volumes they obliterated ranged from outdated school textbooks and government reports to used business, farm, and plantation ledgers" (208, 52). Mecklenburg-Faenger similarly notes of scrapbooks made by Progressive-Era women's organizations that while "some have beautifully bound and embossed covers, others are compiled in ledgers meant for business accounting, and some are even made from unwanted books" (142).

In contrast, the annotated *Progress and Achievement* does not "obliterat[e]" or *replace* the contents of an "unwanted" book. Nor does the rhetor employ a blank or unrelated book. Rather, the relationship between *Progress and Achievement* and its layers is dialogic in terms of the specific, ongoing interplay among the original text, the periodical clippings, and the illustrations. Such interplay is visually evident in the rhetor's pasting strategy in figures 1 and 2, in which only the top edge of the clipping is fixed to the book; a photograph is then inserted (not pasted) atop. The outcome is significant. One can lift, flip, and look both at and beneath these layers to access a more multidimensional narrative about the past.

Layered feminist historiography thus anticipates key aspects of "strategic contemplation" as described by Royster and Kirsch in *Feminist Rhetorical Practices*. Specifically, the rhetor "generat[es] . . . thick descriptions" that "mak[e] the nature of the multiplicities clearer . . . rather than trying to simplify or oversimplify them" (90). Consider, for example, the adjacent placement of two clippings that identify different origin points for the first U.S. woman's club (figure 3). They read:

> <u>*Top*</u>: the first [woman's] club was organized in Jacksonville, Ill., in 1833 . . . This was the "Ladies' Educational Association," organized for self-instruction because no colleges were open to women.
>
> <u>*Bottom*</u>: the first woman's club definitely organized in the United States was The Gleaners, which originated in Boston, Mass., in 1818. Its membership was limited to unmarried women who "met to discuss questions of proper attitude to be maintained toward gentlemen."?

The original text by Hall, Leach, and Smith meanwhile traces the woman's club movement to seventeenth-century Anne Hutchinson and her weekly religious gatherings of women. "We like to call her our first American club woman," they write, "and feel that the little group she gathered about her was the nucleus of the women's clubs we enjoy to-day" (4). These three different origin stories together position "multiplicities" as inherent to history (and history writing). Multiplicity is both visually present through material arrangement and reinforced by reading the different narratives.[7] Together, they provide various vantage points that encourage readers "to resist coming to firmly set conclusions too quickly"—to swap out binoculars in favor of assorted lines of vision (Royster and Kirsch 90).

Another noteworthy annotation is layered over the book's dedication:

Figure 4. 637450, The Huntington Library, San Marino, California.

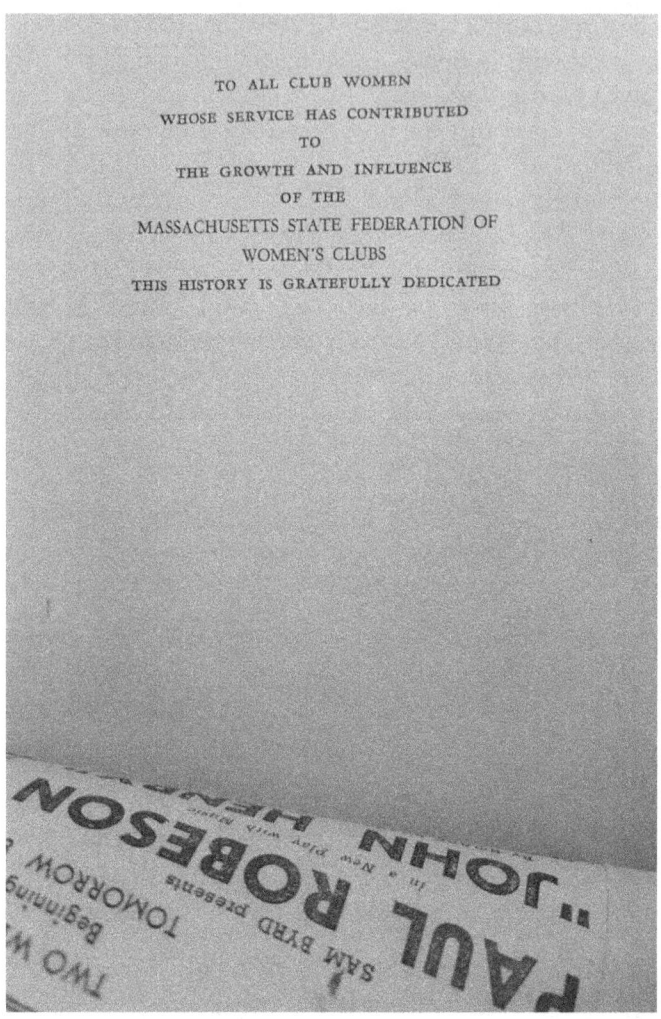

Figure 5. 637450, The Huntington Library, San Marino, California.

The dedication (figure 5) honors the service of past Massachusetts clubwomen; the article (figure 4) meanwhile announces a historical pageant also designed to pay tribute to past Massachusetts Federation members. This pageant—held eight years after *Progress and Achievement*'s publication and representative of a genre that was "wildly popular in America" during the earlier half of the twentieth-century (White 513)—acknowledged influential leaders while portraying early emerging clubs such as the Ladies' Library Association of Randolph.

Two takeaways are key here. First, this rhetor's layering practices seem clearly strategic. She appears to be working deliberately and mindfully—

evidenced by the strong resonance between the book's dedication ("[t]o all clubwomen whose service has contributed to the growth and influence of the Massachusetts State Federation") and the pageant's articulated purpose ("show[ing] how and why the present club woman is beholden to those who have gone before"). The rhetor thereby works in dialogue with the text—here taking up its strains and deepening its resonances—while also acknowledging multiplicities by featuring different origin stories several pages later.

Second, the rhetor introduces new ways of seeing. Specifically, the placement of visuals throughout the text supplies a valuable new sensory dimension. The inserted photograph of the Ladies' Library Association of Randolph (figure 1), for instance, interacts with both the original history as well as the pageant clipping. While the former describes the purpose of the Library Association ("to furnish library books to the women of the community") the latter contributes written imagery of these clubwomen "carrying their huge Webster's dictionary to meetings" (Hall, Leach, and Smith 5). One can thus picture the Randolph clubwomen in the photograph's scene—walking up the pathway to the large colonial house for a meeting with "their huge Webster's dictionary." The photograph in this way animates both the book's description and the clipping's written imagery.

Overall, the rhetor who annotated *Progress and Achievement* orchestrates materially dynamic and textured dialogue with the original record while also shaping new meanings. These DIY practices share notable similarities with contemporary feminist zines. Described by Alison Piepmeier as "self-produced and anti-corporate" booklets by girls and women, zines creatively assemble various cultural materials and are capable of "releas[ing] meanings that challenge, contradict, and go beyond the cultural materials themselves" ("Girl Zines" 2, 11). Their commonly "raw cut-and-paste style" and "multilayered" representations are in fact suggestive of the "multiplicities" that characterize *Progress and Achievement*—signaling how both zines and innovative works like *Progress and Achievement* comprise "part of a significant trend" of participatory media (including scrapbooks) in women's and feminist history (Licona 2; Piepmeier, "Girl Zines" 19; Piepmeier, "Feminism and Zines" 161-62).

This is not to claim that the annotated volume is free of power asymmetries. One is the clear erasure of African American clubwomen's rhetorical practices. This is especially evident when—despite its "multiplicities"—the annotated *Progress and Achievement* (like the original) neglects African American women's achievements in charting the origins and development of women's clubs. Yet this annotated text, in a different respect, helps to diversify perspectives represented in the original volume. This occurs through the rhetor's integration of layers that reveal the influential rhetorical practices of Native American club leader Roberta Campbell Lawson.

In *Feminist Rhetorical Practices*, Royster and Kirsch observe "a growing commitment to shift rhetorical studies away from traditional, imperialist perspectives of rhetorical performance and knowledge to a more democratic and more inclusive one" (111). *Progress and Achievement* offers budding evidence of this commitment at work many years ago. Inserted into the conclusion, we find clippings about State Federation presidents whose service postdated the book's publication. Among those presidents inserted via annotation is Mrs. Herbert F. French, whose picture is flanked by several layers about Native American rhetor and former General Federation president Roberta Campbell Lawson:

Figure 6. 637450, The Huntington Library, San Marino, California.

Figure 7. 637450, The Huntington Library, San Marino, California.

Figure 8. 637450, The Huntington Library, San Marino, California.

The photograph of French (figure 6) appears alongside a 1941 memorial she composed for Lawson. French observes that "Mrs. Lawson was . . . greatly interested in music, and was the author of the 'Indian Music Programs' and the compiler of a collection of Delaware Tribal songs." Deeming Lawson "a shining light to others," French concludes by expressing: "Massachusetts joins with clubwomen throughout the world in paying tribute to her memory." These "glimpses" into the life and rhetorical practices of a Native American rhetor who led the three million member General Federation of Women's Clubs from 1935-1938 deepen as readers peel back the layers (Royster and

Kirsch 126; Sonneborn 131). Nestled behind this text is the article "Granddaughter of Indian Chief is Club Leader" by Lemuel F. Parton which notes: "Mrs. Lawson's grandfather was Charles Journeycake, the last chief of the Delawares" (figure 8). Readers then learn more about Lawson that helps "shift" Western-based conceptions of rhetorical significance (Royster and Kirsch 111):

> . . . Lawson is proud of her family tree and has spent much time and money in tracing its branches. In her Tulsa residence she has three large rooms filled with one of the finest collections of Indian art and handicraft in America. She organized the first women's club in Tulsa . . . She was president of the Oklahoma federation from 1917 to 1919 and General federation director from 1918 to 1922, and was elected national president in June, 1935. She is an accomplished musician, collecting and scoring Indian songs and chants and singing them in costume.

These words appear beside a large captioned picture of Lawson from *The Boston Herald*. Although partially obstructed, the caption visibly describes her as "an expert on Indian music." Altogether, these annotations situate Lawson's indigenous heritage as central to her rhetorical commitments. Ultimately, this reconstructed conclusion helps "shift the ground" of *Progress and Achievement*—expanding "our capacity to see and appreciate a different vista, and mak[ing] more room for human variety" (Royster and Kirsch 113). Having analyzed means by which *Progress and Achievement* anticipates today's feminist rhetorical practices and values, I now turn to a pedagogical application.

Pedagogical Application: The Beneficial Outcomes of Layered Feminist Historiography

The material engagement enriching *Progress and Achievement* offers a dynamic class application: a layered feminist historiography assignment. Layered feminist historiography adopts Kara Poe Alexander's call to "consider the numerous rhetorical possibilities of scrapbooks as a multimodal assignment" and moreover continues the work of feminist rhetoricians and other scholars who have recently employed "varied ways of teaching with archives" (Alexander 20; Hayden 134). As Wendy Hayden observes, scholars including Pamela VanHaitsma, Jessica Enoch and Jordynn Jack, and Tom Keegan and Kelly McElroy have lately "expanded archival research pedagogies to undergraduate students, inspiring us to think about the many ways we can incorporate archives into undergraduate instruction" (134). This article offers one new approach that builds on work by Duncan Koerber, who in the pages of this journal discussed assigning personal narratives (accompanied by critical reflections) to illustrate the "epistemological challenges of doing history" (54). Layered feminist historiography similarly reveals to students "the inherent constructedness . . . involved in historical work"—but in this case by asking them to quite literally reconstruct a historical text or narrative (52). I argue that this assignment expands students' rhetorical capacities as well as their critical reading, multimodal composing, and archival/research skills through DIY annotation practices that inspire "invitational, inclusive, expansive, and playful" narratives (Lunsford "RSA at 50").

I implemented this layered feminist historiography assignment in a writing-intensive women's rhetorical history course taught during Spring 2018 and composed of both English majors and students from a range of other disciplines. Alongside other assignments such as response papers and a researched academic argument, the layered feminist historiography project contributed to these students' development as writers through a unique type of "multi-writing." Multi-writing, Robert Davis and Mark Shadle maintain, is a composing practice in which a wide range of sources and "multiple genres, disciplines, cultures, and media" merge together to permit "various information, mindsets, and ideas—as well as diverse methods of thinking and ways of expressing, arguing, and communicating—to question and deepen one another and together make a greater, but still dissonant, whole" (417, 432). Alexander has already observed that scrapbooks "fit into" this category of writing (1-2). Layered feminist historiography, too, is a form of such "multi-writing" premised on DIY dialogic interplay with the already published. It asks students to construct a dynamically "dissonant" text by way of material annotation practices that involve composing using multiple modes including the visual, spatial, and even haptic (touch).

To illustrate this unique form of composing, I acquainted students with the archival text that had inspired this assignment. Specifically, I projected images from *Progress and Achievement* (including figures 1, 2, and 6) onto the interactive whiteboard to model types of interplay and arrangement conducive to multi-layered composing. Images from *Progress and Achievement* were additionally featured on the assignment sheet, which tasked students with annotating a published history in order to write/revise history with layers. Students were instructed to

> [u]se the previously published history as a "base text." Then, add new dimensions to this history by annotating it with a diverse range of texts from both past and present (e.g., newspaper articles, photographs, press releases, book excerpts, speech excerpts, Tweets, etc.). Your job is to <u>build on, enrich, update, complicate, contextualize,</u>

and even globalize the original document. Readers of your project should be able to lift, flip, and look both at *and beneath* your layers to access a rich multi-dimensional story. (*Note*: feel free to layer upon layer!) **Remember:** *you are not replacing the original text. You are interacting with it in revisionary ways.*

The assignment also included specific instructions "to make most—if not all—of the following rhetorical 'moves'":

- *Contextualize*: expand/deepen the context present in the base text.
- *Complicate*: demonstrate how the story (as told by the base text) is more complex and multi-dimensional than originally represented.
- *Update*: feature material that updates the base text—building from where it left off and drawing connections with the present.
- *Link*: highlight important (and perhaps underexplored) links between people, events, and/or locations.
- *Globalize/Diversify*: "shift the ground" of the original history by telling a more culturally and globally inclusive story (Royster and Kirsch 113).

Finally, students were required to compose a formal reflection paper explaining their base text choice and "what layers [they] selected, how [they] arranged them, and for what rhetorical purposes." Consistent with commitments among archival and feminist rhetorical researchers to acknowledge "positionality," the reflection paper also asked students to "contemplate [their] own situatedness" by considering biases or historical "blinders" that might have shaped their projects (Gaillet 41).

As students embarked on their work, they were supported by a university librarian who shared research strategies and overviewed relevant library databases and primary resource guides. Additionally, I assembled and distributed a related guide to useful archival collections and databases (including the Library of Congress digital collections, Harvard's digital collections, OAIster, ArchiveGrid, and newspapers.com). Students' composing processes were meanwhile supported by a lecture on multimodality and material engagement, a related concept review handout, and an assignment "checklist" (articulating expectations ranging from "proficiency in making effective rhetorical choices" to "a strong form/content relationship"). Freewrite reflections—along with peer reviews of projects-in-progress—also offered students ways to contemplate questions ranging from base text options to the rhetorical functions of potential annotations.

The resulting projects offer evidence that layered feminist historiography builds valuable multimodal composing skills, rhetorical skills, and archival/

research skills anchored in close and critical engagement with texts. Moreover, through DIY material annotation practices, students gain an opportunity to enact important feminist rhetorical research values such as embracing complexity and "multiplicities," illuminating excluded histories and voices, and resisting closure (Royster and Kirsch 90). Several examples, alongside students' written reflections, indicate how this process unfolded.

***

Two opening examples reflect students' attentive interaction with published histories for the purposes of spotlighting excluded histories or recovering new voices. Consistent with the rhetor's practices in *Progress and Achievement*, these students work in dialogue with their base texts while adding to them complexity and rich texture. The first project annotates a chapter from Robert J. Allison's *The American Revolution: A Concise History* published by Oxford University Press. This student aimed to highlight excluded histories through layers that reveal contradictions surrounding the Boston Tea Party. As she explains, this event "is idolized by many Americans as the epitome of revolution and freedom. However, which revolutions of the same period were silenced amongst the patriots cries for freedom?"[8] This is illustrated by the following example:

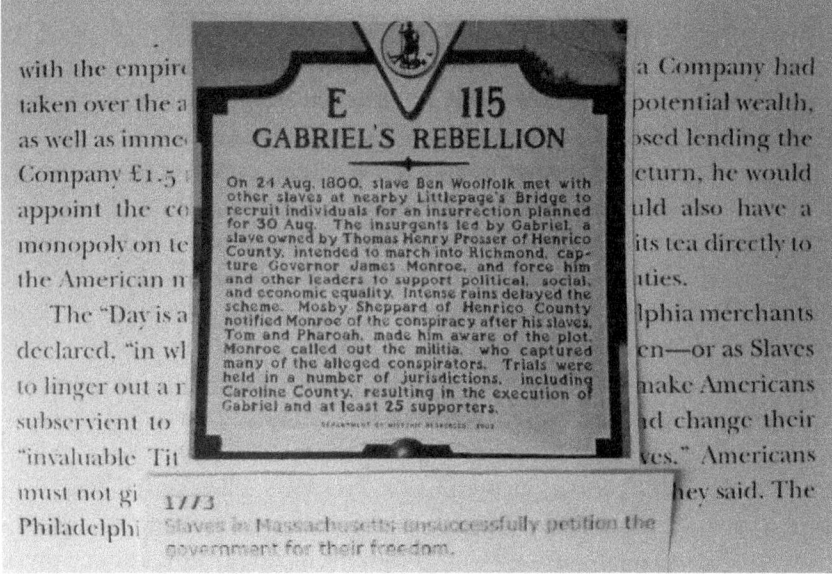

Figure 9.

The top layer describes Gabriel's Rebellion, an attempted 1800 slave revolt. The annotation below reads: "1773: Slaves in Massachusetts unsuccessfully petition the government for their freedom." This year notably coincides with the Boston Tea Party and resistance to the Tea Act by Philadelphia merchants who (as the base text recounts) resolved: "The 'Day is at length arrived . . . in which we must determine to live as Freemen—or as Slaves to linger out a miserable existence'" (Allison 16). This student thus underscores colonists' appropriation of the discourse of slavery to denounce the Tea Act. As she elaborates, "the words of the Philadelphia merchants relating the Tea Act to their slavery is juxtaposed with the actual enslaved people fighting for freedom and failing. Examples of this phenomenon include the rejection of the slaves of Massachusetts petition for freedom and . . . Gabriel's Rebellion."

A second contradiction is also illuminated later in her project: that "the rebelling colonists . . . use the image of people they oppress, the Native Americans" during the Revolutionary era. By layering examples—including the liberty tree's initial connection to the Great White Pine of the Iroquois—over a base text paragraph describing how the Bostonians disguised themselves as native people during the Tea Party of 1773, this student highlights deep contradictions in the colonists' struggle for freedom.

The second project thoughtfully annotates a chapter from Joshua Bloom and Waldo E. Martin, Jr.'s *Black Against Empire: The History and Politics of the Black Panther Party* published by the University of California Press. The annotations shown in figures 10 and 11 interact closely with the base text by supplying richly textured context while also recovering a new voice through archival research.

Beneath these annotations, the base text introduces Huey P. Newton and describes his family's 1945 relocation to Oakland—part of the twentieth-century Great Migration of African Americans from the South to the urban North and West. Layered onto the base text are three annotations: (1) a photograph of W. E. B. Du Bois; (2) a portion of Du Bois's *Crisis* article, "The Migration of Negroes" (1917); and (3) a 1918 letter by Macon Georgia resident Mrs. J. H. Adam to the Bethlehem Baptist Association of Chicago requesting migration assistance. These annotations interact with both the base text and each other in compelling ways. Du Bois's article, for instance, marks the early origins of the Great Migration and speculates that migration may grow. This growth is notably represented in the base text's description of the Newton family three decades later "following the path of many black families migrating from the South" (Bloom and Martin 20).

Further significant is Mrs. J. H. Adam's letter (figure 11) from the Carter Goodwin Collection of the Manuscript Division at the Library of Congress (made digitally accessible through The Phillips Collection Migration Series).

This 1918 message further resonates with Du Bois's article, which outlines "general dissatisfaction with the conditions in the South" due to floods, devastation, Northern labor demands, and "outbreaks of mob violence" in Georgia and South Carolina (63-65). The letter reads:

Macon Ga April 2, 1918

To the Bethlehem Baptist Association reading in the Chicago Defender of your help securing positions I want to know if it is any way you can oblige me by helping me to get out there as I am anxious to leave here & every thing so hard here. I hope you will oblige in helping me to leave here ans at once to 309 Middle St. Mrs. J. H. Adam (Adam)

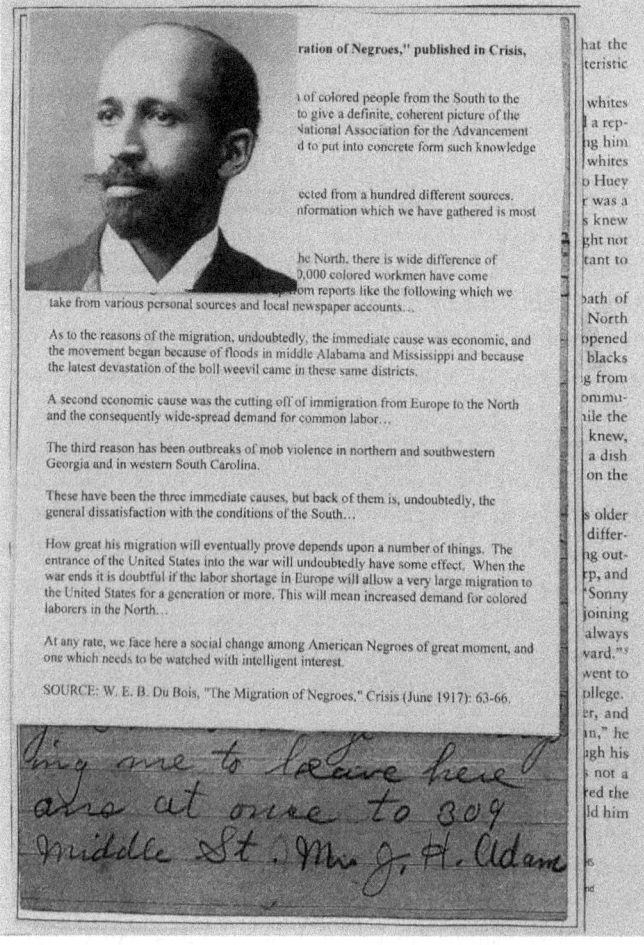

Figure 10.

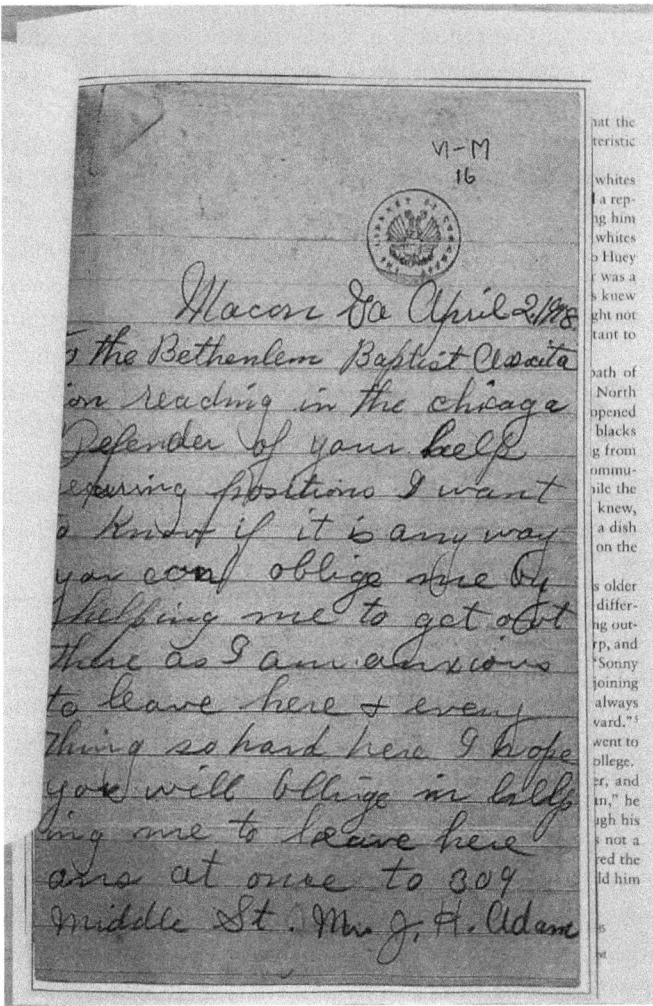

Figure 11.

These annotations and their rhetorically powerful interplay on the page indicate a commitment to multivocality that resembles the rhetor's annotation practices in *Progress and Achievement*. They also reflect this student's close attention to language, multimodal capacities, and ability to draw meaningful connections—in addition to his growing archival research skills. Indeed, similar to students in Hayden's recent undergraduate course on Rhetoric and Composition's archival turn, the student here demonstrates that he has "learn[ed] the feminist value of archival research" and "the feminist research [strategy] of recovering lost voices" (134).

These outcomes are further reflected by other student projects including one that annotates a short biography of Rosa Parks by Mary Hull. This project features digitally accessible archival materials including African American newspaper articles from the *New York Age* and a poll tax receipt from the "Rosa Parks Papers" at the Library of Congress. For this student, layered feminist historiography inspired her to examine "a wider range of sources" than she would have "by simply researching and writing a paper on my chosen topic." She observes particularly that "the newspaper archives in which I looked through were monumental in my understanding of my topic along with my creation of rhetoric." Hayden has recently noted that archival research "requires students to adopt a more nuanced approach to information literacy" and that "[s]ynthesizing . . . primary sources into a coherent narrative involves further development of that nuanced approach" (135). Consistent with Hayden's findings, students in this course gained valuable information literacy skills through their careful archival research—utilized in our case, however, to compose not "coherent narrative[s]" but rather purposefully unsettled ones.

Ultimately, the multifaceted nature of layered feminist historiography inspired students' meaningful archival work and deep research. As one student reflected: "The project itself really makes you dig into research and discover different aspects of a topic. I think the project itself was really symbolic. You are searching for more and more layers," she went on to explain, "and it's pretty cool to actually find the layers and see that sometimes, when you just stick to the first thing you find, you don't get the whole story." This account highlights strong ties between material engagement, feminist historiography, and archival/research skills.

Material engagement also inspired highly creative critical composing. As one student remarked, "having to use physical materials brought a new concreteness and creativity to the project that got me to really think about what I was doing." This point is illustrated by two projects with innovative form/content connections. The first project annotates "Women in 1970" (1971), a record by the Citizens' Advisory Council on the Status of Women recounting women's advancements.

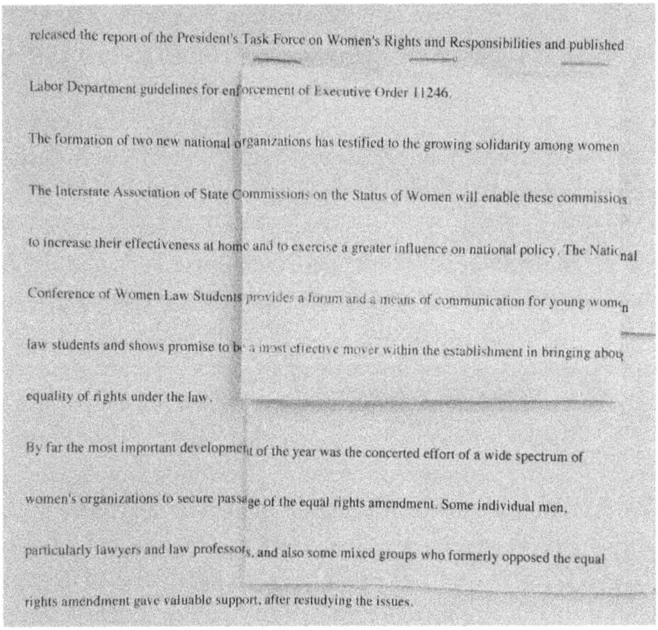

released the report of the President's Task Force on Women's Rights and Responsibilities and published

Labor Department guidelines for enforcement of Executive Order 11246.

The formation of two new national organizations has testified to the growing solidarity among women

The Interstate Association of State Commissions on the Status of Women will enable these commissions

to increase their effectiveness at home and to exercise a greater influence on national policy. The National

Conference of Women Law Students provides a forum and a means of communication for young women

law students and shows promise to be a most effective mover within the establishment in bringing about

equality of rights under the law.

By far the most important development of the year was the concerted effort of a wide spectrum of

women's organizations to secure passage of the equal rights amendment. Some individual men,

particularly lawyers and law professors, and also some mixed groups who formerly opposed the equal

rights amendment gave valuable support, after restudying the issues.

Figure 12.

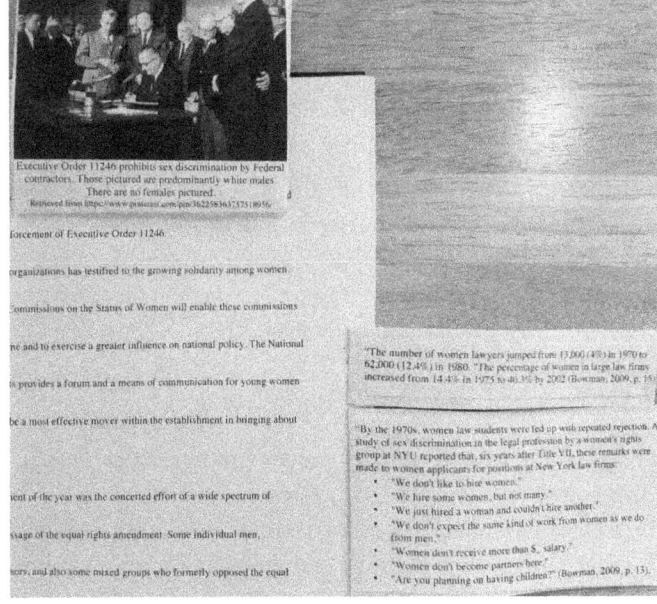

Figure 13.

Layered Feminist Historiography 35

This student pastes "hidden" information on each annotation's underside. While the recto replicate original words from the base text (figure 12), the verso create a more expansive story (figure 13). Consider the bottom annotation, for instance. The recto (the base text) praises The National Conference of Women Law Students as a promising "mover within the establishment in bringing about equality of rights under the law" ("Women in 1970"). The verso then reveals an excerpt from a recent Cornell Law Faculty publication that states "[b]y the 1970s, women law students were fed up with repeated rejection." The publication goes on to reference "[a] study of sex discrimination in the legal profession" during this period that revealed "remarks . . . made to women applicants for positions at New York law firms"; these remarks included "We don't like to hire women" and "Women don't receive more than $__ salary" (Bowman 13). This annotation concretely establishes the discriminatory context within which The National Conference of Women Law Students operated. As a sobering complement to the base text, it also resonates with the project's treatment of the gender pay gap two pages earlier when this student links the base text's discussion of equal pay ("In fiscal year 1970 over $6 million was found due under the Federal equal pay law to nearly 18,000 employees, almost all of whom were women") to more recent findings from a 2016 Pew Research Center study, "Racial, Gender Wage Gaps Persist in U.S. Despite Some Progress" ("Women in 1970").

Overall, the design of this project reflects deliberate rhetorical choices and a strong form/content relationship centered on touch—a modality that Davis and Yancey deem "central to the making of meaning" in scrapbooks and related genres (Davis and Yancey 16). As this student recounts in her reflection paper:

> I chose to cover the top of my layers with the original base text so that it could be read easily (without having to lift up the layers). I did this to demonstrate that though it is easier to read one document (or perspective) on a historical event, it is not enough to get a comprehensive understanding. In order to fully understand a historical event, you must do some digging. Though this is more work, as demonstrated through the lifting of the layers, it is worth doing.

The form/content relationship described here is premised on readers' engagement with their haptic sense (touch). Such composing experience is valuable for students. As Alexander maintains, "[a]lthough our writing classrooms emphasize verbal and visual modes, they do not typically pay as much attention to the haptic"—despite the powerful role of touch in "impact[ing] how readers make meaning" (20, 18). Layered feminist historiography foregrounds the haptic mode by suggesting that history can be more dynamically and complexly composed and read when touch has a role in our stories about the past.

An additional project reinforces the value of the haptic mode through its own unique form/content relationship. Consider the following annotations of Mark Gridley's *College Music Symposium* article, "Misconceptions in Linking Free Jazz with the Civil Rights Movement." These unique annotations take the shape of folded books (figures 14 and 15) and a pop-out accordion (figures 16 and 17). Present on these annotations are also numbers (figures 14 and 17) that correspond with sources in the Works Cited page.

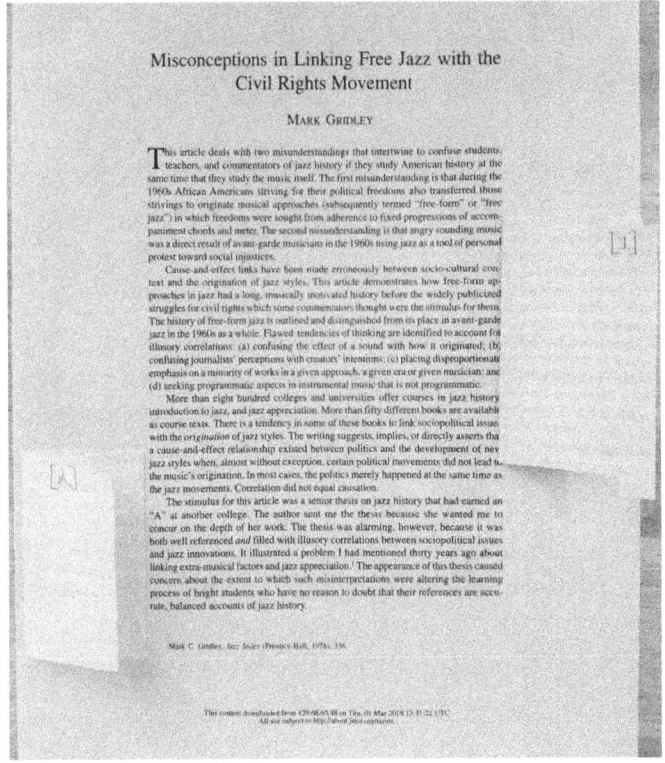

Figure 14.

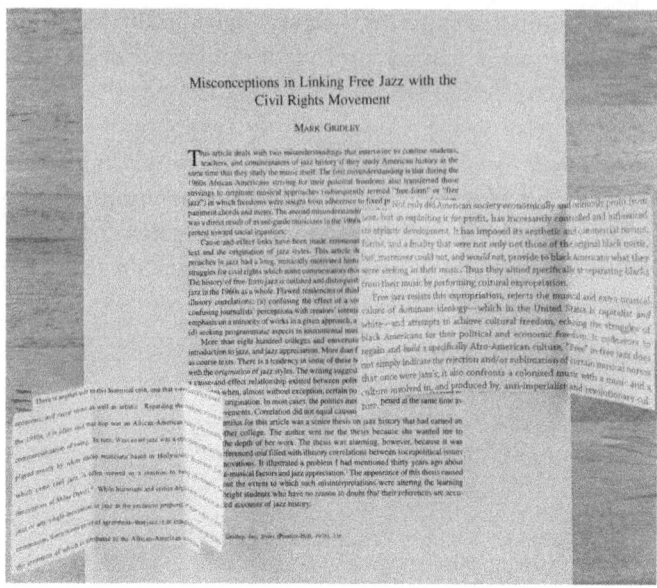

Figure 15.

Both the folded books and the pop-out accordion ask readers to critically engage with the text through haptic interaction. As this student further explains, "I wanted to 'complicate' the base text by constructing layers that require flips and folds just to read the text. Essentially, the complication exists not only in the content of the added layers, but also in their structure." The folded book, for instance, conveys "the symbolic association that there is more than one 'story' being told for free jazz and its relationship to politics/civil rights." The pop-out accordion meanwhile "incorporate[s] three layered texts" through a dialogic "'linking' process."

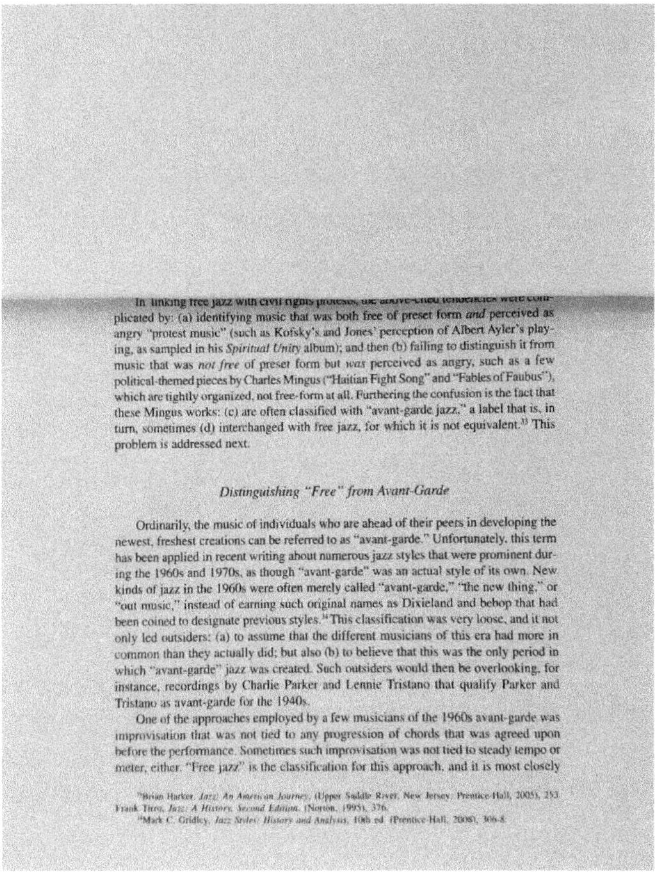

In linking free jazz with civil rights protests, the above-cited tendencies were complicated by: (a) identifying music that was both free of preset form *and* perceived as angry "protest music" (such as Kofsky's and Jones' perception of Albert Ayler's playing, as sampled in his *Spiritual Unity* album); and then (b) failing to distinguish it from music that was *not free* of preset form but *was* perceived as angry, such as a few political-themed pieces by Charles Mingus ("Haitian Fight Song" and "Fables of Faubus"), which are tightly organized, not free-form at all. Furthering the confusion is the fact that these Mingus works: (c) are often classified with "avant-garde jazz," a label that is, in turn, sometimes (d) interchanged with free jazz, for which it is not equivalent.[33] This problem is addressed next.

Distinguishing "Free" from Avant-Garde

Ordinarily, the music of individuals who are ahead of their peers in developing the newest, freshest creations can be referred to as "avant-garde." Unfortunately, this term has been applied in recent writing about numerous jazz styles that were prominent during the 1960s and 1970s, as though "avant-garde" was an actual style of its own. New kinds of jazz in the 1960s were often merely called "avant-garde," "the new thing," or "out music," instead of earning such original names as Dixieland and bebop that had been coined to designate previous styles.[34] This classification was very loose, and it not only led outsiders: (a) to assume that the different musicians of this era had more in common than they actually did; but also (b) to believe that this was the only period in which "avant-garde" jazz was created. Such outsiders would then be overlooking, for instance, recordings by Charlie Parker and Lennie Tristano that qualify Parker and Tristano as avant-garde for the 1940s.

One of the approaches employed by a few musicians of the 1960s avant-garde was improvisation that was not tied to any progression of chords that was agreed upon before the performance. Sometimes such improvisation was not tied to steady tempo or meter, either. "Free jazz" is the classification for this approach, and it is most closely

[33] Brian Harker, *Jazz: An American Journey*, (Upper Saddle River, New Jersey: Prentice-Hall, 2005), 253. Frank Tirro, *Jazz: A History, Second Edition*. (Norton, 1993), 376.

[34] Mark C. Gridley, *Jazz Styles: History and Analysis*, 10th ed. (Prentice-Hall, 2008), 306-8.

Figure 16.

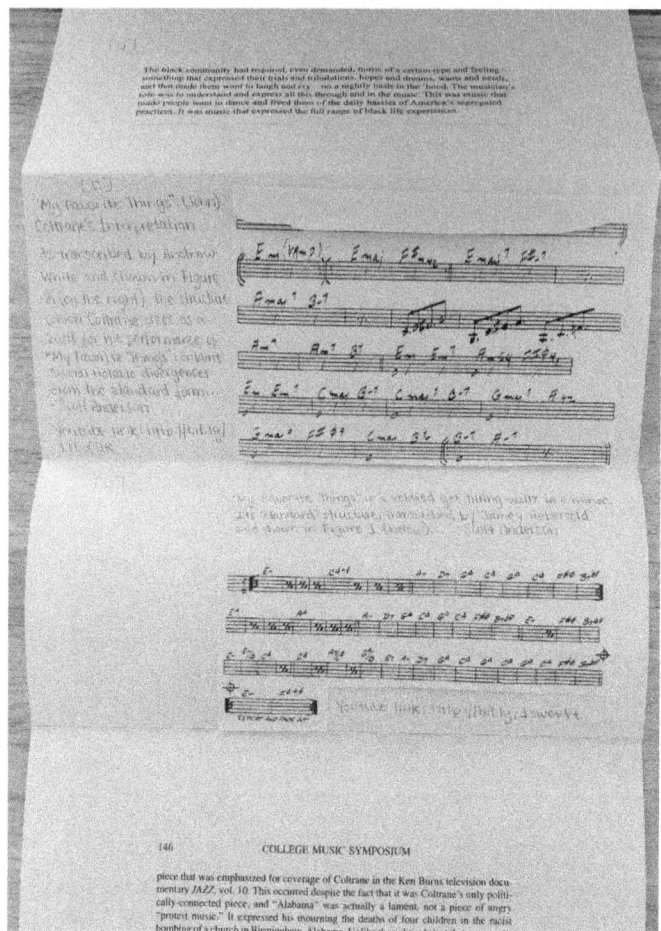

Figure 17.

Alexander has argued that materiality—especially within scrapbook assignments—"affords students a wide range of possibilities for conveying and representing their meaning" (3). This is apparent in this student's creative use of the haptic mode to accentuate "multiplicities" and "to physically and figuratively play with my audience's interpretation/experience." The depth behind such thoughtful rhetorical choices is further indicated by two fascinating pieces of this student's invention process:

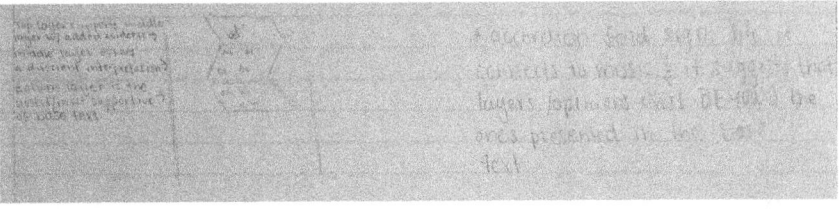

Figure 18.

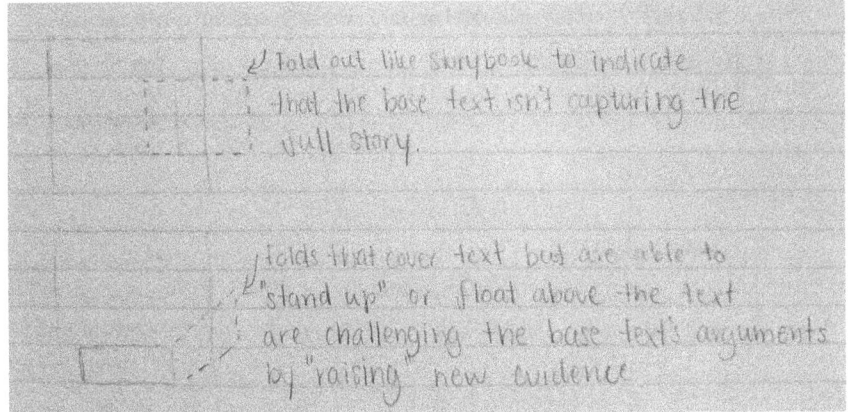

Figure 19.

Ultimately, both student projects reflect sophisticated rhetorical facility and critical composing skills as well as students' overall increased capacity for "expansive" and "playful" storytelling (Lunsford "RSA at 50"). Put differently, these projects "forestall coming to closure too quickly"—an important value of feminist rhetorical research (Royster and Kirsch 139). This emerging commitment is articulated insightfully in another student's reflection. She writes:

> I really enjoyed this project but I don't know if I could ever be fully satisfied with it. It was definitely hard to cut myself off of finding more connections, but I think that speaks to the fluidity of history. It's hard to even comprehend the expanse of voices and narratives I haven't been able to capture. I'd be really curious to see someone undertake the layered historiography of this text in a couple decades' time.

This passage suggests—as Liz Rohan has observed in "Everyday Curators: Collecting as Literate Activity"—that texts can carry "limitless" contexts (59). Quoting Mikhail Bakhtin, Rohan reminds us that "There is neither a first nor a last word and there are no limits to . . . dialogic context (it extends into the boundless past and the boundless future)" (qtd. in Rohan 59).

Overall, students enthusiastically affirmed the value of layered feminist historiography—including the rewards of DIY material engagement. As one student wrote:

> This project was unlike any other project I have been assigned in college, especially in an English course. I feel that the goal of the project could not have been as well presented if it was assigned as a formal English paper. I believe that I benefited from actually interacting with my layers. From the research, to the printing, cutting, folding, and pasting. By physically engaging with my texts I was able to see firsthand how my history had different dimensions to it ... I am a kinesthetic learner, so any project that allows me to physically interact with the material benefits myself as a student.

A second student corroborated the benefits of physical textual engagement while also highlighting its enjoyable aspects. Her below comment (in addition to other student remarks such as one suggesting that constructing layers "demanded an 'artist's eye'") in this way supports Tamar Katriel and Thomas Farrell's observation that scrapbooking arrangement practices "often [take] on the flavor of a pleasurable artistic enterprise" (11). She writes:

> I enjoyed creating this project, despite the amount of work it required. I particularly enjoyed the fact that we had to create it physically with our hands...I think that a project such as this has more benefits than simply writing a paper—in fact, I don't know how we could have achieved the same result if the project was simply a paper.

Noticeably, both of these students posit the distinct value of DIY material engagement in comparison to paper writing. Their comments are suggestive of reasons why many composition instructors have embraced vibrant supplements or alternatives to the traditional research paper. Examples include both Davis and Shadle's "multi-writing" research project (a means of moving beyond "the modernist research paper" in order to "resist, suspend, and/or decenter the master consciousness or central perspective inscribed in the essay") and more recent archival-based assignments such as Keegan and McElroy's "alternative to the five-page paper" involving the crowdsourced DIY History Project (Davis and Shadle 440, 431; Keegan and McElroy "Archives Alive!"). This latter assignment asked students to transcribe, rhetorically analyze, and contextualize archival letters while jettisoning the "arid work" of traditional research papers—which as the authors argue contain "no texture, no hook; nothing animates them" (Keegan and McElroy "Archives Alive!").

Layered feminist historiography brings an animated and decentered perspective to history (re)writing—offering benefits to students across disciplines through dynamically material-based learning. This process encouraged new understandings of history and meaningful appreciation for multivocal stories. As one student recognized, "just because something is published does not mean it is the whole truth. This project helped me realize . . . I am able to interact with a history and deepen my understanding." A second student connected the project directly to feminist rhetorical researchers from our course, writing: "this project helped me change the way I read and understand history. Like Glenn, Ronald, and Ritchie stated in the works we read this semester – there isn't one 'history' and every story or historical account consists of many different histories. This project helped me see that for myself." Perhaps most notably, a final student linked the project to Adichie's TED Talk—anticipating Lunsford's RSA keynote address:

> One TED Talk that I kept thinking about throughout the process of creating my layered historiography was the talk given by Chimamanda Ngozi Adichie entitled "The Danger of a Single Story." The message of this talk aligns with this new thinking that has been developed because of this project. That new way of thinking involves looking at a story from multiple angles . . . but also how we can break down prejudices and barriers amongst people through educating ourselves on every aspect of a given "story" or "narrative."

This comment highlights the value of materially engaged multimodal composition driven by feminist rhetorical practices. If—as Lunsford argues—"[r]hetoric's responsibility" is "to create and sustain just narratives that are invitational, inclusive, expansive, and playful," then layered annotation seems to offer one promising way to approach this goal in the writing classroom ("RSA at 50").

Conclusion

Overall, layered feminist historiography yields valuable pedagogical benefits while calling attention to "the enormous complexity" of the past, the inevitable limitations of history texts, and the importance of approaching history as "inquiry" (Schlereth 340, 342). DIY material annotation practices help students critically intervene in the histories that have been handed to them and in doing so builds multimodal composing skills, rhetorical facility, and archival/research capacities. To conclude, I offer two broader takeaways from this research.

First, I propose using terms such as "scholarly foremother" or "scholarly forerunner" to capture instances in which our research subjects reveal new dimensions of our rich and multifaceted scholarly pasts. This builds on work by Heidi A. McKee, James E. Porter, and Jacqueline Jones Royster who have discussed approaching archival research subjects "as *persons*" and "even co-researchers" (McKee and Porter 77).[9] The budding elements of feminist rhetorical practices and values in the annotated *Progress and Achievement* reveal early seeds of future work in feminisms and rhetorics; in doing so, they more broadly emphasize the importance of attending to a range of scholarly "legacies of thought and action" of various kinds (Royster and Kirsch 23).

Second, this compelling instance of shared research commitments not only helps contribute to an expanded picture of a long-standing feminist scholarly heritage, but also affirms how our research subjects can function as valuable pedagogical mentors. In this case, the rhetor who annotated *Progress and Achievement* inspired one of the most productively rewarding classroom experiments I have pursued in recent years. I am grateful for the mentorship provided through her innovative work. There remains much more to learn from other scholarly forerunners, especially those whose work offers both unique pedagogical applications and exciting new ways of understanding our scholarly pasts.

Notes

1. Lunsford borrows the term "narrative justice" from Lisa Russell, the Dulwich Centre (Adelaide, Australia), and Judithe Registre. See Lunsford's blog post entitled "Can We Achieve Narrative Justice?" for further discussion: https://community.macmillan.com/community/the-english-community/bedford-bits/blog/2018/09/06/can-we-achieve-narrative-justice.

2. I borrow this fitting phrase from Lunsford's description (as shared in her keynote) of her forthcoming *Norton Anthology of Rhetoric and Writing*, which aims "to demonstrate the multivocal, multifocal, multimedia, multiethnic nature of rhetoric" (Lunsford "RSA at 50").

3. Federation histories published during this period include (to name only a few): *The Story of the Illinois Federation of Colored Women's Clubs: 1900-1922* (1922); *A Record of Twenty-five Years of The California Federation of Women's Clubs: 1900-1925* (1927); *History of the Maryland Federation of Women's Clubs: 1899-1941* (1941); *The History of the Woman's Club Movement in America* (1898); and *Lifting as they Climb* (1933).

4. The intricate work and knowledge of this rhetor suggest she was likely a Massachusetts clubwoman. The book's reference to individual clubwomen's libraries also points to this possibility (ix). It is further possible that *Progress and Achievement* was

reconstructed collaboratively. No name(s) or confirming details are available in the book, however.

5. Two indicators suggest the text was reconstructed during the late 1950s or over the years leading up to this time. First, the rhetor updates a list of Federation presidents until the year 1956. Second, there are many inserted clippings from the 1950s, but none I found dated from the 1960s.

6. Building on Royster, my use of the term "feminist" suggests that the rhetor who annotated this volume "take[s] actions that we might recognize and describe as complementary to our goals and actions—ones that we have chosen to call 'feminist' even" if this rhetor "may not have made this terminological choice" (qtd. in Royster and Kirsch 146).

7. Interestingly, one of these "multiplicities" appears twice—the narrative describing the "Ladies' Educational Association" founded in 1833 (see figures 1 and 3). While this could be interpreted as the rhetor's "favored" narrative, I would argue that these similar clippings (considered within the larger context of "multiplicities" in the volume) draw attention to how certain narratives can gain traction through press reprints and circulation.

8. IRB approval was obtained for this study. As requested by the Saint Joseph's University IRB, I quote and share projects from only those students who agreed in writing to the protected use of their data.

9. McKee and Porter discuss "viewing the archives as *persons*—perhaps not persons in the IRB sense of subjects, but persons as research participants, even co-researchers. As Royster describes her own study: 'The women emerge not just as subjects of research but also as potential listeners, observers, even co-researchers, whether silent or voiced, in the knowledge-making processes themselves' (274)" (McKee and Porter 77-78).

Acknowledgments

I would like to thank editors Laura R. Micciche, Matt Davis, and Kara Taczak and the blind reviewers for their helpful revision suggestions. Additionally, I thank Cristina D. Ramírez for proposing the term "historical layering" during an early conversation about this project; from this suggestion, I developed the term "layered feminist historiography." I also thank Rachel N. Spear, Courtney George, and Rachael L. Sullivan for their feedback on earlier versions of this article.

Works Cited

Adam, Mrs. J. H. Letter to the Bethlehem Baptist Association of Chicago. Carter Goodwin Collection, Manuscript Division, Library of Congress, 2 Apr. 1918, uploaded by The Phillips Collection, Washington DC, 2008 https://www.phillipscollection.org/migration_series/flash/print/primary_source_25.pdf

Adichie, Chimamanda Ngozi. "The Danger of a Single Story." TED, July 2009, https://www.ted.com/talks/chimamanda_adichie_the_danger_of_a_single_story?language=en.

Alexander, Kara Poe. "Material Affordances: The Potential of Scrapbooks in the Composition Classroom." *Composition Forum: A Journal of Pedagogical Theory in Rhetoric and Composition*, vol. 27, Spring 2013, pp. 1-25, https://files.eric.ed.gov/fulltext/EJ1003969.pdf.

Allison, Robert J. *The American Revolution: A Concise History*. Oxford UP, 2011.

Bloom, Joshua and Waldo E. Martin, Jr. *Black Against Empire: The History and Politics of the Black Panther Party*. University of California Press, 2016.

Bowman, Cynthia Grant. "Women in the Legal Profession from the 1920s to the 1970s: What Can We Learn From Their Experience About Law and Social Change?" *Cornell Law Faculty Publications*, Paper 12, 2009, https://scholarship.law.cornell.edu/cgi/viewcontent.cgi?article=1011&context=facpub.

Citizens' Advisory Council on the Status of Women. "Women in 1970: '70 Highlights." Washington D.C., 1971.

Davis, Robert and Mark Shadle. "'Building a Mystery': Alternative Research Writing and the Academic Act of Seeking." *CCC*, vol. 51, no. 3, 2000, pp. 417-46.

Davis, Matthew and Kathleen Blake Yancey. "Notes Toward the Role of Materiality in Composing, Reviewing, and Assessing Multimodal Texts." *Computers and Composition*, vol. 31, 2014, pp. 13-28.

Du Bois, W.E.B. "The Migration of Negroes." *The Crisis*, June 1917, pp. 63-66.

Gaillet, Lynée Lewis. "(Per)Forming Archival Research Methodologies." *CCC*, vol. 64, no. 1, 2012, pp. 35-58.

Garvey, Ellen Gruber. *Writing with Scissors: American Scrapbooks from the Civil War to the Harlem Renaissance*. Oxford UP, 2013.

Hall, Mrs. Walter A., Mrs. Joseph S. Leach, and Mrs. Frederick G. Smith. *Progress and Achievement: A History of the Massachusetts State Federation of Women's Clubs, 1893-1931*. The Plimpton Press, 1932, 637450, The Huntington Library, San Marino, California.

Hayden, Wendy. "And Gladly Teach: The Archival Turn's Pedagogical Turn." *College English*, vol. 80, no. 2, 2017, pp. 133-58.

Katriel, Tamar and Thomas Farrell. "Scrapbooks as Cultural Texts: An American Art of Memory." *Text and Performance Quarterly*, vol. 11, no. 1, 1991, pp. 1-17. Communication & Mass Media Complete, doi: 10.1080/10462939109365990.

Keegan, Tom and Kelly McElroy. "Archives Alive!: Librarian-Faculty Collaboration and an Alternative to the Five-Page Paper." *In the Library with the Lead Pipe*, 26 Aug. 2015, http://www.inthelibrarywiththeleadpipe.org/2015/archives-alive-librarian-faculty-collaboration-and-an-alternative-to-the-five-page-paper/.

Koerber, Duncan. "Truth, Memory, Selectivity: Understanding Historical Work by Writing Personal Histories." *Composition Studies*, vol. 41, no. 1, 2013, pp. 51-69.

Licona, Adela C. *Zines in Third Space: Radical Cooperation and Borderlands Rhetoric*. SUNY P, 2012.

Lunsford, Andrea A. "On Reclaiming Rhetorica." *Reclaiming Rhetorica: Women in the Rhetorical Tradition*, edited by Andrea A. Lunsford, University of Pittsburgh Press, 1995.

Lunsford, Andrea A. "RSA at 50: (Re)Inventing Stories." 18th Biennial Conference of the Rhetoric Society of America, 1 June 2018, Hilton Minneapolis, Minneapolis, MN. Keynote Address.

McKee, Heidi A. and James E. Porter. "The Ethics of Archival Research." *CCC*, vol. 64, no. 1, 2012, pp. 59-81.

Mecklenburg-Faenger, Amy. "Material Histories: The Scrapbooks of Progressive-Era Women's Organizations, 1875-1930." *Women & Things, 1750-1950: Gendered Material Strategies*, edited by Maureen Daly Goggin and Beth Fowkes Tobin, Ashgate, 2009, pp. 141-53.

Piepmeier, Alison. "Feminism and Zines: An Origin Story (And the Accidents that Reveal Them)." *Feminist Challenges or Feminist Rhetorics?: Locations, Scholarship, Discourse*, edited by Kirsti Cole, Cambridge Scholars Publishing, 2014, pp. 158-76.

Piepmeier, Alison. *Girl Zines: Making Media, Doing Feminism*. New York UP, 2009.

Ratto, Matt and Megan Boler. "Introduction." *DIY Citizenship: Critical Making and Social Media*, edited by Matt Ratto and Megan Boler, MIT Press, 2014, pp. 1-22.

Rohan, Liz. "Everyday Curators: Collecting as Literate Activity." *Composition Studies*, vol. 38, no. 1, 2010, pp. 53-68.

Royster, Jacqueline Jones and Gesa Kirsch. *Feminist Rhetorical Practices: New Horizons for Rhetoric, Composition, and Literacy Studies*. Southern Illinois University Press, 2012.

Royster, Jacqueline Jones. *Traces of a Stream: Literacy and Social Change Among African American Women*. University of Pittsburgh Press, 2000.

Schlereth, Thomas J. "Collecting Ideas and Artifacts: Common Problems of History Museums and History Texts." *Museum Studies: An Anthology of Contexts*, edited by Bettina Messias Carbonell, Blackwell, 2004, pp. 335-47.

Sonneborn, Liz, ed. *A to Z of American Indian Women, Revised Edition*. Infobase Publishing, 2007.

White, Kate. "'The pageant is the thing': The Contradictions of Women's Clubs and Civic Education during the Americanization Era." *College English*, vol. 77, no. 6, 2015, pp. 512-29.

Unspeakable Failures

Kelly Myers

Failure has become an acceptable, even celebrated, part of innovation, education, and personal growth, a sign of resilience—as long as individuals bounce back in quick and efficient ways; as long as they *fail, fast, forward* (Bartz). On the surface, the popular rhetoric around failure lifts the taboo by reframing failure as a ubiquitous experience and learnable skill; however, without critical engagement and efforts to create counter-stories, failure and resilience rhetorics operate as a discourse of white privilege. Failure experiences that do not make the imperative turn toward success are the unspeakable failures, unspeakable because we lack language or support systems for experiences that do not rebound quickly and consistently into forward movement. By developing responses that are analytical and reflective, and by unpacking the rhetorical construction of the failure stories that are shared publicly, we can explore ways to better understand and voice the unspeakable failures.

As a graduate student, the story of Kairos captivated me—that fickle and fleeting god who offers opportunity, in a flash, to the bold and prepared. Tracing the legend of opportunity through centuries of artwork and literature, I discovered that the god Kairos is often portrayed as the goddess Occasio. As a young white woman and the first in my family to attend graduate school, I felt a kinship with Occasio based in my deepest and quietest desires. Just by attending graduate school, I felt like I had seized the goddess of opportunity, but I constantly feared that she would slip away. I met my fear face-to-face when I discovered Metanoia, the female figure who inhabits the realm of missed opportunity and regret. But the experience of metanoia, I later learned, always involves regret *and* transformation—a "change of mind or heart" catalyzed by regret, repentance, remorse (Liddell and Scott 1115). As a graduate student, the transformative dimension of metanoia sparked feelings of hope and possibility.

Maybe missed opportunities can serve as openings.

Maybe I don't need to carry the weight of fear and shame heavily in my body.

Maybe there is a different story to tell about opportunity.

I spent a decade, in my research and teaching, working to expand the story of Kairos by reclaiming regret and missed opportunity as generative experiences. In earlier work, I framed metanoia as a missing piece in conversations about kairos and I imagined what it could mean to "seize metanoia." I envisioned richly variegated paths of metanoic experience, but the kairos story still dominated my thinking; I could not see my way out of it. I kept defaulting to metanoia as a learning process through which "a rhetor becomes better prepared for the next moment of opportunity" ("Metanoia and the Transformation" 11). I was trying to understand experiences around and beyond kairos, but I failed to question the underlying narrative of success. I stuck to the script, lining the road to success with metanoic moments.

Over time, I started to see the consequences of looping metanoia into kairos. I realized that my metanoia-based pedagogy, aimed at expanding opportunity for writers, risked putting students in an even more vulnerable position. For many of my students, the concept of metanoia is freeing. Amber Sutherland, for example, a student who took my upper-division nonfiction workshop in 2016, shared, "Metanoia allowed me to embrace regret, which opened up a huge new world for me with my writing and the way I think. Embracing the regret that metanoia gives you allows you to be comfortable with where you are, and who you are, and who you were before" (Myers et al.). For Amber, embracing regret opened up new possibilities, but I started to wonder about the voices I was not hearing. And then, as time passed, I started to wonder why the once enthusiastic voices—like Amber's—were fading from the conversation.

What about the experiences of regret that are not generative or transformative? What about the students who are not able to move forward or bounce back, those who get stuck in failure and regret no matter how hard they work?

I have come to understand failure experiences that do not make the imperative turn toward success as the *unspeakable failures*—unspeakable because we lack language or support systems for failure experiences that do not rebound quickly and consistently into forward movement. Unspeakable failure develops out of dangerously simple generalizations: the notion that successful failure is a skill we can all develop if we put our minds to it, and the idea that resilience is an embodied capacity we can all build—again, if we put our minds to it. These assumptions feed a stock story of success in the United States that conflates bootstrapping with resilience and maintains the idea that both success and failure are chosen and controlled by individuals. Unspeakable failure, I argue, stems from the refusal to see, and speak back to, the underlying privilege—distinctly white privilege—that permeates failure and resilience rhetoric.

In the sections that follow, I begin with Scott Sandage's work on the history of failure in the United States, looking specifically at the underlying concept of "obligatory striving" and the nineteenth-century linguistic shift toward "personal failure." From there, I turn to current trends in popular rhetoric, particularly rhetorical strategies that either distance or link failure and the personal or bodily. After examining historical roots and current trends, I emphasize the implications: without critical engagement and efforts to create counter-stories, failure and resilience rhetorics operate as a discourse of white privilege.

[Obligatory] Striving for Success

At Boise State University, many of my students travel winding paths into and through the university. They return to school after time away. They juggle family and financial obligations on top of a full course load. Some students work all night and then go straight to 7:30 a.m. classes. Some are reinventing themselves after a difficult relationship or an unsatisfying career. So, when I begin class on the first day of the semester with the question, "How did you arrive here, in this moment, at Boise State?," my students respond with a collective sigh and a you-don't-even-want-to-know look in their eyes. They all tell really interesting, and vastly different, stories of the paths that brought them to our current moment, but the timeline tends to be laden with shame—too many years ... too many majors ... too many mistakes. Their stories inevitably end with: "I should have figured it out sooner ..." *Successful people figure it out sooner.* With these winding paths and ongoing obstacles, many of my students feel as if they have already failed when they enter the classroom. One student described his day-to-day experience at the university as "living in a suspended state of failure." Even when they are doing well, many students fear that their efforts are never good enough—or just never enough.

Before moving to Boise, I taught at Stanford University, a place where students feel the fear of failure pressing at their backs. During my time there, I heard too many stories of young people committing suicide on the train tracks not far from my office. I quickly learned about the Stanford "duck syndrome"—the idea that students may look calm on the surface, but the "waters" beneath are troubled by a frenzy of movement. Students glide by each other in classes and dining halls, masking the physical and emotional exhaustion of their "paddling" to get or stay ahead. Though the duck syndrome narrative originated at Stanford, the mentality spans campuses across the country. In fact, even before entering college, students experience "college admissions mania," a process where "the treadmill never stops and the stakes can feel impossibly high" (Bennett). The shame of the winding path, the quiet pressure of the duck syndrome, and the mania of the treadmill, all point to an underlying ideal that equates educational success to ceaseless movement.

Scott Sandage, in his celebrated book *Born Losers: A History of Failure in America*, describes this ceaseless movement as "obligatory striving," explaining, "Ours is an ideology of achieved identity; obligatory striving is its method, and failure and success are its outcomes" (265). Through obligatory striving, comprising the power and persistence of thoughts and actions, individuals can propel themselves toward success and away from failure—a mindset that results in sprinting "as much to outrun failure as to catch success" (2). While such movement toward success can feel empowering, it also generates a well of shame at the other end. Pushing forward, pressing onward, and climbing upward frames failure as more than blatant mistakes, as the very act of slowing down can be considered a sign of personal weakness. The duck syndrome narrative allows for failure—as long as students keep paddling; the treadmill metaphor allows for stumbles—as long as students keep running.

Popular failure and resilience rhetorics do not uncouple "obligatory striving" and success; instead, striving-for-success operates as the underlying ideal in failure rhetoric. As a result, it may seem as if failure has become more visible and acceptable on college campuses—the taboo lifted—but the failure stories that circulate most widely are ultimately success stories. Or, as Anne Sobel puts it, "Americans love a nice, meaty failure—as long as it ends with success" ("How Failure in the Classroom"). Popular failure rhetoric, specifically "fail-forward" and "build resilience" messaging, brings failure out of the shadows, but it does not eliminate the shadows. Instead, the elevated ideal of successful-failure deepens the shame around failure experiences that do not conform, feeding the silence around unspeakable failures. In what follows, I begin with the emergence of "personal failures," as a concept, in order to track on-going efforts to collapse and expand the rhetorical distance between failure experiences and personal responsibility. Current trends in popular failure rhetoric seem to create distance between failure and personal responsibility; I will show, however, that failure remains deeply personal.

Personal Failures

The idea that an individual can be "a failure" or "a loser," commonplace to the level of cliché today, was born of the boom-and-bust economy of early American capitalism. Sandage points to the moment in U.S. history when failure transformed from an external event (related to business ventures and bankruptcy) to an aspect of individual identity. As Sandage writes, around 1800 "Americans 'made' failures, but it took a while before failures made—or unmade men … Failure was something made, not someone born—until the market revolution" (11). If a business venture failed, the entrepreneur *made* a failure but was not considered to *be* a failure as a person. According to Sandage, both the 1828 and 1855 versions of the *Webster Dictionary* defined failure as "a breaking, or becoming insolvent," but by 1857 *Webster* explicitly connected failure to an individual's character: "some weakness in a man's character, disposition, or habit" (11-12).

Context plays a large role in this revised definition, as the heartbreaks and triumphs of the market revolution demanded explanations. A new language of failure emerged to describe these swings: "wiping out," "flunking out," "go to smash," "fizzle out," "dead broke," and so on (25). The market revolution created a paradoxical pattern of success and failure where "The ideal was unreachable unless a man pushed uphill—yet, pushing and 'going to smash' or appearing 'hard pushed' exposed his weakness to all" (26-7). Efforts to better understand and control this stream of boom-and-bust experiences led to new perceptions of failure, responsibility, and character. It was not enough to blame circumstances or luck; a failed business venture was now the result of personal mistakes and shortcomings. As Sandage concludes, "This was the legacy of the nineteenth century: failure as an imputed deficiency of self" (259). With this shift, a newfound sense of self-monitoring and self-evaluation enters into the work of achieving and maintaining success (11-12). If failure—like success—can be accepted and rejected, claimed and reclaimed, on a personal level, then any individual who is not perpetually working to overcome failure and strive toward success can be considered *a failure*.

Today, framing failure as a "deficiency of self" clashes with the pace and perception of innovation in business, technology, and education. Innovation, as currently conceptualized, requires failure and risk-taking and thus necessitates a language of failure that, at least on the surface, shifts the emphasis away from personal fault or flaw. To frame and control the new stream of boom-and-bust experiences that come with innovation, we have seen the language of "wiping out" and "flunking" transform into mantras such as "fail fast, fail often," "fail better," and "fail forward" (Asghar). In her 2012 commencement address, former Yahoo CEO Carol Bartz streamlines the message into "fail, fast, forward," instructing graduates to: "Recognize you've failed, try to do it fast, learn from it, build on it, and move forward." In the Silicon Valley, this messaging has become so prolific that failure now represents a "rite of passage," even a "badge of honor," to be presented with pride on a résumé (Martin; Roose).

These trends in popular failure rhetoric allow for the illusion of agency, reframing feelings of shame as a speed bump rather than a signal of flawed character; however, the messaging exists under the umbrella of Neoliberal ideals of individualism, efficiency, competition, and profit. As long as Neoliberalism operates as the default for envisioning and interpreting success, failure experiences will perpetually recalibrate to the obligatory striving response, sweeping the complexities of failure into a fast-forward movement and mantra.[1] In a Neoliberal framework where "[i]ndividuals are regarded as rational

---

1. For an example of how this "recalibration" to Neoliberal ideals plays out in political discourse, see James A. McVey's "Recalibrating the State of the Union: Visual Rhetoric and the Temporality of Neoliberal Economics in the 2011 Enhanced State of the Union Address."

economic actors who are expected to make choices that will maximize their human capital" (Stenberg 5), failure becomes a commodity to be acquired and a skill to be mastered in a quick and efficient way. Gross and Alexander, in alignment with Lauren Berlant's *Cruel Optimism,* argue that the Neoliberal pressure to constantly succeed at failure leaves "everyone feel[ing] like he or she is failing at everything, all the time" (287-88). If failure must be strategically and quickly controlled, even mastered, then instead of erasing the concept of personal failure, a new category of failure surfaces: those who fail at failing successfully. Or, as I show in the next section, the true failures fail at building their personal resilience. The mandate to "fail forward" and "build resilience," predicated on privilege and haunted[2] by whiteness, resituates failure in the bodies of individuals.

The Resilience Muscle

Popular failure rhetoric, as explored above, de-emphasizes personal responsibility for failure, but the parallel emphasis on "building resilience" shifts the focus onto the individual's response to failure. The concept of resilience represents hope and empowerment in the face of difficult situations; resilience rhetoric, however, often focuses on individual bodies and neglects the myriad social inequities, stereotypes, and conditions that prevent people from "failing forward."

Through her speeches and recent book collaboration, Sheryl Sandberg reaches large audiences with messaging that links resilience to the body. In her popular 2016 commencement address at UC Berkeley, she invites students to imagine resilience as an embodied capacity, even comparing it to a physical body part that can be exercised. In the speech, Sandberg shares the devastating experience of losing her husband and offers the lessons that she "learned in death." She tells graduates to go out and "build resilience," assuring them: "You are not born with a fixed amount of resilience. Like a muscle, you can build it up, draw on it when you need it." Since delivering the commencement address, Sandberg partnered with Adam Grant to publish a book and create a website dedicated to building resilience. Their website, *Option B*, offers resilience strategies and stories in response to situations ranging from "grief and loss" to "health, illness, and injury" to "abuse and sexual assault." They also provide "strategies to build everyday resilience," again emphasizing the idea of the "resilience muscle." The "Build Your Resilience" section of their

---

2. When I refer to the "haunting" of whiteness, I am drawing on Kennedy, Middleton, and Radcliffe's collection *Rhetorics of Whiteness: Postracial Hauntings in Popular Culture, Social Media, and Education.*

website announces, "Resilience is like a muscle you can build. It's just a matter of knowing how" (Sandberg and Grant).

Far from an anomaly, Sandberg's description of resilience as a personal, embodied capacity aligns with trends in popular rhetoric. Described by Flynn, Sotirin, and Brady in *Feminist Rhetorical Resilience*, "commonsensical and popular understandings" of resilience "emphasize the self-sufficient, heroic individual" (5). This individual has "the ability to respond positively in the face of adverse conditions and calamities, to gain ground where others might give in to difficulties and obstacles" (5-6). Certainly, it can be invigorating to imagine resilience as a capacity for self-improvement that exists within everyone, a muscle that "heroic individuals" can build and flex—especially when faced with the kind of shattering loss that Sandberg experienced or the debilitating pressure of perfectionism that many students face. At the same time, though, the idea that people are born with something like a "resilience muscle" implies that resilience exists equally and occurs naturally within the bodies of all individuals, as part of the human spirit or anatomy. Working under the assumption that all people are equipped with a resilience muscle, if they can just learn how to build it, allows us to celebrate or dismiss individuals (or praise or shame ourselves) based on efforts to build that "muscle"—a mindset that directs attention away from social conditions and constraints.

Resilience-based support plays a vital role in coping, healing, and growth, but the underlying messaging conveyed through popular resilience rhetoric cannot go unquestioned because even the most dedicated striving or the strongest resilience response cannot guarantee success. There will always be what Kate Losse calls the "less buoyant failure stories." People are positioned to fail in irreparable ways as an imperative of capitalism and a result of inherently unjust stereotypes and systems, but the dominant narrative of success still insists that failure exists as a weakness of character and lack of conviction. We cannot, as Tyler Hallmark urges, "ignore the fact that failure affects people differently, and that privilege plays an important role in who is allowed to fail—and who isn't." We must turn our attention toward new conversations about failure, conversations that move beyond what failure is as experienced by individuals and into the realm of how failure operates on larger systemic levels. These concepts—obligatory striving, failing forward, building personal resilience—are not isolated ideas; they all operate together, quietly and consistently, as defining features in the stock story of success in the United States.

Pulling Ourselves Up by Our Resilience

Stock stories, Aja Martinez explains, "feign neutrality and at all costs avoid any blame or responsibility for societal inequality"; they are "powerful because they are often repeated until canonized or normalized" (38). The American Dream, with its "bootstrap mentality," serves as the long-standing stock story of success in the United States. But the story does not end there. The proliferation of failure and resilience rhetoric, "repeated until canonized or normalized," extends "bootstrapping" into a required stance for responding to all forms of adversity. The concept of "building resilience," absorbed into the stock story of success, becomes a form of bootstrapping. Even though the "bootstraps break before the boots are on" and "too many have no boots" (Villaneuva, *Bootstraps* xiv), the emphasis on resilience—framed as an embodied capacity—reinforces the idea that success, failure, and successful-failure are all a matter of personal strength and work ethic. We should all, as the stock story goes, be able to pull ourselves up by our resilience.

Bootstrapping through failure experiences requires ceaseless movement; however, the ability to sustain steady forward momentum comes from privilege. More specifically, freedom and fluidity of movement—what Sara Ahmed refers to as "motility"—is a key feature of whiteness. Ahmed explains, "If whiteness allows bodies to move with comfort through space, and to inhabit the world as if it were home, then those bodies take up more space. Such bodies are shaped by motility, *and may even take the shape of that motility*" ("A Phenomenology," 159, emphasis in original). Failure and resilience rhetoric, with steady movement through adversity as a core element of the messaging, assumes the ability to "move with comfort through space"—movement that applies to both physical and emotional spaces Those who feel as if they can "fail forward" and "build resilience," if they just put their minds to it, are relying (often unconsciously) on the motility granted to some bodies and denied to others.

Ahmed, drawing on Frantz Fanon, describes the ways in which bodily privilege creates or denies movement:

> If classical phenomenology is about 'motility,' expressed in the hopefulness of the utterance 'I can,' Fanon's phenomenology of the black body would be better described in terms of the bodily and social experience of restriction, uncertainty and blockage, or perhaps even in terms of the despair of the utterance 'I cannot.' Husserl and Merleau-Ponty describe the body as 'successful,' as being 'able' to extend itself (through objects) in order to act on and in the world. Fanon helps us to expose this 'success' not as a measure of competence, but as the bodily form of privilege: the ability to move through the world without losing one's way. (161)

Bodily privilege becomes visible in those who can respond (or who automatically respond) to failure, and "fail forward" messaging, with the "I can" mentality. With this mentality, the correlation between building resilience and achieving success is taken for granted. The distance, or what Ahmed refers to as the "proximity," between failure and success feels small, manageable (155). Instead of acknowledging bodily privilege or proximity, failure and resilience rhetorics stress individual "competence," promoting the message that each (courageous) individual has equal "ability to move through the world without losing one's way." Such messaging frames the ability to fail-forward and stay on track as both individual and universal, reinforcing the perception that failure is a personal deficiency.

Ahmed extends the discussion of bodily privilege even further through the idea of "stopping," elaborating how some bodies flow freely into the movement of failing forward, while others are stopped. According to Ahmed,

> For bodies that are not extended by the skin of the social, bodily movement is not so easy. Such bodies are stopped, where the stopping is an action that creates its own impressions. Who are you? Why are you here? What are you doing? Each question, when asked, is a kind of *stopping device:* you are stopped by being asked the question, just as asking the question requires that you be stopped. (161, emphasis in original)

This "stopping," Martinez explains, occurs in experiences of both failure and success: "[M]y race is continually targeted by colleagues, students, and professors as a personal and professional deficit when I struggle, and as an unfair advantage when I succeed" (34). In both cases, race is used as a form of "stopping"— a way to derail forward movement ("unfair advantage") or explain the halting of forward movement ("personal and professional deficit"). Villanueva speaks to the default assumption of "personal and professional deficit" when he writes, "The disproportionately few people of color in front of the classrooms or in our publications, given the ubiquity of the bootstrap mentality, reifies the conception that people of color don't do better because they don't try harder" ("On the Rhetoric," 650-51). The rhetoric of "failing forward" and "building resilience" functions in a way that privileges steady forward movement and positions "stopping" as a personal choice or a sign of weakness, distracting from the social conditions and systems that create barriers.

In contrast to the experience of "stopping," whiteness can have a "smoothing" effect, easing forward movement on the road to success. Drawing from his personal experience, Ira Shor explains, "whiteness smoothed the often rough road I traveled from the working class to a tenured professorship. However, on this peculiar trip, the advantages of my whiteness were rarely drawn to my attention" (Prendergast and Shor 379). Whiteness must, Shor urges, "be distinctly made visible," and failure and resilience rhetoric offer a concrete site for that critical work (379). We must attend to how whiteness functions to smooth the road to success so that we can begin to complicate and unsettle the mythology of resilience bootstrapping. When, for example, we encourage students to "fail forward" in the writing process or on an exam, or when we motivate colleagues to build resilience in their journey along the tenure track, we must remember that striving-for-success is a privileged position, haunted by whiteness, through which some bodies are propelled forward and others restrained, no matter how hard an individual works. The sections that follow offer two entry points for future work: critical engagement in the middle of failure experiences and strategies for un-resolving successful-failure stories.

In the Middle of Failure

Rather than trying to rush through or brush over failure experiences, we should, as Ahmed argues, focus on *stopping*. She explains, "a phenomenology of 'being stopped' might take us in a different direction than one that begins with motility, with a body that 'can do' by flowing into space" ("A Phenomenology" 161). Unsettling patterns and complicating the messaging in failure rhetoric, then, begins from "a phenomenology of 'being stopped'" rather than an imperative to push forward through all forms of adversity. That means we need to both identify and create *stopping* by attending to how bodies are stopped and intentionally stopping during failure experiences with the goal of understanding failure in new ways.

At the 2015 CWPA conference, Shari Stenberg and Zach Beare offered the idea of working "in the middle of failure," focusing specifically on emotion as an entryway into critical engagement with failure. They expressed the concern that "when we talk about the ways that failure might help individuals develop grit as a post-failure affect, we have a tendency to ignore the complexity of emotions that are involved when one is in the middle of failure." Engaging the emotion that surfaces in the middle of failure can uncover the stories we are telling ourselves about how and why we and others failed, and we can begin to shape new questions and responses. As Stenberg and Beare put it, "While so much work talks about how failure can make one stronger and more calloused and more protected, the way that failure also has the potential to puncture and fracture and expose cracks in foundations might be equally as useful." In other words, critically engaging the emotions of failure involves a simultaneous in-and-out-of-body experience where individuals attend to feelings within the body while also looking beyond their experience.

Turning toward the emotion associated with failure experiences conjures what Daniel Gross and Jonathan Alexander refer to as "the critical power of negative emotion" (290). This turn toward emotion follows the path paved by Queer theorists, like Judith Halberstam, who explore how "unhappiness, dissatisfaction, and even failure might serve as entry points to critique the power structures and normalizing discourses that direct our lives and efforts along certain lines" (Gross and Alexander 288). Such an approach does not discount individual experiences of emotion, but instead seeks ways to "turn such failure, our disappointment and frustration, into critique" (289). Gross and Alexander argue, "The cost of forgetting negative emotion, even the experience of failure, is high. Success feels good, but it does not reorient us against unjust norms. Success, as it trumps personal failure, can also numb us to failures that are structural" (290). Working in the middle of failure, turning toward the negative emotion that we experience and witness, can reveal new questions and complexities. Such reorientation can also help us rethink the source of the emotion—particularly with a feeling like shame that is not just produced within, but is also imposed upon, bodies.

Allison Carr refers to failure and shame as "congenial bedfellows." As she explains it, shame moves experiences into the category of failure: "Shame acknowledges the failure, and in so doing, names the failure *as failure*, causing us to feel isolation while making us painfully aware of our relationality" (emphasis in original). As a default response, people tend to isolate themselves and turn inward because, Ahmed explains, shame "feels like an exposure" and "the bind of shame is that it is intensified by being seen by others *as* shame" (*Cultural Politics*, emphasis in original, 103). Shame marks the difference between an individual experiencing a failure and feeling like *a failure*. The idea that an individual can be a personal failure is only possible under the influence of shame. And shame is highly influential because it is personal and situational, as well as socially bound and constructed. Shame entangles the personal and social—"the biology and biography of a person" (Probyn 82).

While shame feels like personal exposure, it can also function to expose. Experiences of failure and feelings of shame reveal the instability of ideology and the fallibility of stock stories and stereotypes. Halberstam writes, "failure recognizes that alternatives are embedded already in the dominant and that power is never total or consistent; indeed failure can exploit the unpredictability of ideology and its indeterminate qualities" (88). The shame associated with failure stems from an implicit agreement or alignment with social expectations, values, and norms. Shame, in other words, contains the rulebook for appropriate versus inappropriate behavior within a community or situation. In order for emotion to have meaning and power, the rules must be agreed upon; or as Laura Micciche puts it, "[O]nly through collective, implicit assent in communal life does emotion have meaning" (11). According to Ahmed, "Shame can work as a deterrent: in order to avoid shame, subjects must enter the 'contract' of the social bond, by seeking to approximate a social ideal. Shame can also be experienced as *the affective cost of not following the scripts of normative existence*" (106-7, emphasis in original). People can avoid shame by sticking to the "script," and they experience what Carr describes as "the raw sting of shame" when they stray from that script or break the rules.

In the case of failure experiences, there are many ways to break the rules. One of them is to defy the expectations of obligatory striving—to stop or be stopped. If striving exists as the norm associated with success, then those who do not strive or cannot "bounce back" into the movement of striving, are not following the script. Breaking the "social bond" of striving can thus usher in feelings of shame, directing failure into the bodies of individuals (*I am not working hard enough, trying hard enough, doing enough…I am not enough*). Shame sounds an alarm. Or, in Ahmed's words, "When shamed, one's body seems to burn up with the negation that is perceived (self-negation); and shame impresses upon the skin, as an intense feeling of the subject 'being against itself.' Such a feeling of negation, which is taken on by the subject as a sign of its own failure, is usually experienced before another" (103). When individuals feel shame "burn" in the body and "impress on the skin," they often collapse inward, spiraling into accusatory and punishing questions: How could I…? Why didn't I…? Why can't I…?

Turning toward "the critical power of negative emotion" in the middle of a failure experience can transform shame-based feelings and judgements into a spotlight that illuminates the script, creating an opportunity for inquiry that moves beyond self-blame. In other words, an emotion like shame makes the social norms, stereotypes, and rules of the situation visible, and we can respond to feelings of shame in ways that move the emotion out of individual bodies and into new forms of conversation. For Gross and Alexander, negative emotions, at their best, "signal the need for critique and often motivate people who experience the world differently" (286-7). Engaging the negative emotion of failure as a critical tool means changing the emphasis in questions of self-blame, diverting attention away from the "I": *How* could I? *Why* didn't I? *Why* can't I?

Meagan Rogers illustrates the shift away from personal blame when she advocates for "racial awareness narratives" as a pedagogical strategy for surfacing white privilege (223). In her classes, she shares a personal story about a moment in which she was "both unintentionally racist and consciously antiracist" (228). In telling this story, she directly acknowledges the feelings of shame that the story evokes, but she does not focus the narrative on her feelings; instead, she explains, "I placed that shame alongside my conscious choice on how I acted" (229). The idea of "placing shame alongside" failure experiences opens up important avenues for conversation with students and colleagues. First, we can encourage intentional slowing or stopping—when failure is fresh—to place shame alongside the experience in order to situate personal feelings within social circumstances. Shame, read like a text, contains a list of "should" statements that are rooted in values and beliefs. In failure experiences, we can unravel feelings of shame like a scroll: we can spread out the script and read the list of instructions, drawing the values to the surface so that they become a dialogue instead of a directive.

At the same time, we must consider the motility in this emotional self-monitoring. We must understand that such intentional slowing or stopping—as well as *choosing* to put shame alongside an experience—is a sign of white privilege. As such, we must always ask: Who is allowed to make intentional stops in order to work in the middle of failure, and who is not? Who can "place shame alongside" and who does not have a choice? How are bodies and experiences marked with shame?

This invitation to inquiry does not dismiss the importance of behavioral guidelines or the realities of personal responsibility; shame functions in important ways to control destructive behavior and spark personal reflection. The point, instead, is to identify default responses to shame and failure—the impulse to internalize the emotion and absorb the responsibility. When we stop, or pay attention to stopping, in the middle of failure, we can start to unpack the shame and scrutinize the sources of societal ideals and systemic oppression.

Un-resolving Failure Stories

In addition to the analysis that can take place in the middle of failure, we must also turn our attention toward storytelling. When failures are translated into narratives, we tend to see the same storyline over and over. And it makes sense: the failure stories that are shared in public venues emphasize successful-failure because success and failure are bound to individual identity and authority. The storyteller must construct the story in a way that balances vulnerability and strength in order to maintain or advance his or her *ethos*. However, when the failure story begins with a successful outcome, the storyteller inevitably works backwards, recasting failures as bumps on the road to success. The complicated movement of exploration and struggle gets funneled into the progression toward the successful outcome. We can, however, work to un-resolve failure stories. We can unpack existing examples of successful-failure narratives: unraveling the plotlines, identifying the tropes, and unsettling the assumptions.

Fail-forward rhetoric reaches large audiences, on a regular basis, through the commencement speech genre. As mentioned earlier, Sheryl Sandberg launched her resilience message during a UC Berkeley commencement address to a live audience of thousands and, since then, to a YouTube audience of hundreds of thousands. Additionally, two of the most well-known and widely circulated commencement speeches, delivered by Steve Jobs at Stanford and

JK Rowling at Harvard, focus on successful-failure as the central theme. All three commencement speakers—Sandberg, Jobs, and Rowling—are white, and they each addressed audiences at elite institutions. Embodying whiteness at an elite university does not guarantee success; in fact, the ubiquity of success often intensifies the fear of failure. Access to resources and the motility of whiteness does, however, decrease the distance between failure and success. Thus, "fail forward" is more than an inspirational message—it's a viable option. On the other hand, fewer resources and less motility increases the gulf between success and failure, making the forward-failure a larger and larger leap. When commencement speeches are posted online and circulated through social media, the rhetorical situation changes, but the message does not. This implies equal access to successful-failure and reinforces the emphasis on individual resilience and courage, regardless of circumstances.

Steve Jobs' 2005 commencement address offers an example of a speech that was delivered at Stanford University but then reached millions of people through YouTube (32 million views and counting). In the speech, Job shares three stories that were pivotal to his success: each one a failure that transformed into a turning point; each one haunted by whiteness and motility. In the three stories he shares, he has access—access to a college campus; access to financial resources; access to the very best health care. Thus, even though the speech revolves around experiences that seem, initially, to be stopping points, Jobs' stories ultimately have a sense of unfettered movement. He conjures the courage and embodies the resilience to regain momentum, but the undercurrent of movement, the motility, was always there—a stream that he could dip his feet back into. To un-resolve the successful-failure narrative in his speech, we can ask questions such as: What resources are required in order to follow his advice? How and where does his whiteness (and maleness) allow him to move freely where others may be stopped? How is his body read, during and after failure?

Un-resolving failure stories means identifying plotlines that highlight the courageous individual and ignore the privilege that enables movement and rewards courage. Additionally, we can work to un-resolve the genre of "failure story," seeking to identify the many sub-categories that exist under the umbrella. What if, for example, we categorized Steve Job's commencement address as a *racially privileged failure narrative*? How might such a distinction help us imagine different experiences and expand the genre of the failure story?

Commencement speeches provide a large archive of successful-failure narratives to analyze, but the narratives are constructed within tight constraints (i.e., an inspirational message, delivered in a culminating moment, often by someone outside of the community). With the proliferation of resilience programs on college campuses, more and more students and faculty are sharing their failure stories on a regular basis. As failure and resilience discourse gains traction, we must seek productive opportunities to un-resolve the stories that circulate locally, bringing new layers of rhetorical awareness into our campus conversations and resources.

The Stories Alone

Thus far, I have focused on challenging and complicating failure rhetoric; however, I want to pause here to emphasize the important—even life-saving—work that "fail-forward" messaging can do on college campuses. The 2015 *New York Times* article, "Suicide on Campus and the Pressure of Perfection," links "America's culture of hyperachievement" to the increase in "suicide clusters" at high schools and colleges across the country (Scelfo). These "clusters"—a group of 3-6 student suicides in a single year and on a single campus—show the urgency behind the "fail forward" and "building resilience" messaging. Many students live with a constant, often debilitating, fear of falling behind and failing to live up to expectations.

To mitigate the pressure of perfectionism, colleges and universities are developing programs that directly address failure and resilience. The Resilience Consortium, for example, represents the combined efforts of ten elite universities seeking to help students build their "capacities for persistence, creativity, emotional intelligence, grit, cognitive flexibility, risk-taking, agency, adapting to change, delaying gratification, learning from failure, and questioning success." Tulane University offers a program called "The Untold Story of Failure" that encourages students, faculty, staff, and alumni to share their stories as a way to "normalize the idea of failure and setbacks." The Thrive program at UT-Austin offers an app that provides access to student stories and interactive activities to encourage reflection practices and coping strategies. These programs, and many others across the country, are responding to the immediacy of the pain and pressure that students experience. Sharing failure stories can offer a profound moment of catharsis, particularly for students who have struggled in silence. As resilience programs continue to evolve, we must look for ways to extend story sharing to include story shaping.

When faced with the crisis of high suicide rates, providing coping mechanisms and cathartic experiences can feel more urgent than critical engagement with the rhetoric of failure, but we have to consider the long-term effects of the language we use and the storylines we promote. If the stock story of success goes unquestioned, then the coping and catharsis will fade and the fear will return. The invitation to share failure stories, alone, does not make such sharing safe. Martinez describes her time in the academy as full of "barriers of institutional racism, sexism, and classism" (33) and she has faced, as quoted earlier, "unrelenting experiences in the institution in which my race is continually targeted by colleagues, students, and professors as a personal and professional deficit when I struggle" (34). The decision to share a personal failure story in the high-pressure environment of higher education is a sign of bravery; but the freedom to share a personal failure story—without barriers and targeting—is a sign of white privilege.

What, then, does it look like to give voice to a wider range of experiences when doing so can prove vulnerable and unsafe? Critical race theory, and counter-storytelling methodology in particular, offers a starting point for envisioning how we might expose and challenge stock stories of success on our campuses. For example, Martinez models dialogic composite storytelling, placing a stock story and counter-story side-by-side. In Martinez's example, the story revolves around Alejandra, a character who has failed her PhD qualifying exam—a context that Martinez selected because it serves "a programmatic gatekeeping function for graduate students," a form of stopping (40). From the perceived failure, Martinez puts forward two very different conversations. In the stock story, three professors assess "Alejandra's progress and status in the program" (40) and whether or not she is a "good fit" (42). The stock story contains a restrictive rubric for success, full of assumptions about how a "successful student" should operate in academia. The counter-story, presented as a phone call between Alejandra and her mother, takes place after the program director has advised Alejandra to leave the program. Their conversation is full of questions, and, as such, models the work of slowing down to unpack assumptions in the face of a perceived failure.

As college campuses continue to develop resources and conversation around failure and resilience, we need to uncover the underlying stock stories and map the parameters around "speakable" and "unspeakable" failures on our campuses. From there, we need to integrate counter-storytelling practices into the collection, distribution, and discussion of failure stories. Composite storytelling offers a starting point, a way to begin surfacing a wider range of stories and experiences without asking students to risk the vulnerability of the spotlight.

Conclusion

During the 2005 commencement season, the same year that Steve Jobs took the stage, David Foster Wallace delivered the address at Kenyon College. He started with a "didactic little parable-ish" story about two young fish who happen to pass by an older fish. As they pass each other, the older fish nods at them and says, "Morning, boys. How's the water?" After they swim on for a bit, one fish turns to the other and says, "What the hell is water?" Wallace immediately assured the audience that he would not assume the role of "wise, older fish explaining what water is to you younger fish"; instead, "The point of the fish story is merely that the most obvious, important realities are often the ones that are hardest to see and talk about." At the end of the speech, he returned to the fish parable to describe the "capital-T Truth," as he saw it:

> It is about the real value of a real education, which has almost nothing to do with knowledge, and everything to do with simple awareness; awareness of what is so real and essential, so hidden in plain sight all around us, all the time, that we have to keep reminding ourselves over and over:
> This is water.
> This is water.

When power and privilege go unquestioned, when whiteness goes unnoticed, the successful-failure narrative—the idea that all courageous and resilient individuals can and should fail-forward—becomes the "water," the stock story of success that is "hidden in plain sight all around us, all the time."

Seeing the "water," for me, started with the realization that I was stuck in a thought pattern that perpetually looped metanoia back into kairos, failure into success. But it's not just a "loop" in my thinking: it's my privilege, my white privilege in particular, that defaults to the perception of successful-failure as an open road for the brave and hard-working. I have come to realize that the story of Kairos, the one that captivated me as a graduate student, is a story of motility. The god of opportunity, with wings on their back and feet, embodies constant and unfettered movement, and I was projecting that motility onto the concept of metanoia. Instead of questioning the freedom of movement embedded in kairos, I tried to extend that movement, that motility, into the realm of missed opportunity. I encouraged students to reimagine regret as a gateway and to mobilize failures into stepping stones. But then, when I started listening to my students' silences and struggles, the underlying privilege in my pedagogy surfaced.

When I turned toward failure to seek understanding instead of answers, the quick and efficient pace of striving slowed into the layered work of inquiry. I focused on surfacing questions and stitching together ideas: obligatory striving, the rhetorical construction of "personal failure," resilience bootstrapping, the haunting of whiteness, the middle of failure, and unresolved plotlines. Instead of a solution or formula, these pieces illustrate a process—a snapshot of one person's effort to unravel a stock story to see how it's built. To avoid replacing one stock story with another, we have to not only deconstruct stock stories but also acknowledge the ways in which we contribute or comply. That is the work, messy and slow, that will bring new light and language to the unspeakable failures.

Acknowledgments

This article came together like a puzzle, constructed over several years, and I am grateful to the many people who helped me find pieces and make connections: Bruce Ballenger, Kim Cross, Whitney Douglas, Jim Fredricksen, Stephanie Hartselle, Andrea Lunsford, Laura Micciche, Kathy Myers, Michelle Payne, Shari Stenberg, Glenn Stout, and the anonymous reviewers. I feel particularly grateful for the feedback I received from Asao Inoue. I appreciate every word he wrote, but there was one particularly transformative sentence: *You miss at every turn any discussion of race.* I carried that sentence into my revision process, and I carry it with me every day, at every turn.

Works Cited

Ahmed, Sara. "A Phenomenology of Whiteness." *Feminist Theory*, vol. 8, no. 2, 2007, pp. 149-68. doi: 10.1177/1464700107078139
—. *The Cultural Politics of Emotion.* Routledge, 2004.
Asghar, Rob. "Why Silicon Valley's 'Fail Fast' Mantra Is Just Hype." *Forbes*, Forbes Magazine, 14 July 2014, www.forbes.com/sites/robasghar/2014/07/14/why-silicon-valleys-fail-fast-mantra-is-just-hype/#2dc66a0724bc.
Bartz, Carol. "UW—Madison 2012 Spring Commencement." *YouTube*, uploaded by UW-Madison, 20 May 2012, www.youtube.com/watch?v=AYWHVv4vRVU.
Bennett, Jessica. "On Campus, Failure is on the Syllabus." *The New York Times*, The New York Times, 24 June 2017, www.nytimes.com/2017/06/24/fashion/fear-of-failure.html?mcubz=0.
Carr, Allison. "In Support of Failure." *Composition Forum*, vol. 27, 2013, n. pag. compositionforum.com/issue/27/failure.php.
Flynn, Elizabeth A., Patricia Sotirin, and Ann Brady. "Introduction: Feminist Rhetorical Resilience—Possibilities and Impossibilities." *Feminist Rhetorical Resilience*, edited by Elizabeth A. Flynn, Patricia Sotirin, and Ann Brady. Utah State UP, 2012, pp. 1-29.
Gross, Daniel M. and Jonathan Alexander. "Frameworks for Failure." *Pedagogy*, vol. 16, no. 2, 2016, pp. 273-95. *Project Muse*, doi: 10.1215/15314200-3435884.
Halberstam, Judith. *The Queer Art of Failure.* Duke UP, 2011.
Hallmark, Tyler. "When 'Failure is OK' is Not OK" *The Chronicle of Higher Education.* 11 February 2018. www.chronicle.com/article/When-Failure-Is-OK-Is/242489.
"Home." Resilience Consortium. *Harvard University*, resilienceconsortium.bsc.harvard.edu/.
Jobs, Steve. Stanford Commencement Address. *Stanford News*, 12 June 2005, news.stanford.edu/2005/06/14/jobs-061505/.
Kennedy, Tammie M., Joyce Irene Middleton, Krista Ratcliffe, editors. *Rhetorics Of Whiteness: Postracial Hauntings in Popular Culture, Social Media, and Education.* Southern Illinois UP, 2017.
Liddell, Henry George, and Robert Scott. *A Greek-English Lexicon.* Oxford UP, 1948.

Losse, Kate. "The Art of Failing Upward." *The New York Times Sunday Review*, The New York Times, 5 Mar. 2016, www.nytimes.com/2016/03/06/opinion/sunday/the-art-of-failing-upward.html?mcubz=0.

Martin, Claire. "Wearing Your Failures on Your Sleeve." *The New York Times*, The New York Times, 8 Nov. 2014. www.nytimes.com/2014/11/09/business/wearing-your-failures-on-your-sleeve.html.

Martinez, Aja Y. "A Plea for Critical Race Theory Counterstory: Stock Story versus Counterstory Dialogues Concerning Alejandra's 'Fit' in the Academy." *Composition Studies*, vol. 42, no. 2, 2014, pp. 33–55.

McVey, James A. "Recalibrating the State of the Union: Visual Rhetoric and the Temporality of Neoliberal Economics in the 2011 Enhanced State of the Union Address." *POROI*, vol. 11, no. 2, 2015, pp. 1-24, doi: 10.13008/2151-2957.1231.

Myers, Kelly, Herman Davis, Dillon Haws, Frieda Johnson, Alex Lierman, and Amber Sutherland. "Metanoic Movement: The Transformative Power of Regret." *College Composition and Communication Videos*, March 2017, cccc.ncte.org/cccc/ccc/videos.

—. "Metanoia and the Transformation of Opportunity." *Rhetoric Society Quarterly*, vol. 41, no.1, 2011, pp. 1-18, doi: 10.1080/02773945.2010.533146.

Micciche, Laura R. *Doing Emotion: Rhetoric, Writing, Teaching*. Heinemann, 2007.

Prendergast, Catherine and Ira Shor. "When Whiteness Is Visible: The Stories We Tell about Whiteness." *Rhetoric Review*, vol. 24, no. 4, 2005, pp. 377-85, *JSTOR*, https://www.jstor.org/stable/20176678.

Probyn, Elspeth. "Writing Shame." *The Affect Theory Reader*, edited by Gregory J. Seigworth, Melissa Gregg, Lauren Berlant, Elspeth Probyn, Brian Massumi, and Sara Ahmed, Duke UP, 2009, pp. 72-90.

Rodgers, Meagan. "The Pedagogical Role of a White Instructor's Racial Awareness Narrative." *Rhetorics of Whiteness: Postracial Hauntings in Popular Culture, Social Media, and Education*, edited by Tammie M. Kennedy, Joyce Irene Middleton, Krista Ratcliffe. Southern Illinois UP, 2017, pp. 222-34.

Roose, Kevin. "The Failure Fetish in Silicon Valley." *New York Magazine*, New York Media, 25 March 2014, nymag.com/daily/intelligencer/2014/03/silicon-valley-failure-fetish.html.

Sandage, Scott. *Born Losers: A History of Failure in America*. Harvard UP, 2006.

Sandberg, Sheryl. "Sheryl Sandberg Gives UC Berkeley Commencement Keynote Speech." *YouTube*, uploaded by UC Berkeley, 16 May 2016, www.youtube.com/watch?v=iqm-XEqpayc.

Sandberg, Sheryl and Adam Grant. "Build Resilience." *OptionB*, optionb.org/build-resilience.

Scelfo, Julie. "Suicide on Campus and the Pressure of Perfection." *The New York Times*, The New York Times, 27 July 2015, www.nytimes.com/2015/08/02/education/edlife/stress-social-media-and-suicide-on-campus.html.

Sobel, Anne. "How Failure in the Classroom Is More Instructive Than Success." *The Chronicle of Higher Education*, 5 May 2014, www.chronicle.com/article/How-Failure-in-the-Classroom/146377?cid=at&utm_medium=en&utm_source=at.

Stenberg, Shari J. *Repurposing Composition: Feminist Interventions for a Neoliberal Age.* UP of Colorado, 2015.

Stenberg, Shari and Zach Beare. "If at First You Don't Succeed: Considering Failure as Critical In(ter)vention," Sustainable Writing/Program/Administrators, CWPA, 17 July 2015, Boise Centre, Boise ID. Panel presentation.

"The Untold Story of Failure." *Tulane University*, success.tulane.edu/node/2826.

Villanueva, Victor. *Bootstraps: From an American Academic of Color.* NCTE, 1993.

—. "On the Rhetoric and Precedents of Racism." *College Composition and Communication*, vol. 50, no. 4, 1999, pp. 645-61, http://www.jstor.org/stable/358485.

Wallace, David Foster. "Kenyon College 2005 Commencement Address." *YouTube*, 21 May 2005. www.youtube.com/watch?v=8CrOL-ydFMI.

"I Can't Do Cartwheels, So I Write": Students' Writing Affect

Amy D. Williams

This article uses an ethnographic case study of high school writers preparing for college to explore students' writing experiences in and outside of school. In each domain, students experience affects related to embodiment, relationships, and movement, but the study reveals qualitative differences in those affective experiences. These differences seem to underlie students' overall orientation toward personal, out-of-school writing and away from in-school writing. Interpreting students' orientations as affective responses or consequences, the author offers suggestions for writing pedagogies that might arouse the embodied, relational, and movement affects students prefer within the domain of academic writing. The article thus positions the study of affect as integral to composition theory, research, and teaching.

Within Composition as a post-1960 discipline, intimations of bodily affect appear as early as Sondra Perl's 1980 work on composing processes. Borrowing a term from philosopher Eugene Gendlin, Perl labels hesitations in students' writing processes as "felt sense," which she applies to writing in this way: "The move is not to any words on the page nor to the topic but to feelings or non-verbalized perceptions that *surround* the words, or to what the words already present *evoke* in the writer. The move draws on sense experience . . . . The move occurs inside the writer, to what is physically felt" (364-365, italics in original). Perl's use of felt sense bears striking similarities to contemporary affect theory, which grounds subjective experience in embodied sensory perceptions that may precede or exceed conscious recognition. In the nearly forty years since Perl, it has become almost commonplace to theorize writing as an affective relationship between writers and writing environments, which scholars describe metaphorically as ecologies, networks, matrices, and rhizomes. Marilyn Cooper's assertion that writing is not "the product of minds somehow separated from bodies" points to the importance of a writing body's affective experience and, indirectly, to affect's breadth—its ability to incorporate both mind and body (18).

Despite the field's apparent comfort with affect theory, the use of affect in research and practice "remains very much in progress" (Micciche, "Material" 489). There is more to learn about how students affectively experience writing. This article contributes to that work by using an affective lens to explore students' composing experiences in and outside of school. I conducted this

IRB-approved research in an elective, writing-intensive workshop designed to prepare high school students—particularly students who are underrepresented in higher education—for success in college writing. These questions guided my research:

- How do students affectively experience writing in academic settings, including a literacy program designed to help them develop academic writing skills?
- How do students affectively experience writing outside of school?

The findings reveal affective dimensions of students' self-chosen and academic writing practices, particularly their affective orientations toward personal writing and away from academic writing. Importantly, these orientations appear to be rooted in experiential differences that exceed common emotional labels—"like" or "hate," for example. Rather, those labels seem to function as shorthand for affects related to embodiment, relationships, and movement.

Because students often use the language of emotion to describe their writing experiences, some researchers accept affect as reducible to emotion.[1] For example, Joanne Addison and Sharon McGee describe the "truly affective" component of their research: asking high school and college students to identify their "feelings" about writing by selecting from options that include "enjoy," "look forward to," and "like" (166, 168). The authors correctly assert the importance of understanding students' emotional responses to writing. "After all," they say, "if people just do not like to write, [writing teachers] have an entirely different battle to wage" (166). However, to say a student likes or dislikes writing or that students find some writing pleasurable and other writing painful fails to fully account for their affective experiences.

Drawing on interviews and student-authored freewrite journals, I offer a more complete affective understanding of what students mean when they say that they like (and hate) certain kinds of writing. In interviews, I asked students to describe all the writing they do—where they write, what their bodies and minds do while writing, and what sensations and stimulations they experience. Understanding students' writing affect in this more expansive way—beyond just emotions and feelings—is vital because, as Julie Nelson argues, "repeated experience with similar affects grow together to create an underlying disposition and, in turn, our own affective capacities" (par. 12). Through repeated experiences, affects stick to bodies. Thus, the negative affects that students in my study associate with academic writing present a challenge for teachers of the college composition classes they may enter. Importantly, however, some scholars argue that affect can also be unstuck or, as Jenny Edbauer Rice says, be "disarticulate[d]" and "rearticulate[d]" (210). This quality of affect—its ability to be both tenacious and loose—points to affect's pedagogical potential. After laying a theoretical foundation for my research and explaining my methodology, I explore the affective differences students describe in personal and academic writing and suggest how understanding affect can transform pedagogy in ways that draw students toward academic writing.

Theorizing Affective Bodies, Relationships, and Movement

In its broadest sense, affect concerns bodies and how they perceive, respond to, resonate with, interpret, and evaluate the forces and objects they encounter. Though intrinsic to Rhetoric and Composition, the body's status as an object of scholarly and pedagogical interest in both fields has waxed and waned. Affect theory insists that it be a focal point.

Affect privileges a body that is not self-contained and independent, but unavoidably entangled in an assemblage of forces, energies, practices, objects, and other bodies. While Perl described "sense experience" that occurs "inside the writer," affect scholars today focus on affect as a phenomenon that emerges between bodies and material and immaterial objects, ranging from the obvious (pens, paper, keyboards, desks, teachers, assignments, and readers) to the unexpected (animals, feelings, and locations). These, Laura Micciche notes, are not mere accompaniments to writing but rather "partnerships that constitute the very condition of writing itself" ("Material" 499). The objects writers respond to include anything that has the capacity to affect writers, even "objects in the sense of values, practice… as well as aspirations" (Ahmed 41). Thus, writing itself—as a practice, a value, and an aspiration—forms part of the assemblage in which a writer is embodied.

This emphasis on writing as interactions links embodiment to a concern for relationships. Gregory Seigworth and Melissa Gregg locate affect in "intensities that pass body to body (human, nonhuman, part-body, and otherwise), in those resonances that circulate about, between, and sometimes stick to bodies and worlds" (1). Affect is "how we are touched by what we are near" (Ahmed 30). Affective connections include those between a writer and reader, a writer and a text, and a writer and writing itself, as Victor Vitanza elaborates: "What writing or composition wants is a writer! To invite someone to become a writer! . . . A body filled with tics that cannot but (not) write! Twitchings." Notice that writing invites and wants, and writers respond through ineluctable tics and twitchings. Vitanza's complication of agency underscores again that writing is not an autonomous cognitive act. Writing's wild, insatiable desiring that provokes voluntary and involuntary affective responses in the writer.

A third affective concern, movement, affirms the body as always in motion within an assemblage of swirling elements. Incompatible with stasis, affect is not interested in what a thing is, but in its "becomings"—its potential for change and for new ways of being (Deleuze xxx). Becomings unfold within and across relationships through intentional and haphazard movements. "The drama of contingency" characterizes affective movement, suggesting that everything is both possible and provisional (Ahmed 30). At the same time, affect moves bodies in ways that are not purely random. Sara Ahmed clarifies: "To be affected by something is to evaluate that thing. Evaluations are expressed in how bodies turn toward things…Those things we do not like we move away from" (31-2). The evaluation of an object as good or bad relates to immediate affective responses and also to the future happiness (or unhappiness) that we assume will result from our proximity to that object. Thus affect includes at least three kinds of movement: sensations of motion, processes of changing or becoming, and orientations toward and away from other bodies and objects. Together, concerns of embodiment, relationships, and movement provide some definitional integrity for my research; however, they are not the discrete categories my language may imply. Rather, the data shows considerable interplay and overlap between and across these concerns.

Researching Affect

Its emergent and fluid nature makes affect an unwieldy research topic, yet my study shows how ethnographic methods can be used to trace and describe affect. My research site is a collaboration between a public school district and a university College of Education.[2] The annual summer workshop is designed for secondary students, some identified as "struggling" writers because they have failed a language arts class, scored below proficient on standardized tests, or been identified by a teacher as potentially benefitting from additional instruction. Pedagogically, the workshop uses a self-regulated strategy development model (Graham et al.) intended to provide students explicit instruction about writing skills and strategies, help them develop positive attitudes about and confidence in their own writing abilities, and teach them methods for monitoring and regulating their own writing development. During the two-week workshop, students write an argument essay and daily freewrite journal entries. This article draws from my analysis of the freewrite journals and interviews in which I asked students about all writing they do, not just their writing in the workshop. I spent three summers in the workshop. During the first two years, I observed the workshop and worked with a few students on their essays. I also obtained IRB approval to analyze anonymized texts students produced in the workshop (diagnostic essays and freewrite journals). During the third year, I undertook an IRB-approved research project to compile fieldnotes and interview that year's participants.[3] The research methods and questions about writing affect I used in the final year emerged from my participation during the first two years and my analysis of the journals, as I describe below. When I interviewed students during the last three days of the

2016 workshop, I asked them about their writing experiences and affect generally, as I had not yet anticipated the themes of embodiment, relationships, and movement that emerged as I coded the data (Appendix A).[4]

Because my interest is students' composing experiences, I do not say much about the quality of the texts (journals and essays) they write in the workshop. Faculty and peers give students abundant feedback on drafts of their essays, but no one grades the final copy; students receive academic credit just for attending the workshop and completing the essay. The freewrite journals are designed to help students develop "fluency," which faculty believe will help them on computer-assessed essays where length is a predictor of score. Students write in the journals for a timed period each day, trying to increase the amount of text (measured in number of written lines) they produce. Workshop faculty do not record number of lines written and do not read the journals. Because students composed the journals as part of the regular curriculum and not for my research and because I did not ask for journals until the workshop's end, the students who contributed their anonymized journals wrote with no anticipation that their journals would be assessed or analyzed.

As I have shared my research, some have objected that students' texts (especially the freewrite journals and other out-of-school writing they describe) would likely be "a mess" by conventional assessments. That may be true, but at the same time textual quality does not reveal much about the writer's affective experience. In fact, from an affective standpoint, the quality of students' texts might matter only if evaluations of those texts become part of the affective ecology—a C grade on a paper may provoke different affects than an A grade, for example. For workshop students, evaluations of their final essays and their personal writing are mostly self-appraisals (students' own sense of the text's effectiveness or an audience's probable response). Thus in the context of the workshop, the affective impact of assessment is more muted than it might be in traditional academic settings.

Using a grounded theory approach, I first read the freewrite journals, interview transcripts, and fieldnotes holistically to identify salient patterns, themes, and issues related to affect. I applied preliminary codes to chunks of discourse, for example, *describes the body or a bodily sensation*. Those preliminary themes guided additional rounds of coding, in which I created more detailed and refined codes and concepts, for example, *uses positive language to describe embodiment*. Axial coding (Corbin and Strauss) allowed me to put the data back together as I noticed connections and relationships between codes regarding affective responses, writing domains, and writing tasks, and as I gathered these around what emerged as core phenomena: relationships, embodiment, and movement. I coded freewrite journals from twenty students (40% of 2015 population) and interviews with thirty-one students (75% of 2016 population).

Tracing Affect across Data Sets and Writing Domains

The following discussion of the two data sets (journals and interviews) illustrates both how my research evolved and how that evolution led me to trace students' affect across writing domains (in- and out-of-school). Again, the journals were a daily exercise in "keep[ing] your hand moving." Students knew they could write about anything they chose, but faculty provided prompts as a source of invention. The prompts served both expressivist and self-regulating functions related to the curriculum's goals:

- Who am I as a writer?
- What do I like or dislike about writing?
- What do I need to do to get better at writing?

When they write about themselves as writers, students primarily describe experiences with writing *outside* the workshop. In fact, of the sixteen journal writers who claim to "like" or "love" writing, fifteen describe enjoying writing tasks and writing topics that seemed unlikely to be required in school. For example, students say they enjoy writing to "get my expressions out," "to vent," to "say my problems," to record "my crazy hectic complicated life," to express "whatever comes to my mind, sometimes about my feelings or my day," and to describe "people who are more fucked up than I am."

Furthermore, students seem to enjoy non-academic genres most, those written outside of school. Only two students (10%) who "like" or "love" writing mention writing in academic genres such as argument papers, persuasive essays, and reports. It is not surprising that these students enjoy self-directed writing but dislike required writing. Addison and McGee report a similar finding, with nearly half of high school students in their study claiming to enjoy personal rather than academic writing. The higher percentage (75%) of happy journal writers in my study perhaps reflects the context: an elective summer writing program. Students who attend may be more interested in and committed to writing than a general high school population. On the other hand, my study included a lower percentage of writers who claimed to enjoy all writing tasks (10% compared to Addison and McGee's 28%). Importantly, in my study, students' out-of-school writing often resembled what might happen in classrooms that use expressivist pedagogies to encourage "self-sponsored, imaginative, contemplative, and exploratory" writing (Harris 79). Proponents of these pedagogies have long contended that students find such writing therapeutic, satisfying, and joyful, and my data supports that position.

An important moment in the research process occurred early in my reading of the journals when I encountered this response to the prompt asking about writing "like" and "dislike":

> I like fictional writing. It is, to me, the immense joy of creating entire worlds derived from a single mind, a single entity. You exist as if you were a god from the tales of theology in your own universe. Nonfiction, however, presents itself as a hassle. Your limiters exist in the concepts of logic and facts, and you exist as a dot, trapped in a swarm.

The evocative metaphors, the stark contrast between fiction's virtual possibility and nonfiction's confinement, the acknowledgment of writing's affective power over and on a writer, and the tremendous agency afforded nonfiction writing—resulting in the writer's embodiment as a "dot"—all captivated me. I returned to this passage again and again. Clearly, this student understood writing genres and writing domains as distinct affective experiences, but what about other students? How did their affective writing experiences vary across domains? What role did affect play in their writing enjoyment? Armed with these questions, I returned to the workshop in 2016. I asked this new group of students to describe their experiences with writing inside and outside of school: "Think about the writing you do [inside school/outside of school] and try to describe what that feels like for you—maybe describe where you are when you write and your feelings or thoughts or how your body feels."

Perhaps the most surprising finding in interviews was how much writing these "struggling" writers do outside of school. Of the thirty-one students I interviewed, 77% write regularly outside of school, and another 16% report writing at least occasionally. The occasional writers include three students who initially answered "no" or "not really" when asked if they write outside of school. In follow-up questions, I asked about texting and social media platforms like Facebook and Twitter. These students then acknowledged their SMS and social media use but seemed surprised that I considered these forms of writing.[5] Only two students (7%) claimed to only write in school. This means that despite having abundant non-writing recreational options, 93% of students choose to spend at least part of their leisure time writing. This impressive number suggests that personal writing "affects [them] in a good way" (Ahmed 38). One said it makes her "feel free," another that it "lifts weights off my shoulders." Overwhelmingly for students in my study, to use the words of one, personal writing is "more of a want than a need."

Equally impressive, the interviews show that outside of school, students write in a variety of genres, across multiple media, and for different purposes. Students compose in many creative genres—poems, plays, stories, fan fiction, novels, and character sketches—as well as transactional genres—takeout orders, applications, instructions, letters, and email. Overall, these genres represent writing that fulfills practical, therapeutic, and recreational purposes and that helps these young writers feel competent in outside-of-school domains. Altogether, it is an impressive list that speaks to the generic range, literacy, and rhetorical ability of students who have been identified as "struggling" writers.

Importantly, students' out-of-school writing falls primarily in "creative" genres while their in-school writing is done in genres typically thought of as academic—argument, expository, and literary analysis papers. In 2008, researchers at the University of Washington identified school as the dominant domain for fiction, poetry, freewriting, and even journaling (Rounsaville et al.). Perhaps due to the adoption of Common Core standards, this is not the case for the students in my study. One student says of her high school curriculum, "All we do in high school is argumentative for four years, and it really kills the students' love of writing to just do essays. I feel like if there were opportunities to work on poetry, stories, creative anything, it would make writing so much easier for students who struggle with it." But another student expresses "serious doubts" that poetry would ever be rewarded in school. School, he says, is full of "negative energy and pressure to advance, because you won't make it in the world if you don't make it in school. There is not that pressure with leisure things like poetry." So creative writing gets a back-handed compliment: students prefer it, but it is not something that is going to help anyone "make it in the world."

In dismissing creative writing's value, this student tacitly accepts academic writing's status as a social good—something widely accepted as promising well-being, contentment, and happiness. If you can write well, then good things (academic success, college degree, rewarding employment, prosperity) will follow (Ahmed 41, adapted). Thus, students who turn to academic writing because it affects them in a good way are in harmony with a community that "shares an orientation toward [writing] as being good" (Ahmed 38). But most of the students I interviewed are not affected by academic writing in a good way; it is not the writing they turn toward. To understand why this is so, I trace students' affect across the two writing domains: personal and in-school (especially their regular secondary classrooms). In both domains, students experience affects that map onto the theory described above. In fact, relationships, embodiment, and movement seem key to understanding students' orientations. Again, for ease of discussion, I attempt to separate these concerns, though they overlap. Even so, I hardly capture the complex and messy interplay between affective elements.

Personal Writing

Perhaps most prominently, students describe their personal writing as deeply relational. Students repeatedly use the word *out* in their descriptions of personal writing. Fifty-five percent of students see personal writing as a way to move emotions, ideas, thoughts, concerns, and problems outside of themselves. Referencing both embodiment and movement, the spatial orientation of "out" appears to be not about discarding emotions, etc., but rather about separating them from the writer in order to allow a new perspective on, stance toward, or aesthetic response to them.

For example, one student says, "It's really nice to take something that's bothering me [and] create it into like, make it, mold it into something that I think is beautiful and release it in a way that takes something very ugly and makes something beautiful. . . . It's really nice to get it out there and to make it something better than frustration or anger." Out also affords writers a different relationship to past and future selves. One student says, "I like leaving something for myself to find…And then my writing as well, they [previously written texts] showed me how far I've come, how far I've changed, and it makes me a stronger person." Students also write things out to work through challenges in interpersonal relationships or to compensate for lack of relationships. As one student says, "I have a whole bunch of ideas just like in my head and like I don't have anyone to talk to about it . . . so it's kind of good here [in a journal] to write them."

The students' "out" language may seem to index a Cartesian duality that is at odds with the idea of an affective ecology. Karen Barad's notion of agential realism provides a framework more coherent with my affective lens. In Barad's conceptualization, "out" can be read as referencing temporary boundaries generated by the body's participation in intra-active writing phenomena. Rather than describing the body itself, "out" functions as, in Barad's terms, a "cut" that momentarily marks and divides objects and bodies, opening new opportunities for knowing and being.

This kind of "out" differs, of course, from the externalization that Charles Bazerman and Howard Tinberg posit as one of writing studies' "threshold concepts." For them, externalization creates a text that can "be examined, revised, or otherwise worked on by the writer, collaborators, or other people" (61). Externalization and connection are linked, in this view, to textual improvement. In contrast, students in my study externalize and connect for reasons that are less, or at least differently, instrumental. As described above, students write for insight, self-awareness, conflict resolution, catharsis, therapy, and relationship maintenance or repair. Connection, rather than textual perfection, appears to be the primary motivation for writing things "out." In fact, one student suggests the value of personal writing's textual flaws. "It's not like I have to write to please someone," she says, "it's just kind of what I want to put out there." Free from evaluative concerns, her writing "just kind of flows."

Second, students represent personal writing as pleasurable embodiment. Many students described their writing spaces—often bedrooms—in sensory detail: "When I'm in my room alone, I set a candle. I have like water or tea, a little bit of, like, calm violin music—like classical music—on. I'm in my pajamas." Others describe feeling sensations of release, calm, or cool breezes, hearing the sound of water running or birds chirping, experiencing a "lightning storm," or being "enthralled" or transported to different conscious states or other worlds. Even negative bodily sensations evoke positive evaluations. For example, one student interprets an aching hand as evidence that writing can "suck you in" to the point that "you kind of forget you exist." Another student compares the embodiment of writing to running: "I'm not an athlete at all really. But if I could imagine what I think some sprinters feel like, I think it'd be similar to that, because I'm sure—like my hand will cramp up, but it's just like you're so in the zone that it just kind of fades away." This student's experience resembles what psychologist Mihaly Csikszentmihaly terms "flow" moments, "when a person's body or mind is stretched to its limits in a voluntary effort to accomplish something difficult and worthwhile" (3). During flow experiences, positive affects related to meaning, purpose, and motivation overwhelm negative affects, in this case the pain of a throbbing hand. That students may enter a flow state while composing makes their descriptions of personal writing as "just kind of flow[ing]" even more apt.

My third concern—movement—intersects with writing's relational and embodied qualities. Again, these three concerns work in the rhizomatic fashion affect theory suggests; rather than separate and independent elements, they act as nodes in a shared affective structure. For example, movement is essential to the "out" that anchors students' relational affect since "out" moves emotions, thoughts, and ideas through networks of paper, screens, and bodies. Even when the circulation of the writer's thoughts does not include other human bodies, the movement to paper or screen seems affectively important. For example, one student writes a lengthy and articulate letter to her dad and his partner in her freewrite journal. Chafing under their rules for internet and phone use, this student apologizes while skillfully defending her disobedient behavior. Yet early in the next day's entry she writes that she did not share her thoughts with them, and she does not mention their rules again. The movement to the page alone appears to assuage her affective need.

Students similarly weave movement into their descriptions of embodied sensation, as in the above description of running. One student likens writing to an embodied expression of joy, akin to doing cartwheels. "But," she says, "I can't do cartwheels, so I write it instead." Many students experience writing as a sensation of moving through places they create in writing. Such movement seems to be a key element of personal writing for the student (quoted above) who described writing fiction as the sensation of "exist[ing] as if you were a god," since the student contrasts that with the sensation of being "limit[ed]" and "trapped" while writing nonfiction. For other writers, writing movement is literal as they act or speak things out in the process of composing. In summary, relationships, embodiment, and movement appear to be key affective components that compel students' outside-of-school writing.

In-school Writing

In school, where their writing consists primarily of argument and literary analysis essays, students have a different affective experience. Most identify a purpose for this kind of writing: the opportunity to get their voice, opinion, or ideas "out." One student says, "It's letting out what you learned." Again gesturing to both embodiment and movement, this spatial conception mirrors students' personal writing, but it is important to note that when this student talks about his academic writing going out, he does not envision it forming relationships with other objects in a writing assemblage—the move out does not forge new connections to other bodies, objects, or forces. "Out," in this case, appears to be merely a mental exercise in which knowledge is transferred from the brain onto the paper without transforming either the writer or the knowledge. Both remain static.

Another student says, "It feels empowering because you're finally getting it out there and you're showing that you have an opinion and so you feel strong. You like have a connection to it, and so it just feels really good to have it out there." While emphasizing the empowerment associated with getting something "out," this writer mostly reaffirms her original connection to her opinion. She does not indicate what—if anything—her opinion might do "out there" or what other objects or audiences might be affected by her "show." Another student says that academic writing is "to get your opinion out so that you can be heard." Here the passive construction of the dependent clause raises questions about the relational force of her writing. Across interviews, this pattern was typical—most students describe academic writing as an important means of "put[ting] my voice out in the world" but do not seem to imagine their writing as part of a relational network. When, rarely, students mention an audience, they use vague descriptors—"the world," "someone," "people"—that belie authentic relational intentions or results. However, one student points to the relational potential of her academic writing by comparing it to a story. She says:

> The whole point of writing is to take someone somewhere, to make them see things from your perspective. . . . You can't immerse someone in a story if you can't make what you're writing feel real or important, and so being able—even in informative essays—it's everything to be able to explain what you're seeing in your story so they can see it too.

Significantly, this writer demonstrates academic writing's affective capacity by highlighting its similarity to the out-of-school writing she prefers, namely the embodiment ("seeing") and movement ("take someone somewhere") of stories.

Still, most students express limited relational value "out there" for their academic writing. More troubling is that academic writing may disrupt a writer's intrapersonal affect. The workshop lets students choose the topics they will write on, and many students express appreciation for that agency. But in answer to questions about in-school writing in general, students describe academic writing and affect as incompatible. One student seemed surprised when I asked her to describe how in-school writing feels: "Um, I don't, I don't really feel anything . . ." Another student characterizes academic writing this way: "You detach yourself from the essay." And the student who described academic writing as "pretty much you are just letting out what you learned" followed that statement with a definitive "It's not like feelings." One student suggests that this need not be the case for academic writing. The problem, she believes, is not the academic genre, but the lack of choice:

> When it comes to school, it's like, um, it's assigned by the teacher . . . and it's not the same feeling as doing a paper on something you know you like or you want . . . even though I still can get it done. But it's not the same, like, it can be the same effort, but it doesn't come out the same, kind of, what would you call it, like, good I guess. Like it doesn't come out the same way. Like you can tell the feeling of a paper than the other one.

For these students, then, academic writing can index a double relational void. Severed from a personal connection to the text, students see their writing moving "out" but not necessarily toward other objects. It is textualization without relational purpose or affect.

Students' experiences of embodiment with academic writing are likewise discouraging. Students use words like *forced*, *rushed*, *livid*, *focused*, *bound*, and *pressured* to describe the experience of writing in school. The students' diction emphasizes both the energy that in-school writing exerts on students and their evaluation of that energy. Thirty-nine percent of students describe academic writing in terms of necessity, but only four mention being compelled by the teacher, the assignment, the grade, or the due date. One student describes forcing himself to write. More commonly, students assign agency vaguely to the writing itself, its structure, or the work it demands: "When I'm writing essays, I'm more focused because I have to be." Many students, echoing

Vitanza, acknowledge academic writing's capacity to affect them, but mostly in negative ways.

For example, a student who experiences a sensation of flying while writing poetry describes academic writing this way: "Not like against a wall, but like I'm climbing a wall. I'm bound by force, but I'm scaling it to a destination. If I keep climbing I will eventually finish." In his descriptions of both writing domains, we see the interplay of embodiment and movement, but the language here suggests the imperative force academic writing inscribes on his body and some uncertainty about the point of it all. The student does not clarify what the "destination" is or why one would want to "finish" climbing the wall. Thus, the problem of in-school embodiment may be less the pain and exertion writing requires and more the absence of purpose or reward.

After all, even unpleasurable affects can spark writing. Micciche ("Trouble") describes the generative potential of troubling affects such as agitation, disturbance, interference, interruption, and exertion. In fact, much of the self-chosen writing students describe as affectively pleasurable originates in unpleasant affects. It is often emotional trauma, family stress, and personal crises that provoke students to write and not just in creative or expressivist genres. The one student in my study who wrote an essay outside of school did so in response to classroom activities and assignments about identity and immigration that disturbed her and precipitated her later voluntary writing. As a Mexican-American student, she "really got into" the idea of marginalized or "in the shadows" identities. That idea produced an affect of agitation that provoked her elective essay. Furthermore, even when students negatively evaluate the exertion academic writing requires, that exertion—when linked to a meaningful purpose—can provide affective motivation, as it did for the student who enjoyed the feeling of an aching hand in out-of-school writing.

Finally, movement. Except for the movement of "out" described earlier, only the "climbing" student above and three other students associate academic writing with movement. One student laments that writing shuts down his movement because it is too "complicated" and "stressful." Another student describes the "really repetitive and routine" movement academic essays requires: "Here's one point, here's a supporting quote, here's why it works, here's my ending to that paragraph. And then over and over again." Only one student gestures toward the kind of curious, generative, exploratory movement we might hope to see in students' descriptions of writing: "When I first start writing and like the idea is there and it's just like BOOM all of these connections. It's like a giant Venn diagram . . . like a word web, and it just all fits together. And then I actually have to, like, put it into sentences . . . That's where it gets, like, shaky." Here academic writing curtails inventive movement.

Another student admits she is "a lot more enthralled" with personal writing done by hand than with an argument essay written on a computer, where "I try to sit up straight and kind of like, 'K we gotta do this.'" But later in the interview she expresses a more favorable view of using a computer for academic writing. "One nice thing about computers is that it's still all there, but you can move it around," she says. The computer makes writing "kind of like a puzzle," where she can rearrange, add, and discard pieces. She concludes, "So [writing the essay] was not like [writing in her journal] where it's on the page, it's on the page, and it's over. It's a lot of revision, and I think I like the revision part of it even more than I actually like the writing part of it." Though this student disavows academic writing in general, like other students she seems drawn to affective dimensions of movement and relationships. While not changing her overall affective orientation, the affordances of the computer that allow her to move and reorder relationships in her essay draw her to revision.

Affective (Dis)Harmony

This research complements and elaborates scholarship that theorizes writing as an affective phenomenon. To understand students' writing affect, I have focused on an affective triad of relationships, embodiment, and movement, but these concerns do not exhaust the bodily responses, sensations, impulses, thoughts, and emotions associated with writing. Rather, they provide a starting point for understanding the affects writing provokes. Attention to these categories reveals the experiential differences that underlie students' orientations toward out-of-school writing and away from in-school writing. My goal in interpreting these orientations as affective consequences is more than just a critique of academic writing. Rather, I offer some implications of the research for both pedagogy and research.

My study affirms the value of expressivist and creative writing both in and outside of school. While the idea of expressivist pedagogies is not new, my research contributes a more nuanced explanation for why expressivist writing matters. We expect students to prefer expressivist writing because it "places the writer in the center" (Burnham 19). Unlike academic tasks that ask students to research and write about subjects about which they may have little interest, expressivist writing "assign[s] highest value to [the student's] imaginative, psychological, social, and spiritual development" (19). Additionally, students may feel less restrained by the conventions of creative writing genres than by those of academic genres. And much expressivist and creative writing includes no assessment or accountability. Though all of these factors contribute to students' affective orientation toward expressivist and creative writing, my research shows that students also value the relational, dynamic, and embodied affects such writing elicits—affects they do not typically experience while fulfilling academic writing assignments.

Because students associate positive affect with expressivist and creative writing, composition instructors might seek ways to include more of this writing in the curriculum. Speaking appreciatively of the freewrite journal, one student described it as a place for creative expression before turning to the work of "serious writing." Yet, we might also reimagine the "serious writing" we require in our classrooms, perhaps dissolving the strict boundaries between academic genres and more expressivist and creative genres, as some scholars are beginning to do in their own writing. For example, in a recent *CCC* article, Chris Anson "repurpose[d] the case-study genre into a reflective analysis of a completely personal experience" (544). He admits that he was only able to perform this kind of deviation because "he had earned the confidence and authority to do so" (544). We can help students earn confidence and authority in our classrooms by introducing them to work like Anson's and encouraging generic experimentation. Finding ways to couple academic and personal writing in composition classrooms may positively shape both individual student affect toward in-school writing and the overall affective ecology of our classrooms.

A second approach to reimagining "serious writing" is to design writing tasks that arouse the affects of embodiment, relationships, and movement students prefer but still require students to follow standard academic conventions. Mary Soliday and Jennifer Trainor suggest that assignment descriptions are a key way teachers can encourage what Arlene Wilner calls "bounded openness"—creative, exploratory, and unexpected movement within academic conventions. Assignment descriptions that ask questions, hedge, avoid listing dos and do nots, and include language such as "'consult,' 'imagine,' 'consider,' or 'you may probably find'" allow students to experience writing as a complex and uncertain unfolding of connections (137). Likewise, Wendy Hayden proposes the benefits of archival assignments that allow students "wiggle room" to experience novel (for an academic context) sensations of embodiment, relationships, and movement (146). The work of these scholars illustrates the possibility of creating affectively enjoyable writing experiences within traditional academic conventions. Additionally, we might consider assigning digital genres or multimodal genres that can do academic work but may feel less like "school writing" for our students. My research provides a heuristic for evaluating the affective consequences of the writing we assign.

Finally, I believe my research suggests the value of making affect visible in writing classrooms. Thinking about how bodies respond to other bodies, objects, and ideas fascinates many students. Most participants in my study answered my questions about writing affect easily, offering rich and full stories of their writing experiences. One participant described her affective experience in detail even before I asked the question. Still, seven students struggled to articulate their affect, despite additional probing on my part. In my composition classes, I have found that most students eagerly participate in conversations about affect. They readily describe their own affective responses to movies, music, food, and other people. They can identify and articulate affective orientations toward or away from—among other things—sushi, puppies, chewing noises, or Beyoncé. These general conversations about affect provide a lens and a vocabulary that can be transferred to talking about affective responses to writing and may help students, like the seven in my study, who initially hesitate to talk about affect. I encourage my students to reflect on their writing experiences, both orally and in writing. This allows them to recognize positive and negative affects they experience while writing. Sometimes the most beneficial result of this is the realization that they do, indeed, enjoy some kinds of writing. As we talk about negative affects associated with writing, we consider how students might rework those affects in productive ways (as Micciche suggests), rather than falling into well-worn tropes about not liking writing or not being able to write. For example, when students say that they feel constrained by the rules of academic writing, we talk about the moves that are available to them even within academic genres and how they might play with their writing even within constraints that sometimes seem immutable.

These pedagogical suggestions derive from, and are therefore limited by, my research, which offers just one way of studying and theorizing writing affect. While I observed the workshop's affective ecology, I can only guess at the affective environment of other spaces where these students do most of their writing. In interviews, many students described out-of-school scenes of writing, but few detailed their high school classroom environments, perhaps assuming that this information was self-evident. Additionally, I know little about the complex web of affective influences that make up these students' writing histories. My research would benefit from sustained attention to writing environments and writing pasts. Future research could more fully situate the embodied writer in an affective milieu and could examine other elements of the writing ecology—in- and out-of-school. Still, my research does suggest that affect should be integral to Composition theory, research, and teaching. If we want students to both succeed in our classrooms and to persist as writers long after they leave, then it behooves us to understand what draws them to writing.

Acknowledgments

I wish to thank Casey Boyle for early guidance and Deborah Dean and Brian Jackson for generous reading of and feedback on late drafts. I also wish to thank the anonymous *Composition Studies* reviewers for their insights.

Notes

1. Others have done excellent work addressing the affect/emotion dilemma (Nelson). My purpose is not to propose a resolution. Rather, I employ a capacious understanding of affect as a multiplicity of responses, including but not limited to those we call emotions.

2. The College of Education provides funding and facilities for the workshop, and the workshop's co-director is a faculty member in the college. All other workshop faculty are district employees.

3. My activity during my first two years in the workshop—mentoring students—and my age, gender, and professional background may have caused students to view me as part of the workshop rather than as an outside observer. Even in the third year, when my involvement consisted of furiously typing fieldnotes and conducting interviews, some students thought I was affiliated with the workshop or College of Education in some way. For example, after one interview, a soft-spoken senior said, with apparent relief, "I thought I was in trouble!" Thus my own affect—my embodiment, my relationship with students and faculty, and my movement within the workshop—may have impacted the data. As evidence of this, students rarely criticized the workshop in interviews. In the journals, which were not composed for my research, students complain freely about the workshop.

4. I acknowledge the limitations of my ethnographic case study, which provides anecdotes and starting points for thinking about affect rather than generalizable results. I also acknowledge the limitations of any research that seeks to represent affect. Inspired by the philosophies of Gilles Deleuze and Brian Massumi, most affect theorists accept affect as virtual—a plane of immanence where anything can happen. Empirical research, in contrast, attempts to identify, harness, and isolate the object of study, as I do here. I present my research as a compromise. It allows me to say some things about students' writing affect without pretending to have captured affect's pure potentiality.

5. Amanda Lenhart et al. report similar findings.

Appendix A

1. When you aren't in school or at this workshop, what do you like to do?

    Probe: Hobbies? Interests?

2. Why did you decide to come to this workshop?

3. What kind of writing do you do outside of school?

    Probe: How often do you do this kind of writing?

    Probe: What motivates you to do that writing?

    Probe: How comfortable are you sharing that writing with other people?

4. Think about the writing you do outside of school and try to describe what it feels

like for you—maybe describe where you are when you write or your emotions or thoughts or how your body feels.

5. How good do you think you are at this kind of writing?

6. How important do you think this kind of writing is?

7. How do you feel about the writing you do in school compared to the writing you do on your own?

8. Let's do that same thing I asked you to do with your writing outside of school. Think about writing in school and try to describe what it feels like while you are writing—your body, emotions, thoughts, etc.

9. How good do you think you are at this kind of writing?

10. How important do you think it is to be able to write argument essays like the one you are writing here at the workshop?

   Probe: Where else do you think you might write an essay like this?

11. What kinds of writing do you see yourself doing in the future?

12. How important do you think writing is to your future?

Works Cited

Addison, Joanne, and Sharon James McGee. "Writing in High School/Writing in College: Research Trends and Future Directions." *College Composition and Communication*, vol. 62, no. 1, 2010, pp. 147-179.

Ahmed, Sara. "Happy Objects." *The Affect Theory Reader*, edited by Melissa Gregg and Gregory J. Seigworth, Duke UP, 2010, pp. 29-51.

Anson, Chris M. "The Pop Warner Chronicles: A Case Study in Contextual Adaptation and the Transfer of Writing Ability." *College Composition and Communication*, vol. 67, no. 4, 2016, pp. 518-549.

Barad, Karen. *Meeting the Universe Halfway: Quantum Physics and the Entanglement of Matter and Meaning*. Duke UP, 2007.

Bazerman, Charles, and Howard Tinberg. "Text Is an Object Outside of Oneself That Can Be Improved and Developed." *Naming What We Know: Threshold Concepts of Writing Studies*, edited by Linda Adler-Kassner and Elizabeth Wardle, UP of Colorado, 2015, pp. 61-62.

Burnham, Christopher. "Expressive Pedagogy: Practice/Theory, Theory/Practice." *A Guide to Composition Pedagogies*, edited by Gary Tate, Amy Rupiper and Kurt Schick, Oxford UP, 2001, pp. 19-35.

Cooper, Marilyn. "Being Linked to the Matrix: Biology, Technology, and Writing." *Rhetorics and Technologies: New Directions in Writing and Communication*, edited by Stuart A. Selber, U of South Carolina P, 2010, pp. 15-32.

Corbin, Juliet, and Anselm Strauss. *Basics of Qualitative Research: Techniques and Procedures for Developing Grounded Theory*. 3rd ed., Sage, 2008.

Csikszentmihalyi, Mihalyi. *Flow: The Psychology of Optimal Experience*. Harper & Row, 1990.

Deleuze, Gilles. *Essays Critical and Clinical*. Translated by Daniel W. Smith and Michael A. Greco, U of Minnesota P, 1997.

Edbauer Rice, Jenny. "The New 'New': Making a Case for Critical Affect Studies." *Quarterly Journal of Speech*, vol. 94, no. 2, 2008, pp. 200-212. doi: 10.1080/00335630801975434

Graham, Steve, et al. "Improving the Writing Performance, Knowledge, and Self-Efficacy of Struggling Young Writers: The Effects of Self-Regulated Strategy Development." *Contemporary Educational Psychology*, vol. 30, no. 2, 2005, pp. 207-241. doi.org/10.1016/j.cedpsych.2004.08.001

Harris, Joseph. *A Teaching Subject: Composition Since 1966*. Utah State UP, 2012.

Hawhee, Debra. *Bodily Arts: Rhetoric and Athletics in Ancient Greece*. U of Texas P, 2004.

Hayden, Wendy. "And Gladly Teach: The Archival Turn's Pedagogical Turn." *College English*, vol. 80, no. 2, 2017, pp. 133-158.

Lenhart, Amanda, et al. "Writing, Technology, and Teens." *Pew Internet & American Life Project*, The National Commission on Writing, 2008.

Massumi, Brian. *Parables for the Virtual: Movement, Affect, Sensation*. Duke UP, 2002.

Micciche, Laura R. "The Trouble With Affect," *Journal of Advanced Composition*, vol. 26, no. 1/2, 2006, pp. 264-276.

—. "Writing Material." *Reimagining the Social Turn*, special issue of *College English*, vol. 76, no. 6, 2014, pp. 488-505.

Nelson, Julie D. "An Unnecessary Divorce: Integrating the Study of Affect and Emotion in New Media." *Composition Forum*, vol. 34, 2016, compositionforum.com/issue/34/unnecessary-divorce.php. Accessed 5 Jan. 2018.

Perl, Sondra. "Understanding Composing." *College Composition and Communication*, vol. 31, no. 4, 1980, pp. 363-369.doi:10.2307/356586

Rounsaville, Angela, et al. "From Incomes to Outcomes: FYW Students' Prior Genre Knowledge, Meta-Cognition, and the Question of Transfer. *WPA: Writing Program Administration*, vol. 32, no. 1, 2008, pp. 97-112.

Seigworth, Gregory J., and Melissa Gregg. "An Inventory of Shimmers." *The Affect Theory Reader*, edited by Melissa Gregg and Gregory J. Seigworth, Duke UP, 2010, pp. 1-25.

Soliday, Mary, and Jennifer Seibel Trainor. "Rethinking Regulation in the Age of the Literacy Machine." *College Composition and Communication*, vol. 68, no. 1, 2016, pp. 125-151.

Vitanza, Victor J. "Abandoned to Writing: Notes Toward Several Provocations." *enculturation*, vol. 5, no. 1, 2003, enculturation.net/5_1/vitanza.html. Accessed 5 Jan. 2018.

Wilner, Arlene. "Asking for It: The Role of Assignment Design in Critical Literacy." *Reader: Essays in Reader-Oriented Theory, Criticism, and Pedagogy*, vol. 52, 2005, pp. 56–91.

Writing Workshops in the Public Turn

Charles N. Lesh

In this article, I model an approach to writing workshops grounded in collaborative design and a sensitivity to the multiple writing locations and identities that students inhabit within and outside the classroom. In redirecting our attention to the potential of designing workshops with students as an enactment of their own writerly ecologies, I situate the workshop as a location for the public work of Composition: protopublic spaces in which writers design, experiment with, and reflect on various forms of circulation and publicity. I ground this discussion in a teacher-research study conducted in an upper-level writing course focused on the specious distinctions between workshops inside and outside classroom walls. This article describes how this pedagogy took shape, explores findings from my research, and examines the value of spatial multiplicity and collaborative design in academic writing workshops.

Introduction

Office hours:

A student walks in to discuss a draft of his final project. After about five minutes he grows visibly upset, that place past the verge of tears but not quite crying. He apologizes for "cheating." His transgression: having trouble writing his essay and unhappy with feedback he had received in class, he called a friend from home, a high school classmate. They spoke on the phone, viewing the document on Google Drive (where students in my classes submit writing), making changes as they discussed potential revisions.

"Uh oh," I think. "What happened next?"

"So, yeah, I'm really sorry," the student conclude*s*.

At the time, I took this meeting as little more than a miscommunication about writing ethics. It was only when designing syllabi for the following semester that I began to reflect on this student's suggestion that by workshopping a text with a friend outside of class he was committing plagiarism (see Spigelman). If a workshop is, as Maggie Debelius writes, "a meeting that focuses on a piece of student writing and generates feedback," then what this student produces is undoubtably a workshop (156). And yet while he misunderstands this for cheating, what he does understand is that workshops, as conceived within composition classrooms, are—in design and execution—often tethered to academic spaces. It is true that scholars have done considerable work documenting writing groups outside of academic spaces (Gere; Moss et al.; Spigelman); yet, in the process, we have largely kept those models of workshops separate, or at least distinct, from the routinized practices of our classrooms. This type of spatial partitioning can lead students to believe that any form of self-organized, self-sponsored, or self-designed workshop that *moves between* academic and non-academic spaces is transgressive in the geographic sense of the word, something that is "out of place," something that crosses a perceived boundary (Cresswell).

There is something exciting in this student's story, a sort of boundary testing opening up the work of the classroom to a previously unaffiliated reader to spur more writing. In this way, it reminds me of Michael Warner's understanding of publics as produced "only in relation to texts and their circulation ..." (66). Though I don't see here the sort of public-making that Warner envisions—particularly his emphasis on public writing being oriented toward strangers (74-76)—I do see productive circulation at work: a student, recognizing the limitations of the classroom, circulates a text to a specific reader with the intent of generating a particular type of response.

Rosa Eberly's work has taught me to view writing classrooms as protopublic spaces in which students write not to "ideal, prefabricated, homological audiences," but rather "experience writing as wholly processual and as practiced within and for real groups of people who need their discourses" (175). A protopublic space is an environment in which students are encouraged to reflect on the concrete ways that writing finds readers while envisioning alternatives, all with the intent of better preparing them to be productive participants in broader publics (175). At their core, protopublics destabilize neat distinctions between academic and non-academic spaces through situated analysis and practice of public writing. Understood as a protopublic space, the new workshop this student produces seems largely successful. Circulating his writing outside of university-sanctioned channels (class, writing center, etc.), he considers what benefits or consequences might arise from this circulation, and reflects on the asymmetrical but interconnected relationship between the writing environment of the classroom and that produced with his extracurricular reader. It *is* exciting, and yet, transgressive.

In this article, I model an approach to writing workshops that contends with that transgression, one grounded in collaborative design and sensitivity to the multiple writing locations and identities that students inhabit within and outside the classroom. In redirecting our attention to the potential of designing workshops *with* students as an enactment of their own writerly ecologies,

I situate the workshop as a location for the public work of Composition. As Beverly J. Moss, Nels P. Highberg, and Melissa Nicolas note, classroom writing groups can often transcend institutional spaces, and in the process, "extend classroom boundaries, making the boundaries more fluid, broadening the sites where writers interact" (6) This tendency to move beyond the classroom motivates me to frame workshops as protopublic spaces where writers not only share, critique, and generate writing, but also where they might design, experiment with, and reflect on the various ways that texts find readers and readers produce more texts. I ground this discussion in a teacher-research study I conducted in an upper-level writing course focused on the specious distinctions between workshops inside and outside classroom walls.[1] This article describes how this pedagogy took shape, explores the findings from my research, and examines the value of spatial multiplicity and collaborative design in academic writing workshops.

What Is a Writing Workshop?

It seems odd starting here, so ubiquitous is the term in the hallways, classrooms, and other institutional locations that have traditionally constituted our discipline. Indeed, even in the earliest issues of *Composition Studies*—when the journal was called *Freshman English News*—there are traces of the workshop emerging as the dominant model of composition pedagogy. For example, in the winter 1973 issue, an advertisement for *Writing without Teachers* explains Peter Elbow's belief that, because "peer group reactions are essential to the development of good writing," we should strive to construct a "'teacherless' class, one in which the teacher becomes a participating member" (5). This desire for collaborative pedagogy took hold, of course. As Joseph Harris writes, "Indeed, I would argue that the workshop has been the default mode for talking about student writing since about 1973—when Peter Elbow described it with such conviction and grace in *Writing without Teachers*. We've even turned it into a verb: *to workshop*" (146). It is not difficult to account for this sustained presence. As Harris implies with his reference to Elbow, the workshop connects us to a particular history, a potent connection point between our disciplinary past and our potential future. It consolidates many of our animating ideas about writing (process, revision, audience, collaboration) and our hopes for students as writers beyond the classroom (Cahill 305; Debelius 155; Reid 219-20). The workshop is more than what we do. It is who we are as a field, as instructors, and as writers.

This ubiquity is the cause of some definitional anxiety. Terms related to workshops (peer review, peer response, writing groups, etc.) are broadly used, sometimes in meaningfully different ways (Armstrong and Paulson). With this in mind, I define writing workshops as *c*ollaborative socio-spatial locations that orient writers and readers to texts in meaningfully different ways. Writing workshops are produced in a diverse range of interconnected academic and non-academic spaces and always already exist at the intersection of these locations of writing. In advocating for this spatially integrated and expansive definition, I am indebted to Anne Ruggles Gere's work on the histories of "writing groups," first outside and then within the curriculum. Based on a belief that writing groups enact theories of collaborative learning, Gere's work directs our attention to the practices of workshops as diverse curricular and extracurricular spaces where writers come together under different conditions to share and revise writing.

Within this larger landscape of workshops, my definition is similarly influenced by Kory Lawson Ching's revision of Gere's historiography, a revision that traces writing groups "from recitation and correction to overwork to the redistribution of labor in the composition classroom" (312). Ching's historiography is compelling, but most significant here are the ways that this alternative lineage reframes authority within the context of workshops. Ching writes that Gere's descriptions of writing groups figure authority as "a resource that one either does or does not possess." To contrast this, Ching argues that "we might more profitably think of authority not as something one *has*, but rather as something one *does* or *enacts* in practice" (313). Ching envisions a workshop environment in which teachers and students do not engage in a struggle for or an abdication of authority, but one in which teachers and students collaborate in the production of dynamic pedagogical spaces where student writing is shared, read, and revised (316).

In "The Politics of Peer Response," Mark Hall argues that the shape these peer-response groups take—the literal models of workshops themselves—have grown so entrenched in writing classrooms that instructors may introduce them "without thoroughly evaluating underlying assumptions and beliefs about how such groups operate" (1). Despite the fact that scholarship on the subject has explicitly considered group dynamics in a range of different workshops (e.g. Bloom; George), our pedagogical models can grow so routinized that discerning their underlying assumptions, values, and politics becomes difficult. In viewing peer response as an artifact rather than an activity, Hall argues that the politics of peer-response groups arise not only from their usage, but also from "their constitutive properties":

> What's more, their politics are not merely contingent upon their *uses*; rather, *they are inherent in their design* . . . Rather than view peer response groups as neutral tools that can be used well or poorly, for good, ill, or something in between, a careful examination of the ways peer groups are designed reveals that they produce a set of conse-

quences—power relationships in particular—*beyond* their immediate use. (2)

When we design a workshop we design a particular type of classroom, a particular type of space infused with power, politics, and implications for writing. Once we understand this, we might view models of workshops not just as things we do, but as things we build and as opportunities to invite students into the production of pedagogical spaces.

But how do we operationalize all of this in our classrooms? What would it mean to develop writing courses that begin from an assumption that workshops are produced in a range of different but connected academic and non-academic spaces? How can we develop a pedagogy that explicitly invites students into the sharing of authority so foundational to writing workshops? How might we employ workshops to discuss the politics implicit in the ways that writers produce and circulate texts to interested readers in a variety of spaces?

One way to address these questions is to approach writing workshops as protopublic spaces that exist within the boundaries between academic and non-academic spaces. In this framing, students are tasked with producing, practicing, critiquing, and revising different models of workshops, thus rendering the workshop itself a point of rhetorical production and analysis. If publics are, as Warner and others have argued, conjured into being and given character through the circulation and uptake of texts, then workshops might serve as an ideal location for students to experiment with existing or imagined ways to write to, and produce, various publics and counterpublics (see Green 154). Workshops are, after all, one of the primary spaces within schools where students discover interested readers. They are the locations where student writers often "[r]un it up the flagpole and see who salutes" (Warner 114).

Our contemporary disciplinary moment seems an opportune time to reframe workshops as protopublic spaces. Within the "public turn" (Mathieu), scholars and teachers of writing have engaged with a range of communities and literacies beyond the university (e.g., Ackerman and Coogan; Deans, et al., eds; Holmes; Kynard; Mathieu, et al.; Rivers; Royster; Weisser; Welch; Wells). At the core of this work has been spatial multiplicity, or the idea that significant writing events occur in spaces as diverse as street papers (Mathieu and George), zines (Farmer), and prison workshops (Jacobi). As Christian Weisser notes, an important consequence of this remapping of disciplinary boundaries has been a shift in our understanding of productive public writing through an increased attention to the local, specific conditions by which writers cultivate (counter)publics:

> In addition, public writing does not necessarily need to address a diverse audience. In fact, student discourse is often most effective if it is aimed at individuals who share common perspectives and goals. Enabling students to connect with counterpublics comprised of like-minded individuals is an important component of a successful public writing assignment or course. In specific counterpublics, students often find that they can generate effective public discourse in a climate that is supportive and nurturing, which prepares them to enter larger public debates in the future. (107)

The workshop, I argue, might serve as a laboratory where students not only discuss and revise writing, but also discuss and revise the channels by which writing is circulated to and encountered by readers.

"The Writing Workshop(s) and Space"

In the summer of 2017, I taught a course titled "English 4010: The Writing Workshop(s) and Space" at Auburn University. English 4010 met Monday through Friday, 9:45 to 11:15am, from May 18th to June 21st. Ten students enrolled, a small number, but not uncommon for an upper-level summer course. Described in the University catalogue as "Topics in Writing," an "in-depth study of a specific topic in writing," the course can reflect an instructor's interests. In designing the summer iteration, I was inspired by Maggie Debelius's discussion of a "metaworkshop," in which workshops themselves become both the routine and topic of the course (154). Taking collaborative design and spatial multiplicity as its starting point, two primary goals of my course were to have students: 1) write, offer feedback, and revise within workshop spaces of their own design; and 2) have students write about, analyze, and revise those workshops spaces.

The course was organized around four central units. Each unit began with a series of reading and writing assignments dealing with the interrelationship between writing, publics, and spatial identity. Students wrote literacy narratives identifying and theorizing a particular literacy activity and the corresponding space in which they participate in that activity (academic, community, and digital). As students composed these narratives, they were asked to develop writing webs, simple visual representations of the various writing spaces they inhabit. These webs were shared with the class on a voluntary basis, and no students were required to divulge any (counter)public memberships.

These webs served as the foundation for the central innovation of the course. For each literacy project, students introduced, practiced, revised, and reflected on workshop models that they had encountered within the writing spaces described in their webs. Inviting students into workshop design allowed them to experiment with crafting discursive environments sensitive to their rhetorical goals. For each literacy project, students identified or invented two models of workshops (figure 1), theorized how each facilitated the circulation of writing, practiced and revised the model when workshopping their literacy narratives, and then reflected on the process in the form of an Author's Note. Throughout this process, we kept three questions written on the board:

- What arguments do these workshop models make about (academic) space?
- What do they imply about writing and writing processes?
- How do these models sustain or refigure student relationships to texts and to one another?

Project Name	Student Writing	Workshop Models
Academic Literacy Project	Academic Literacy Narrative Author's Note	Peer Review Whole Class Workshop
Community literacy Project	Community Literacy Narrative Author's Note	Graffiti Cyphers Choral/Improvisational
Digital Literacy Project	Digital Literacy Narrative Author's Note	Social Media Commenting Synchronous Google-Drive Commenting
Reflection Project	Reflection Essay	Choral/ Improvisational Synchronous Google-Drive Commenting

Figure 1. Workshop Models

Unit two (community literacy project) is a representative example of collaborative design in practice and how various forms of workshops invited conversation on public writing and public building. Students were asked to compose a literacy narrative detailing their participation within a community scene and compose an Author's Note that reflected on the workshop models practiced within this unit. In order to begin generating different workshop models, I first introduced my own: the graffiti blackbook cypher. I first came upon this model in high school but refined many of my ideas during an ethnographic study with graffiti writers in Boston. Blackbooks are notebooks that, while individually owned, are collaboratively written as they circulate within communities of graffiti writers. Sometimes referred to as piecebooks or sketchbooks, blackbooks offer graffiti writers a stable place to practice writing; a method of textual circulation, as writers share their books with other writers; and a community-curated archive that preserves an otherwise ephemeral rhetorical act (figure 2).

Figure 2. BOWZ and MYND, Author's Blackbook

While blackbooks are used in a variety of spaces, cyphers were particularly interesting to me in the context of this course. Quite literally, a cypher is a rough assembly of writers in a circle, passing around blackbooks, commenting on writing, and composing new texts on the spot (often in other writers' books, as in the examples above). This textual circulation is one of the primary ways that graffiti writers sustain a counterpublic.

As I was planning this course, I was drawn to the blackbook cypher as a workshop model that emphasizes revision, the free sharing and circulation of feedback, and perhaps most significantly, improvisation, a recursive loop of feedback and writing. I introduced the cypher to students through an overview of my research and foundational counterpublic texts like the 1983 documentary film *Style Wars*. Recognizing the specific material, historical, and cultural conditions out of which graffiti culture arose, students and I discussed how we might learn from—as opposed to appropriate—the blackbook's emphasis on fluidity and improvisation as we constructed something new within academic space.

Based on these discussions, we devised a tentative set of timed guidelines to be repeated for the duration of the class meeting. We felt these approximated the public and rhetorical work(shop) we observed in cyphers. They included:

- Fifteen-minute exchange with reader, writing suggestions and modeling revisions;
- Ten-minute group discussion, explaining feedback and responses;
- Fifteen-minute writing session, based on feedback;

- Fifteen-minute exchange with new reader, writing suggestions and modeling revisions;
- Ten-minute group discussion, explaining feedback and responses; and a
- Fifteen-minute writing session, based on feedback.

I observed the workshop in action as students formed groups of three or four, assembling their chairs in rough circles. I listened in on discussions, not just about the texts being read and revised but about the constructed space of this workshop. Periodically, groups would call me over as they discussed and executed revisions to their writing *and* to their cyphers. One group shortened the timing of the circulations. Another resisted the atomization that resulted from exchanging with a single partner and instead focused, as a group, on one text at a time. This focus on both the writing and the workshop is significant because students were simultaneously revising their texts and the methods by which these texts circulate to readers. That is, students revised how texts moved, inflected how they were read, and considered how those shifts resulted in different forms of feedback and, eventually, revision and recirculation.

Once I introduced the blackbook cypher as a viable workshop, students began to open up about the various locations where they write and share writing with readers, seeing these situations not as necessarily distinct from the class but as valid sites of rhetorical work. After class one day, John explained his history as a singer for a variety of school music groups. He explained how members would receive new sheet music and, in self-formed groups, "perform" the new piece to one another as listeners offered feedback and suggestions for vocal revision, which would be immediately incorporated into the composition.

The "Choral Workshop" was born. After discussing the model with the class, students formed into groups and went to various spaces on campus, finding locations where they felt comfortable openly sharing their writing with group members. Based on my conversations with John, I was influenced to forego guidelines like those we designed for the cypher. However, I suggested to students that they take turns "performing" their papers to one another. By performing, we decided that we meant much more than reading aloud. Students were invited to read their work while also filling in other details, gestures, or emphases in order to achieve their desired rhetorical effects. Listeners would interject, offering immediate suggestions to be incorporated into the performance and, eventually, the revision.

For each unit, students and I designed and revised different workshop models gleaned from the spaces of their own writing experiences. Students posted their papers to our course Google community page using the comment function to offer feedback across multiple drafts, mimicking the way they interact with texts on social media. We collaborated on what a productive whole-class workshop might look like, making the unavoidable authority of the teacher within these settings more transparent through *in situ* reflections on the relationship between power, authority, and responses to writing. Across models, the workshop became a location for designing, practicing, and critiquing different ways to circulate texts to interested readers. The classroom space became an object of revision and a point of convergence, and students began to feel emboldened to see workshops as permeable and potentially responsive to their identities and rhetorical needs inside and outside of the classroom.

Teacher-Research

In order to capture student insights on workshops and the course more generally, I designed a teacher-research study. According to Marilyn Cochran-Smith and Susan L. Lytle, teacher-research is defined as "systematic, intentional inquiry by teachers about their own school and classroom work" (23-4). As a methodology, teacher-research offered me an opportunity to both participate in the collaborative design at the core of this class and, in the regular process of teaching, collect data: transcripts of classroom discussion; student writing; and a teacher journal. Throughout the course and once it had finished, a research assistant and I transcribed all collected data. The analysis of this data was iterative. Once data was transcribed, the research assistant went through and did first-pass qualitative coding and identified emerging patterns and tensions. After discussing these themes and testing them against data streams, I systematized a codebook and did second-pass coding.

The Patterns

From this coding, three distinct patterns emerged.

(1) Students began to see diversity, spatial multiplicity, and collaborative design as important factors in productive writing workshops.

In his final reflection, Chuck considers his own history with workshops in academic spaces:

> Up until this class, the only workshops I have ever done were the traditional peer review workshops where students get in groups of 3 or 4, read one another's paper, and take turns discussing each one, or the whole class review, where the entire class reads the paper and usually gives constructive feedback only when prompted by the professor. I have never really found these workshops helpful.

Here, Chuck articulates two things. First, he identifies how the introduction of multiple workshop models led him to identify the homogeneity and routinization of his past experiences. On their own, students began referring to academic models previously practiced as "traditional," a term that, to my mind, not only signals routinization, but also an embeddedness in a particular disciplinary history. Students argued that this formation of "tradition" runs counter to the goals of workshop pedagogy: to heighten rhetorical awareness and to improve writing. In the midst of course discussion, Annie admits that while entrenched models might allow students to feel "prepared" and "less anxious," they would also "get old and you'd get the same results over and over again if you kept doing it the same way. You'd have to change at some point to make it better, improve." Students saw tinkering with normalized models as a productive, defamiliarizing pedagogical practice, one necessary to uncover the strengths and weaknesses of traditional models.

Defamiliarization of existing models leads to the second point: a benefit in introducing diverse models of workshops to a single writing classroom. As the class started to reflect on their histories with routinized models, they began to see them not as static structures that spit out feedback, but rather as produced, dynamic, and malleable rhetorical locations in which writers are oriented and reoriented to texts in meaningfully different ways. Students began to call for a range of models in order to obtain a diverse array of rhetorical experiences and feedback. Seth articulates this perhaps most clearly in his project three Author's Note on the benefits of introducing social media commenting into our classroom:

> The digital workshop adds another dimension to the workshop. It adds one more space to the multiplicity of our workshop. And I advocate expanding that multiplicity as much as possible. Though I'm unfamiliar with the cold hard data that studies have probably mined on this subject, both my personal experience and intuition incline me to believe that a workshop inducing the widest variety of mental states and the most interaction between those spaces will likely achieve its goals most effectively.

Students began to tie this multiplicity to their ability to improve a piece of writing and to improve as writers.

This desire for multiplicity was widespread; yet, it is important to note that multiplicity did not simply mean different workshops or other models of instruction, as it has in other studies (e.g., Irvine). Here, multiplicity means diversity *through* collaborative design, workshops born from collaboration between teacher and student. This co-performance of authority is evident in John's final course reflection on designing the choral workshop:

> Moreover, the opportunity to take part in research and experimentations through being asked to design a workshop model for my class was not only humbling and a great honor, but it was also refreshing, because there was no longer an oppressive sense of hierarchical dichotomy between professor and student. The professor and student were collaborating . . .

Within this collaborative environment, one question continually emerged: Are some workshops simply more effective than others? After sustained discussions, students eventually rejected the desirability of ranking workshops. Rather, the risk of workshop inferiority was outweighed by the benefits of rhetorical dexterity, a necessity in public writing. During class discussion, Seth advocates for this view:

> It actually reminds me of strategy games. I saw a guy who, [to] another really successful chess player, asked, "Here is a board state. What would you do?" He says, "Well, any strategy, no matter how good it is, if it is just a set strategy, then it's predictable and exploitable." So, 50% of the time, I would make this move and 25% of the time, I would make this move, and 25% of the time, I would make this move. Just so you can't, I guess, lock into what I'm trying to do. I think in the same way: having variation brings in some kind of—even though it's maybe a less good move, it brings *that* in.

Students began to see workshop diversity as essential for creating space to practice various forms of textual circulation and strategies in order to secure a range of responses.

And students were successful securing different forms of response. We learned that different workshops not only produced different feedback, but also differently attuned readers to texts. While the cypher workshop produced readings that dealt with local aspects of the text—a reflection of the fast-paced temporality and style of the workshop itself—the choral workshop, according to John and his group (Lorraine and Annie), produced readers focused more holistically on the text and its relationship to other topics. In course discussion, John explains:

> The next thing we noticed was that our discussions of our narratives were a lot more in-depth, qualitative, and philosophical than they were when we would workshop each other's narratives [in the

cypher]. Also, we noticed the connections we made, concerning each other's pieces, were more creative than the connections we made while we were inside—that is, we would discuss each other's pieces from the perspectives of environmentalism, sociology, economics, and psychology.

To scholars of public writing, this makes some sense. By changing the method of circulation and context of protopublic discourse, students learned they could provoke different reactions and, eventually, produce different protopublics, each with their own individual character.

Of course, viewing individual workshops as protopublic spaces is not without classroom limitations. Public discourse, as Warner reminds us, relies on a sustained temporality (97), and the limitations of a semester seem to preclude this type of circulation through time. Students recognized this tension during class discussion reflecting on social media commenting as a form of workshop:

Annie: When I commented on Sylvia's paper, she commented and asked me a question. This morning, I commented back to her question. But most of the time [with academic workshops], most people don't go back and look at it. It is what it is. It's just there.

Charlie: So, you're saying you like the temporality of this one? Because it extended outside of the class?

Annie: Well, I like that it has the possibility to.

While Annie did "not expect a conversation to continue forever on one essay," she thought it "would be interesting to see a discussion continue after the class is finished or outside the classroom conversations about the writing." Academic temporality is, no doubt, a limitation, but a generative one. What Annie sees as a weakness of traditional academic workshops is requisite of productive public writing, and thus the class began to question how to design models that facilitate sustained circulation. In this way, the models described in this article are constitutively different than traditional models. They are spaces where *students* have to strategize how to design textual environments that achieve desired rhetorical effects and responses.

(2) Students developed an expansive framework for identifying writing workshops within and outside of academic spaces. They began to see this diversity as inextricably tied to the process and product of writing.

While Gere and others have expanded our disciplinary understanding of writing workshops, connecting writing in and for the discipline to other writing locations has been a problem historically. Yet centering the workshop as the topic and routine of the class allowed students to see the classroom as only one location within a larger writing ecology. While discussing Gere's work, Tiffany and Sylvia began to make connections between the goals of workshops in academic spaces and how their writing is circulated in other environments.

> Tiffany: This is really about what you said, but I feel like Twitter kind of is a writing workshop. That's really weird, but you have likes, retweets, people comment on it.
>
> Sylvia: So Twitter itself is a workshop platform?
>
> [Class discussion on working within a 140-character limit, how tweets are saved as "drafts" before being sent, how revision occurs in these drafts]
>
> Tiffany: And how many times have you been sitting there, saying to a friend, "Is this funny? Should I tweet this?"

This moment represents not only a blurring of the line between workshops and public writing, but also an expansion of what it means to compose and where and when students are acting as public-rhetorical actors. In her final course reflection, Laura considers this more expansive rendering of workshops and writing:

> This revelation must seem obvious: the term 'workshop' has been used outside writing workshops for a long time. Various types of creators—musicians, artists, writers, carpenters, mechanics, smithies, etc.—have called their personal working spaces a "workshop."
>
> The workshop does not belong to writing, so going forward, I argue that a class concerning the writing workshop should also consider other forms of workshop: choir workshops, costuming workshops, auto repair shops, and so on. How do these spaces and contexts change, and how are they similar? How might they give insight on the *writing* workshop? Perhaps starting somewhere different at the beginning of class—discussing a broad definition of workshop without the "writing" modifier—will give students (and teachers) a more situated and thoughtful notion of the writing workshop when they begin to consider all the ways that people who create obtain and give feedback among others in their skillset, career, or hobby.

Impressive and provocative, Laura's reflection points to something essential: workshops are not preexisting but, like publics, in constant states of production and reproduction. As Tiffany puts it, "This class not only taught me different workshops, it has given me the confidence to create my own."

This rendering of the workshop—expansive and continually (re)produced by, as Laura puts it, "students (and teachers)"—led us to consider the relationship between process and product in each workshop we practiced. Regarding process, students considered how workshops encouraged or conditioned revision within the space of the workshop itself or how it deferred revision until the workshop ostensibly ended. Students noted a distance between the workshop models they had practiced in academic spaces and in their writing processes elsewhere. In reflecting on the cypher's emphasis on improvisation, Lorraine notes:

> Going back to John's point about the mundane and the routine, I like it in a way that it did, like, it pushed me to do something I don't like to do which is write on the spot with people telling me, you know, what I need to change.
>
> That makes me uncomfortable. Normally in workshops you can just give feedback and then go home and change it. But here you're pushed to do something that *you're not supposed to.*

Thinking of the workshop as something to revise, as a site of protopublic experimentation, allowed us to interrogate the ways models encourage different rhetorical work; one model can prompt a particular writing behavior that previously seemed outside the bounds of the activity, something *you're not supposed to* do.

Students also began to consider different workshop models in relation to the writing being workshopped. That is, through reading about and discussing the inherent spatiality of texts—how writing circulates and functions in different spaces—students began to question the relationship between workshop models, the texts they are designed to circulate, and writing in various spaces. If a text has an intended spatiality, then shouldn't the model of workshop reflect that spatiality? Shouldn't the ways we workshop texts in academic spaces approximate, or at least make plain, how these texts might circulate to invested readers elsewhere? In a discussion on the feasibility of a course incorporating only one workshop model, John and Laura consider this relationship:

> Laura: I think we wouldn't have had all the topics that we talked about. Because if we're just doing a digital workshop, then we're not worried about any other spaces. We'd be talking a lot more about digital rhetoric and stuff like that. Or it seems like that.

John: … Just having one model, our conversations would be oriented to just that one model. You know, because [we had] the different models in different places and spaces to draw from and have conversations about. I felt like that was very generative and productive.

Laura: What I like about this class is that it's talking about workshops. We're learning various ways of workshopping, the rhetoric behind it, and also the spatial difference.

Articulated here is the value of viewing workshops as embedded in the rhetorical work of the classroom and the genres of writing we ask students to produce (Hall 6-7). It was during this discussion that students sketched an integrated theory on the board, advocating for workshop design sensitive to the texts being workshopped and the spaces through which they (might) circulate (figure 3).

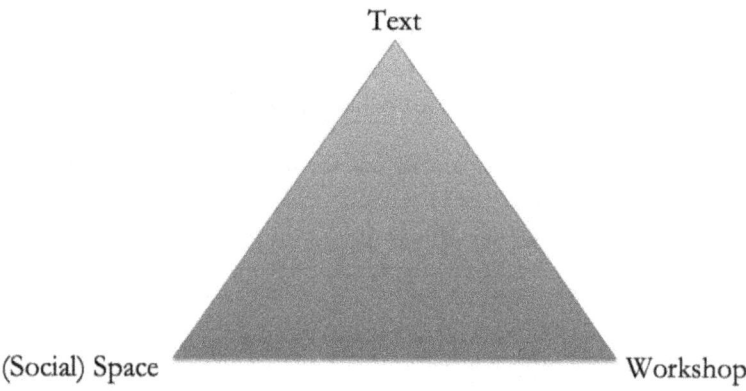

Figure 3. Student Drawing

A workshop can teach us something about both about a text and about the spaces through which it will or could circulate. "OK," students would ask, "we need to workshop a tweet. How can we design a workshop that circulates this genre in instructive ways?"

(3) Students began to reflect more generally on the relationship between writing and space, viewing workshops as locations in which to model and critique environments for public and counterpublic writing.

By considering the spatial politics surrounding and produced by different iterations of the writing workshop, students interrogated how writers and writing are always already emplaced (Reynolds; Rule). Sylvia, in her final reflection, argues that the workshop, though central to the course, was ultimately a means to consider how writing and space are mutually constitutive. She notes, "I know that the place I am writing always influences the text I am writing . . . All-in-all, this class really made me consider space in relation to texts and how they may influence one another." As we experimented with different workshop models, we unpacked the politics of various public spaces available to writers. Research has shown that digital spaces are inhospitable to people of color, women, and other marginalized groups (e.g., Gruwell); what does this mean for our theories of digital workshops and publics? Students discussed constructing alternative, more equitable digital spaces and attempted to model them on our course Google community page. They posed questions like: should these spaces allow anonymity? What role can moderators play in instances of hate speech? How can we acknowledge and negotiate difference within these spaces? The workshop became more than a pedagogical practice; rather, it became a locus of multiple spatialities and an impetus for exploring—and potentially changing—the relationship between space, place, and writing.

As students began to reflect more directly on this relationship between writing and space, the course morphed into an interrogation of spatial division more generally. We discussed and debated the ways that Composition, and other fields, function from locations of constructed spatial singularity.

Following the election of Donald J. Trump, there was a demonstration on campus to protest the new administration's proposal for a travel ban on several predominately Muslim countries. During class discussion that summer, Tiffany described her experience of the protest:

> I was in a class last semester and it was around the time everything with the protests was happening . . . I remember I was in one class and it was so loud. It was right outside the window, and my teacher, he kept on teaching like he was so upset about the protest. He just kept on teaching and it was such a disconnect.

The workshop served as a means through which to critique and potentially destabilize how academic and non-academic spaces are divided in politically meaningful ways, often at the expense of particular groups. Laura reflects on this in her final reflection:

> I also propose that writing workshops do not exist in isolation and are certainly not the only types of *workshops* we should be considering, particularly in a class that concerns itself with the rhetorical and geographical space of a writing workshop. Earlier in the mini-mester, we discussed the fact that our lives do not exist in isolation—the classroom, academic space, does not exist in isolation. What a radical idea! All my life, professors and instructors ask in the unspoken

way of convention and pedagogy that we must leave our personal lives at the classroom door. Yet, this is an impossible demand. Illness, fatigue, stress, memories, follow a student around as much as they do a teacher.

This movement between the idea of a writing workshop and a consideration of spatial politics more generally emerged as a dominant theme of the course. Laura's writing recalls Julie Drew's work on the classroom and students' multiple spatial identities, where she argues that pedagogy "is not located exclusively within the classroom; rather, the classroom is one location in which pedagogical moments occur" (61).

Taking the public turn seriously requires us not only to send our students from the classroom into public spaces or invite them to write about public issues—though I do think it can be both of those things—but also to reimagine and revise curricula and classrooms, including the constitutive pedagogical practices we all share. As a produced and spatially multiple protopublic location, the workshop might serve to enact a classroom sensitive and responsive to the identities and writing spaces that students already occupy.

Conclusion

I recognize some limitations in this research. The findings here are gathered from one class taught in a short window of time. Further, the size of the class allowed me to more easily integrate student-generated workshops, a practice that would be more difficult in a larger section. This was not lost on the students, as Anton notes in his course reflection: "I feel like the small class size not only greatly benefited the course, but also made it possible." Indeed, walking into class and asking students to collaborate with me on something as fundamental as workshop design was stressful and difficult to plan. It also takes time. Yet our students have things to say about workshops. They have experience with various forms of review, academic or otherwise (Reid 221). They have thoughts on how workshops might better connect to their goals as writers. We should listen.

They, like me, do not think that we should eliminate "traditional" peer-review models or stop teaching productive response practices. Chuck, with tongue in cheek, titled his final course reflection, "In Defense of the Classroom," cautioning against throwing out the things we have learned about writing in academic spaces. Other students expressed concern that the professor was too often sidelined in these alternative models. Situating workshops as protopublic spaces asks a considerable amount from students. It asks them to move outside of the workshop spaces that we have built for them, and to produce new ones.

Yet it is within this very movement and production that I hope the value of this study lies. My intent here is not to offer rigid prescriptions or new models of workshops to replace old ones, but to agitate for a consideration and potential revision of the workshop as a site for students to participate in the production of new spaces through writing. At its best, the workshop can serve as a point of convergence between academic and non-academic spaces, a "thirdspace" (Grego & Thompson; Mauk) in which students and teachers experiment with strategies around the shaping, reshaping, and circulation of texts. In his work on the shifting spatialities of composition, Johnathon Mauk writes, "While workshopping and peer editing may always be valued practices in the composition classroom, instructors will have to prompt students into new kinds of reflection, invention, and planning. These behaviors will fundamentally include all facets of the students' lives" (386). This is crucial. As part of our broader public turn and the shifting spaces of Composition, we should consider the workshop, consider the ways that different workshops produce different readers and writers, different circulations, and perhaps less isolated iterations of academic space.

Note

1. This study is approved by the Auburn Institutional Review Board (IRB), protocol #17-130. The class met in the Lab for Usability, Communication, Interaction, and Accessibility (LUCIA) at Auburn University. LUCIA is a "communication-research laboratory" that integrates audio, video, and interactive sensory equipment designed to capture communicative processes for a range of academic and nonacademic clients (Lab). Students were asked to sign consent forms after the first day of class, and all but one student agreed to participate in the study. To accommodate that student, none of their contributions to the class were transcribed. All students are referred to here by self-selected pseudonyms.

Works Cited

Ackerman, John M., and David J Coogan, editors. *The Public Work of Rhetoric: Citizen-Scholars and Civic Engagement.* U of South Carolina P, 2010.

Armstrong, Sonya L., and Eric J. Paulson. "Whither 'Peer Review'? Terminology Matters for the Writing Classroom." *Teaching English in the Two-Year College*, vol 34, no. 3, 2008, pp. 398-407.

Bloom, Lynn Z. "Writers' Workshops and Writing Groups: The Real Deal or Just Friends?" *Writing on the Edge*, vol. 28, no. 1, 2017, pp. 74-85.

Cahill, Lisa. "Reflection on Peer-Review Practices." *Strategies for Teaching First-Year Composition*, edited by Duane Roen, et al., NCTE, 2002, pp. 301-07.

Ching, Kory Lawson. "Peer Response in the Composition Classroom: An Alternative Genealogy." *Rhetoric Review*, vol. 26, no. 3, 2007, pp. 303-19.

Cochran-Smith, Marilyn, and Susan L. Lytle. *Inside/Outside: Teacher Research and Knowledge.* Teachers College P, 1993.

Cresswell, Tim. *In Place/Out of Place: Geography, Ideology, and Transgression*. U of Minnesota P, 1996.

Deans, Thomas, et al., editors. *Writing and Community Engagement: A Critical Sourcebook*. Bedford/St. Martin's, 2010.

Debelius, Maggie. "What Do We Talk About When We Talk About Workshops? Charting the First Five Weeks of a First-Year Writing Course." *Teaching with Student Texts: Essays Toward an Informed Practice*, edited by Joseph Harris, John D. Miles, and Charles Paine, Utah State UP, 2010, pp. 154-62.

Drew, Julie. "The Politics of Place: Student Travelers and Pedagogical Maps." *Ecocomposition: Theoretical and Pedagogical Approaches*, edited by Christian R. Weisser and Sidney I. Dobrin, SUNY P, 2001, pp. 57-68.

Eberly, Rosa. "From Writers, Audiences, and Communities to Publics: Writing Classrooms as Protopublic Spaces." *Rhetoric Review*, vol. 18, no.1, 1999, pp. 165-78.

Elbow, Peter. *Writing without Teachers*. Oxford UP, 1973.

Farmer, Frank. *After the Public Turn: Composition, Counterpublics, and the Citizen Bricoleur*. UP of Colorado, 2013.

George, Diana. "Working with Peer Groups in the Composition Classroom." *College Composition and Communication*, vol. 35, no. 3, 1984, pp. 320-26.

Gere, Anne Ruggles. *Writing Groups: History, Theory, and Implications*. Southern Illinois UP, 1987.

Green, Chris. "Materializing the Sublime Reader: Cultural Studies, Reader Response, and Community Service in the Creative Writing Workshop." *College English*, vol. 64, no. 2, 2001, pp. 153-74.

Grego, Rhonda C., and Nancy C. Thompson. *Teaching/Writing in Thirdspaces: The Studio Approach*. Southern Illinois UP, 2008.

Gruwell, Leigh. "Writing Against Harassment: Public Writing Pedagogy and Online Hate." *Composition Forum*, vol. 36, 2017.

Hall, Mark. "The Politics of Peer Response." *The Writing Instructor*, 2009, pp. 1-13. Retrieved from https://files.eric.ed.gov/fulltext/EJ890609.pdf.

Harris, Joseph. "Workshop and Seminar." *Teaching with Student Texts: Essays Toward an Informed Practice*, edited by Joseph Harris, John D. Miles, and Charles Paine, Utah State UP, 2010, pp. 145-53.

Holmes, Ashley J. *Public Pedagogy in Composition Studies*. NCTE, 2016.

Irvine, Colin. "'Its Fine, I Guess': Problems with the Workshop Model in College Composition Courses." *Does the Writing Workshop Still Work?*, edited by Dianne Donnelly, Multilingual Matters, 2010, pp. 130-45.

Jacobi, Tobi. "Speaking Out for Social Justice: The Problems and Possibilities of US Women's Prison and Jail Writing Workshops." *Critical Survey*, vol. 23, no. 3, 2011, pp. 40-54.

Kynard, Carmen. *Vernacular Insurrections: Race, Black Protest, and the New Century in Composition-Literacies Studies*. SUNY P, 2014.

The Lab for Usability, Communication Interaction, and Accessibility (LUCIA). Auburn University, 2016. www.cla.auburn.edu/lucia. Accessed 17 Aug. 2018.

Mathieu, Paula. *Tactics of Hope: The Public Turn in English Composition*. Boynton/Cook Publishers, 2005.

Mathieu, Paula, and Diana George. "Not Going It Alone: Public Writing, Independent Media, and the Circulation of Homeless Advocacy." *College Composition and Communication*, vol. 61, no. 1, 2009, pp. 130-49.

Mathieu, Paula, et al., editors. *Circulating Communities: The Tactics and Strategies of Community Publishing*. Lexington Books, 2011.

Mauk, Johnathon. "Location, Location, Location: The "Real" (E)states of Being, Writing, and Thinking in Composition." *College English*, vol. 65, no. 4, 2003, pp. 368-88.

Moss, Beverly J., et al., editors. *Writing Groups Inside and Outside the Classroom*. LEA Publishers, 2004.

Reid, E. Shelley. "Peer Review for Peer Review's Sake: Resituating Peer Review Pedagogy." *Peer Pressure, Peer Power: Theory and Practice in Peer Review and Response for the Writing Classroom*, edited by Steven J. Corbett, Michelle LaFrance, Teagan Elizabeth Decker, Fountainhead Press, 2014, pp. 217-31.

Reynolds, Nedra. *Geographies of Writing: Inhabiting Places and Encountering Difference*. Southern Illinois UP, 2004.

Rivers, Nathaniel A. "Geocomposition in Public Rhetoric and Writing Pedagogy." *College Composition and Communication*, vol. 67, no. 4, 2016, pp. 576-606.

Royster, Jacqueline Jones. *Traces of a Stream: Literacy and Social Change Among African American Women*. U of Pittsburgh P, 2000.

Rule, Hannah J. "Writing's Rooms." *College Composition and Communication*, vol. 69, no. 3, 2018, pp. 402-32.

Spigelman, Candace. *Across Property Lines: Textual Ownership in Writing Groups*. Southern Illinois UP, 2000.

Style Wars. Directed by Tony Silver, Public Art Films, 1983.

Warner, Michael. *Publics and Counterpublics*. Zone Books, 2002.

Weisser, Christian. *Moving Beyond Academic Discourse: Composition Studies and the Public Sphere*. Southern Illinois UP, 2002.

Welch, Nancy. *Living Room: Teaching Public Writing in a Privatized World*. Boynton/Cook Publishers, 2008.

Wells, Susan. "Rogue Cops and Health Care: What Do We Want from Public Writing?" *College Composition and Communication*, vol. 47, no. 3, 1996, pp. 325-41.

Literacy as Threshold Concept: Building Multiliterate Awareness in First-Year Writing

Amanda Sladek

> The contextual nature of literacy is a threshold concept that one must move through to better understand composition as a discipline. A nuanced understanding of this concept enables students to critique dominant literacy ideologies and appreciate the diverse literacies present in everyday life. The literacy narrative, a genre that sometimes reinforces reductionist views of literacy, can push students to move through this threshold concept when students are encouraged to think beyond reading and writing in their essays. This article presents the results of a quantitative and qualitative study of 111 first-year writing students' literacy narratives, composed in response to a multiliteracies-focused prompt. Students indicated their developing understanding of literacy's context-boundedness in the diverse topics they chose, the definitions of literacy present in their narratives, and their overall rejection of the "literacy myth." These results are reinforced by interviews with students about their experiences writing their literacy narratives.

The word "literacy" is one of the most evocative and contested terms not only in writing studies, but in the culture at large. In popular discourse, literacy is a core value that is constantly under attack. This mindset is illustrated in a 2018 *Newsweek* editorial by Newt Gingrich and Gerard Robinson, which warns that inadequate standardized test scores in reading and math should make Americans "ashamed of how we are condemning our children to a future of economic insecurity and social decay." Those of us who teach writing know that this rhetoric is nothing new. From the 1874 emergence of composition studies as a "response to the poor writing of upperclassmen" (Rose 342), to the publication of *Why Johnny Can't Read* in 1955, to our contemporary concerns about texting leading to the downfall of writing standards, each generation has been characterized by its own perceived literacy crisis.

Bronwyn Williams argues that this crisis mentality stems in part from the public's incomplete understanding of what literacy has come to mean. A term that once referred to the basic ability to read and write has evolved with the culture's needs and values. The rise of the New Literacy Studies movement in the 1980s and works such as Shirley Brice Heath's *Ways with Words* called for a more inclusive understanding of literacy that includes a range of practices related to orality and performativity. In 1989, James Paul Gee defined literacy as mastery of the values, communication, and ways of being of a community, and noted that this does not need to involve print (7-9). More recently, scholarship on digital writing and multimodality has expanded our understanding of literacy even more. This understanding allows us to see the complex literacies of populations "in crisis," meaning that instructors do not need to "scare [students] with tales of the literacy crisis of their generation but instead teach them how to understand how language, culture, and identity work together" (Williams 181).

As our definition of literacy has moved further from the public perception that literacy is simply the ability to read and write, this relationship between literacy and context has become a threshold concept for composition studies. Jan Meyer and Ray Land define threshold concepts as "'conceptual gateways' or 'portals' that lead to a previously inaccessible, and initially perhaps 'troublesome,' way of thinking about something" (373). These threshold concepts are often key to understanding a field of study, and crossing these thresholds enables "a transformed internal view of subject matter, subject landscape, or even world view" (373). The idea of threshold concepts has been used to frame many of the key tenets of writing studies, most notably in Linda Adler-Kassner and Elizabeth Wardle's collection *Naming What We Know: Threshold Concepts in Writing Studies*. To their list I would add the concept that the definition of literacy is dependent on context. Thinking of literacy as something beyond decontextualized reading and writing skills is certainly troublesome for many students who have had the importance of print-based literacy instilled in them since childhood. Furthermore, understanding the social and contextual embeddedness of literacy brings about a new and more thorough understanding of composition as a discipline and the world at large, as it allows us to see the complex literacies embedded in all communities.

Students can begin to understand the threshold concept of literacy's dependence on context by examining their own histories in literacy narratives. The literacy narrative is, traditionally, a short autobiographical essay describing the author's development in reading and writing. Many versions of this assignment ask students to consider the impact their cultural context has on their literacy (Beaufort; Wardle and Downs) and encourage students to interrogate myths that reinforce literacy as a static construct (DeRosa). For example, the literacy narrative prompt included in Elizabeth Wardle and Doug Downs's *Writing about Writing* reader includes a series of questions for students to consider as they write, including, "What are some institutions and experiences in your life that have acted as literacy sponsors?" (263).

However, the narratives students produce often reinforce common cultural narratives related to literacy. In her analysis of sixty students' literacy narratives, Kara Poe Alexander found that all but one enacted what she calls the "literacy-equals-success master narrative" ("Successes" 608). Similar to Harvey J. Graff's "literacy myth" (xvi), this master narrative positions literacy acquisition as a necessary step toward achieving economic success. This fails to recognize the complex roles literacy plays in different contexts, as well as the power structures embedded in and reinforced by academic literacy ("Successes" 616).

The fact that this belief shows up in student writing is perhaps unsurprising. As Alexander acknowledges, students' understanding of literacy is shaped by a larger culture that portrays literacy (meaning the ability to read and write) as unquestioningly positive and uplifting. This idea can be reinforced by the readings instructors assign to prepare students to write their narratives. Literacy narratives like Malcolm X's "Learning to Read" (included in Wardle and Downs's literacies unit and quoted in their previously-referenced literacy narrative prompt) and George Orwell's "Why I Write" (included in Anne Beaufort's literacy narrative unit plan in *College Writing and Beyond*) portray literacy as liberating and even life-saving. When we are socialized into this belief, it is difficult to recognize that print-based literacy is not enough to guarantee one's success or even survival. It is even more difficult to recognize how judgments of literacy can serve as fronts for racism, classism, and sexism, and that different individuals and groups possess their own unique literacies that may go undetected in academic settings.

The literacy narrative, when properly framed, can help students understand the relationship between literacy and context by encouraging them to engage with the cultural and community forces that influence their literacy development. Some instructors encourage this engagement by asking students to use their alternative literacies to produce multimodal literacy narratives (Chandler and Scenters-Zapico). However, the same understanding can be achieved with a print-based personal narrative. The key is for literacy narrative assignments to emphasize the threshold concept that the definition of literacy is context-dependent. This threshold concept challenges the academy's position as the ultimate judge of literacy, broadens the range of practices that can be considered "literate," and moves students closer to a deepened understanding of literacy.

Yet, focusing students' attention on the relationship between literacy and communities may not be enough to move students across the threshold to a more contextual understanding of literacy. This was the case when I taught a version of Beaufort's literacy autobiography assignment as a new teacher. This assignment asks students to:

> . . . Consider [your] discourse communities . . . Analyze how those discourse communities have shaped you as a writer and analyze your writing rituals . . . in order to gain greater insight into the things

that have influenced your development as a reader/writer. (*College Writing* 190)

While this assignment encourages students to contextualize their literacy development, many of my students chose to focus on their academic communities and reproduce versions of Alexander's "literacy-equals-success" narrative.

The issue as I saw it had to do with the assignment's explicit focus on reading and writing. The literacy narrative prompts presented in both *College Writing and Beyond* and *Writing about Writing* ask students to include the events that shaped them as readers and writers. Wardle and Downs's prompt, for instance, includes specific instructions to begin by "considering your history as a reader and writer" (262). For many students, these early memories are school-centered and include at least some degree of success, evidenced by their presence in a college writing class. When I specifically encouraged students to write about a wider range of literacies (including, as Gee specifies, those that do not involve print), students took the opportunity to define literacy for themselves, showing more critical thinking than I had previously observed in the assignment. Moreover, their narratives, for the most part, did not equate academic literacy with economic success.

Here, I examine how students used their literacy narratives to interrogate the nature of literacy in their own communities. In a study examining eleven sections of introductory composition, I show how giving students space to write about a range of literacies can help them grapple with a new understanding of literacy and approach the threshold concept that literacy's definition changes with cultural context. By engaging with the complexities of their own literacy practices, students can begin to approach the complexities of literacy's role in their lives and in the larger society.

Methodology

This study uses data from a larger project that took place during the fall 2015 semester at a large public research university in the Midwest. I studied work from 111 students enrolled in "Introduction to Composition," the first of two courses in the English department's first-year writing (FYW) sequence. These students were enrolled across eleven sections taught by six instructors, including myself. While I did not control for age, gender, ethnicity, or other demographic factors (opting instead for the largest possible sample), my interactions with the students and instructors suggest that almost all participants were young adults, typically in their first semester of college.[1]

Each instructor taught a unit with a combined focus on the literacy narrative and multiliteracies. I provided each instructor with a unit schedule, homework assignments, and lesson plans along with the assignment prompt for the literacy narrative project.² Students worked with several texts that push the limits of literacy, including Gloria Anzaldúa's "How to Tame a Wild Tongue" and Tony Mirabelli's exploration of the literacies in food service work. Students also explored the literacies embedded in different cultural groups through a short assignment based on the BBC documentary series *Stephen Fry in America*.

The literacy narrative prompt gave students the option to focus either on academic literacy or an alternative literacy. Those who chose to write about alternative literacies were instructed to "think about how [they] learned the 'unwritten rules' of a certain community, subculture, skill, or activity" and explain how their topic can be considered a literacy. Adapting some of Beaufort's language, the prompt also stated that one of the assignment purposes was to prompt all students to "examine [themselves] as a reader and writer of texts (written or otherwise) in multiple contexts." My hope was that the addition of "written or otherwise" would encourage students to look beyond printed texts to the social aspects of literacy, even if writing about academic experiences. I also encouraged this by including an opening epigraph from Anne Ruggles Gere: "…literacy means joining a specific community through understanding the issues it considers important and developing the capacity to participate in conversations about those issues" (120).

As part of my larger study, I examined student work across all participating sections, conducted classroom observations of each instructor, and interviewed all instructors and five randomly selected students.³ Here, I focus specifically on students' written literacy narratives and oral interviews. My study corpus included 111 student narratives.⁴ I used QSR's NVivo program to sort narratives according to topic and to isolate and sort passages of interest in students' writing.⁵ I also rhetorically analyzed each narrative (described below in the appropriate sections). In the following discussion, I use insights gained through these quantitative and qualitative methods to demonstrate how students' definitions and discussions of literacy showed them grappling with the threshold concept that literacies are plural and context-bound.

Multiliteracies in Students' Topic Selections

One way students showed an awareness of literacy's dependence on context was through the topics they selected for their narratives. Participants submitted projects focusing on a wide variety of subjects, including sports, Greek life, and military service. To get a sense of the range of topics, I classified each narrative according to theme. In an initial pass through the corpus, I made note of commonly occurring topics. Then, using NVivo, I created categories for each topic and tagged each narrative accordingly. Those that did not fit a topic category were first tagged as *other*. Finally, I repeated this process with only the *other* category, creating a separate category for any topic that occurred five times or more. Eight categories emerged. Each category is described in table 1.

Table 1
Multiliteracies in Student Narratives

Topic Category	Number of Papers	Percentage of Corpus	Examples (Essay Titles)
LITERACY OF SPORT Describes the literacies involved in playing a sport, often as part of a high school or college team (counted separately from literacy of a subculture due to the topic's popularity).	25	22.5%	"The Complicated Etiquette of Softball"
READING, WRITING, AND ACADEMIC LITERACY Corresponds most closely to the "traditional" literacy narrative. Describes the author's experience learning to read and/or write and typically focuses on school experiences.	19	17.1%	"Learning to Read and Write"
RELATIONSHIP LITERACY Describes the author's experience learning the literacies involved in maintaining interpersonal relationships, including romantic relationships and friendships.	16	14.4%	"Early Lesson about Lying for a 5 Year Old Boy"
LITERACY OF A SUBCULTURE Relates the author's literacy development in a subculture, such as a fan community, Greek organization, or religious community.	13	11.7%	"Joining a Fraternity"
OCCUPATIONAL LITERACY Describes the author's experience learning the literacies of a job they've held.	11	10%	"Working at a Pharmacy"
LANGUAGE AND CULTURE Centers on either the process of learning a new language and/or culture (often, international students moving to the United States or U.S.-born students travelling abroad) or the process of learning slang terms or specialized terminology in one's native language.	9	8%	"English" (about learning English as a second language)
ARTISTIC LITERACY Describes the author's development in an artistic pursuit such as music or graphic design.	6	5.4%	"Animation Communication"
LITERACY OF A NEW SCHOOL Describes the author's experience learning the values and "unwritten rules" of a new school. Unlike academic literacy narratives, these center on the social and cultural dimensions of adjusting to a new school.	5	4.5%	"Here Come the Nuns" (about attending a Catholic high school)
OTHER Narratives that did not have a clear theme or centered on a theme found in fewer than five narratives.	7	6.3%	"A Life Changing Experience" (about the author learning to manage her epilepsy)
	111	100%	

When looking at the literacies students chose to describe, academic literacy is positioned as one of several literacies up for discussion and is not given a privileged position. In fact, most students chose not to focus their narratives on their experiences with academic literacy. Though "reading, writing, and academic literacy" is the second most popular single topic, combining the non-school-focused topics (separating the topics based on whether they focus on academic literacy) shows that 92 of the 111 narratives (roughly 83%) do not center on academic literacy. This shows that students are situating literacy in contexts other than the school system, which indicates that they are developing an awareness of the contextual nature of literacy. Even when combining the "language and culture" category with the academic literacy category, eighty-three narratives (roughly 75%) do not place sole (or, in some cases, even primary) focus on reading, writing, or verbal language.

Most narratives position reading and writing as part of an array of behaviors and practices that the author had to master to become literate in a specific context. For example, Courtney explains that to become literate in serving at the local Mexican restaurant where she was employed, she had to "learn the menu, learn to read the customer and learn how to manage [her] time so that [her] customers are always happy." Only one of these skills, learning the menu, involves reading a printed text. The others require knowledge of a complex range of constructs and behaviors including verbal communication, social cues, and self-regulation. In Courtney's narrative, the processes of reading and writing are discussed alongside the interpersonal and bodily aspects of her literacy as a restaurant server. Facility with print is just one of several skills needed to become successful or "literate" in this context.

Similarly, Stacey draws an extended analogy in her interview between working as a barista at a campus coffee shop (the focus of her narrative) and learning a language. As described in her narrative, gaining literacy in this environment involves learning the unique names for the prepared drinks (many of which reference campus buildings and traditions, which a literate barista would need to understand), the processes for making these drinks, and the abbreviations different employees use for the drinks. It also involves mastering the process of "translating" the customer's order and making the drink, a process she compares to dialect development in her interview:

> … each of these people who are working in the stores were taught by different people, and so that's kind of how a dialect for a language works, too. They're taught different languages by other people … learning how to be a barista [is] a giant allegory for . . . learning the language, since … how you grew up is where you were trained and how you were trained. And so, I mean, we do have an official guide-

book ... Sort of a dictionary and set of rules ... but oftentimes we don't actually follow it and just go with what's instinctively natural for us.

With this analogy, Stacey explains that complex language-learning processes occur in settings that can go unrecognized in the school system and in some academic discussions of literacy. While her understanding of dialect development may be incomplete, she shows an awareness of the contextual nature of literacy and argues for the complexity and legitimacy of alternative literacies, both in terms of dialect and in the embodied literacies required of baristas. For a first-year student whose only college English experience is introductory composition, this is a fairly advanced analysis of the literacy of barista work.

Exposure to multiliteracies led even the students who wrote about academic literacy to explain what, beyond reading and writing, they had to learn to be academically literate. For instance, several writers described how knowledge of their learning disabilities enabled them to become literate by their schools' standards. Another student, Martha, explains in her narrative how writing a successful college paper involves more than the skill of putting words on a page:

> Now that I'm in college, I realized that being literate in writing is knowing what you have to talk about. When we are handed essays for class, yes we are given a prompt we must talk about, but I also know that most professors want you to write to what they want to hear rather then what you want to talk about ...

Though most of her narrative focuses on reading and writing, Martha does seem to have a developing awareness that academic literacy extends beyond these skills. Moreover, her use of the phrase "literate in writing" positions writing as one among a range of literacies. To her, the word "literate" does not imply knowledge of reading or writing; literacy is contextual, and the context must therefore be identified. Again, her understanding of academic literacy is not perfect—most professors would likely quibble with her assertion that they want students to write what they want to hear—but this passage shows that she is working her way through the threshold concept of literacy as a contextually bound social practice. Students' progress toward this threshold concept is perhaps even more apparent when they offer their own definitions of literacy.

Definitions of Literacy in Student Narratives

As noted earlier, I asked students in the literacy narrative prompt to explain or illustrate how their topic can be considered a literacy. While a definition of literacy is not typically a convention of the literacy narrative genre, some writers chose to define the term explicitly within their narratives. These definitions provide arguably the clearest insight into how students framed their own understanding of literacy and how this knowledge developed. In my first reading of the corpus, I sorted the narratives into two categories based on whether they explicitly defined literacy. Using NVivo, I then isolated the definitions present in the thirty-four papers that did offer an explicit definition. Finally, I sorted the definitions according to content. For the sake of comprehensiveness, I placed definitions into multiple categories where appropriate. Four major themes emerged and are described in table 2.

Table 2
Definitions of Literacy by Theme

Theme	Description	Occurrences	Example
LITERACY AS COMMUNITY PRACTICE	The author attempts to define literacy solely within the context of a specific community or provides a general definition that specifies that literacy must be considered within communities.	25 occurrences, 20 papers[6]	David: "In order to be considered a literate member of the United States Army there are fundamentals for addressing a superior or subordinate soldier, specific terminology and acronyms used on a day to day basis, and proper customs and courtesies of the Army."
LITERACY AS "READING AND WRITING PLUS"	Literacy is defined as the ability to read and write, plus some other ability, definition, or restriction.	15 occurrences, 12 papers	Courtney: "A few weeks ago if you asked me to define the word 'literacy' I would tell you that it is having the ability to read and write. While this is true there is more to that word than I thought. Because of this unit I was able to learn that literacy is also having knowledge in a specific area."
LITERACY AS COMMUNICATION	These definitions emphasize the communicative aspects of literacy.	14 occurrences, 12 papers	Luke: "Soccer literacy is . . . being able to discuss with anyone who enjoys the sport and have a detailed conversation with them."
LITERACY AS READING AND WRITING	Literacy is defined as the ability to read and write and is not placed in any community or cultural context.	6 occurrences, 5 papers	Maria: "To me, literacy is about learning and being taught to read and write."
OTHER		6 occurrences, 6 papers	Emily: "Literacy is competence or knowledge in a specialized area."

As shown in the table, twenty of the thirty-four students (roughly 59%) who chose to define literacy in their narratives defined it at some point as a community practice. Most of these statements defined what literacy means specifically in the author's chosen community, such as David's definition of literacy within the United States Army (see table 2). Six of these definitions set their focus more broadly, explaining that in general, the definition of literacy must be placed in some sort of context. For example, Linus writes: "An essential part of communication, literacy is the ability to express your knowledge to a specific audience in a manner that will be meaningful to them." This definition, which was also placed in the "literacy as communication" category, specifies that a literate person must be able to participate effectively in a specific community context.

Definitions in the "reading and writing plus" category often use the author's changing understanding of literacy as a framing device, as with Courtney's definition in table 2. An equal number of students emphasized communication in their definitions of literacy; this theme of "literacy as communication" occurred fourteen times over twelve texts. Examples include Luke's definition of "soccer literacy" (table 2) as well as David's previously-discussed explanation of literacy in the Army. As with the "literacy as community practice" category, these statements all attempted to contextualize literacy rather than discussing it as a set of isolable skills such as reading and writing.

Only five students referenced the definition of literacy solely as the ability to read and write (often in those exact terms). These five students represent 14.7% of the students who defined literacy in their narratives and .045% of the total number of student participants. Notably, they all qualified their definition in some way. Two students used phrases indicating that the definition was their own personal definition ("To me, literacy is . . ." and "My definition of traditional literacy is . . .," respectively). In positioning their definitions as personal to them, they are implicitly acknowledging that other people can have different definitions. Whether this is a genuine belief or an attempt to placate the instructor, it shows some degree of grappling with the troublesome knowledge that literacy is contextual and can extend beyond reading and writing.

Another student in the "reading and writing" category, George, defines literacy in the first line of his narrative: "Literacy is known as the quality or state of being literate, especially the ability to read and write." Though uncredited, it is likely that George took this definition from dictionary.com, as it appears to be an exact quote. Though this may be an instance of the "open with the dictionary definition" trope, it is worth noting that he does not choose to open with the simpler definition of literacy as "the ability to read and write." Instead, the circularity of the first half and the use of the qualifier "especially" position reading and writing as one of several abilities that can be considered "literacy." In a similar vein, Susannah indicates that her definition of literacy is one of many by specifying that the term is "traditionally understood as the ability to read and write," implying that there are other, less traditional understandings of the term. Later, she refers to writing letters as "an universal literacy,"[7] using the indefinite article to indicate that it is one of several literacies. These cases suggest that even when students choose to focus their definitions on reading and writing, some still position the conventional definition of literacy as one of many possible definitions.

Students who did not include an explicit definition of literacy illustrated their understanding by telling stories about lessons they had learned and knowledge they had acquired, then explaining how each bit of knowledge contributes to their literacy. For example, Amir, who wrote his narrative about his experience as a sneaker collector, explains some of the terminology that a person would need to know to be literate in "sneaker culture": "… the correct term to call the shoe enthusiast are 'sneaker heads'… people that buy shoes, not because they like them per say, but because it's the newest thing out are called 'hype beasts'."

While many students centered their implicit definitions of literacy on language, not all did. Rather, several students' explanations view literacy in a similar way as Gee, as mastery of a community's communication and values. Such statements occurred 331 times in the corpus, over five times as often as explicit definitions of literacy. Moreover, these statements were present in 91 narratives, roughly 82% of the corpus. For example, Hamid describes the embodied literacies of soccer: "… you need to make quick decisions on what you should do whenever you have the ball. For instance, you are supposed to decide whether to pass the ball or shoot it as quickly as possible." He then goes on to explain one of the most important attitudes a literate soccer player must adopt: "[My coach] advised me to keep my dreams ahead of me when I play. He said, 'Look at the goal you want to reach, look forward to accomplish new things, and seek to break the previous records and put your own records'." While these aspects of soccer literacy do not focus on language, they are for him as essential as language and communication to developing full literacy in soccer. Explanations like this one show that, even when the students chose not to explicitly define literacy within their narratives, most still understood the knowledge, communicative norms, and behaviors that constituted their chosen literacies.

Working with a prompt that explicitly encourages students to write about alternative literacies led them to define (and, in many cases, redefine) what literacy means in their own communities. In doing so, they demonstrated that their literacies are valid, complex, and worthy of bringing into the writing classroom. They also showed their understanding of literacy's nuances and the many ways literacy can be defined; this level of awareness requires some critical thought. While not all students made their way through the threshold concept of literacy's multiple, context-bound definitions, most appeared to be getting there. In approaching literacy from this perspective, students also produced narratives that differ in an important way from the ones that dominated Alexander's above-referenced study: for the most part, they did not reproduce the myth that equates academic literacy with economic success.

Challenging the "Literacy Myth"

In expanding their discussions of literacy beyond the realm of printed text, students challenged the "literacy myth" or the "literacy-equals-success master narrative" that has been analyzed as a defining feature of student literacy narratives. Most narratives did not conform to this narrative pattern that Alexander found in almost all literacy narratives in her study. To test this observation, I isolated each instance of the "literacy-equals-success master narrative" present in my corpus using NVivo. While 59 out of Alexander's 60 students (98%) enacted this cultural narrative at some point in their texts ("Successes" 613-19), only 26 of my 111 (23%) did. This seems to suggest that a multiliteracies-focused literacy narrative does not prompt students to access this common cultural narrative in the same way the traditional literacy narrative can.

Interestingly, of the twenty-six students who included some form of this narrative, eighteen did not write narratives focusing on acquiring academic literacy. For instance, Stephen concludes his narrative about developing literacy in Boy Scouts by sharing how his experience has prepared him for later success:

> Boy Scouts is a fantastic organization that has taught me so many things over the years that I would never learn in school. It has opened my eyes to all the amazing opportunities I could take advantage of in the future ... Personally, I think that every child should experience scouting. It teaches leadership, perseverance, discipline, and it made me the young man I am today.

In some ways, this passage reflects the "literacy-equals-success master narrative" Alexander describes. Stephen points to unnamed opportunities that his literacy has made possible, a statement that perhaps views literacy "as utilitarian and practical, a means to an end" and that certainly "emphasizes future outcomes of literacy" rather than the role it serves in the present ("Successes" 623).

However, he pushes back against this dominant narrative by grounding this claim in a non-print-based literacy and by not equating his literacy with *economic* success. The equation of literacy with economic success is problematic partly because of academic literacy's entanglement with issues of race, culture, and access. Though the Boy Scouts are certainly not immune to these issues, Stephen equates the possibility of future success with the character traits he learned through this literacy: "leadership, perseverance, [and] discipline." Though he learned these values through scouting, they are values that could be instilled through other means as well. And while he does recommend scouting for all children, he does not position his literacy (or literacy in general) as sufficient for or the only path to success. This works against the "literacy-equals-success" trope and allows for the possibility of other literacies or forces leading to one's success or fulfillment. This understanding would be nearly impossible to achieve without first understanding that literacies are multiple and context-bound. Combined with the relative infrequency of the "literacy-equals-success narrative," the fact that most of the students who invoked a version of this narrative did not do so in relation to academic literacy is significant. While not every student was able to undo a lifetime of cultural influence and wholly reject the literacy myth (perhaps an impossible goal for a one-semester introductory writing course), many do seem to be at some stage in moving through this threshold concept and acquiring a more nuanced view of literacy.

Conclusions and Implications

When exposed to the New Literacy Studies and multiliteracies, most students demonstrated some degree of understanding of the contextual nature of literacy in their narratives. Framing students' own knowledge and community affiliations in terms of literacy gave them a framework though which to approach literacy as a construct. Whether they limited their definitions to specific communities or specified that literacy is context- or community-dependent, very few students wrote about literacy as the decontextualized skills of reading and writing. Even this small step enabled them to adopt a more inclusive, just understanding of literacy and to see the intelligence and expertise involved in a wider range of community practices. This resists the simplification inherent in the literacy myth.

This multiliteracies-focused unit also seems to accomplish Susan DeRosa's goal of using literacy narratives to help students critically reflect on literacy. However, students need to be guided in their reflection, especially early in their college writing careers. In a study conducted after her above-cited literacy narrative analysis, Alexander argues that instructors need to be more explicit in describing the types of reflection they want to see in their students' narratives: "For instance, if we see it as a particular goal of literacy narratives for students to examine and reflect upon certain ideological positions, we could explicitly discuss such values and ask students to articulate how events in their literacy lives lead them to embrace, reject, or appropriate these values" ("From Story" 61). Specifically asking students to think beyond reading and writing seemed to make them think more specifically and critically about literacy, which enabled them to write richer, more original literacy narratives. Very few students reproduced the simplistic, decontextualized myth that equates literacy acquisition with professional or social mobility. Instead, they were more often able to articulate the complexities of literacy and their relationship to it, working their way through the threshold concept of the context-boundedness of literacy. By crossing the threshold into a more contextual definition of literacy, some students began to question the assumption that academic literacy is a necessary and sufficient condition for success, critically evaluate the ways in which this literacy works to maintain power relations, and see the literacies practiced by a wider variety of people, including themselves.

This is perhaps most vividly illustrated by June, who frames her narrative around developing "literacy in cultural sensitivity." She opens her narrative with the following:

> I was always one to consider myself intelligent and educated … When it came to reading and writing, I was not only proficient, but enjoyed it … My junior year of high school, I became increasingly more aware of my vulnerable position in society by being black, and being female. I was naïve, ambitious, and ignorant of what the world held beyond my shallow world views. As I was exposed to more and more of the real world through media outlets, and community gatherings, I began to question my ideals and my morals until I thought I had a decent composite of my identity and what it meant, especially what it meant in relation to other people, and societal denominations … At that point in my life I didn't consider being black or female bad, but I wasn't to a level of education in cultural sensitivity that allowed me to recognize or acknowledge my disadvantages and realize that there was an establishment that promoted and enabled my detriments. I openly sought education and I realized that as far as school went, there were no classes or organizations that could teach me what I wanted to know. I knew plenty of American and World history, but I did not know my own.

As she begins to educate herself on social justice issues, she becomes more and more aware of the societal limitations placed on her because of her race and gender. She continues:

> I have the privilege of being educated, able bodied, and cis-gender. But, I have the disadvantages of being black, being female, being low class, having unacknowledged mental health restrictions, being outspoken yet disregarded among my predominantly white community, having my features mocked and criticized, while simultaneously praised on other races, being too young to have a say, and being trivialized to the point of invisibility. It does make me angry. It makes me angry that somehow I am a part of a society that has taught me

> and at one point made me believe that … other people are not only superior to me, but that they should be, and that as long as people have tried to initiate change, there has been little, if any, change.

Here, June clearly has a deep understanding about how her education—her academic literacy—does not make her immune from the forces of institutionalized racism, sexism, ableism, and classism. Yet, her burgeoning social justice literacy puts her in contact with equality-focused, pro-Black people and communities both local and distant. She closes her essay with: "Because of my literacy, there is nothing that could convince me that I am inferior. There is no other skin tone that I would prefer on my body, there is no end to the self-love that I have gained … I have the will of contention, I write my own slam poems, and as long as that literacy, that knowledge, that rekindling of sensitivity remains, I will maintain a firm and resolute faith in my beliefs."

Another example, Will, author of "Here Come the Nuns" in table 1, writes about his experience as a non-Catholic at a Catholic school. Several times, he uses the phrase "tyranny of Catholicism" when discussing his educational experience. He describes his feelings of oppression at his Catholic school, noting that people at the school would tell him that he is "going to hell" for not following the teachings of the Catholic church. Will also describes the pushback he received from classmates about his decision to take the Eucharist as a non-Catholic (a practice prohibited by the church):

> Imagine a school gym filled with a few hundred of your fellow class mates …They stare at me expecting me not to reach out to fathers hand and take the bread. As I reach out and grab the bread and put it in my mouth you can see the eyebrows of some raising in curiosity, "Did he really just do that?" "He's not even Catholic." I can hear the whispers as I walk past in the isle of kids … a friend of mine Sarah would always ask me every mass, "Why do you always go up and take communion if you're not Catholic?" I would simply tell her "Just because I was never confirmed doesn't mean I don't believe in God."

Will is repeatedly questioned, stared at, and even told he's "going to hell" for refusing to participate as a fully literate member of his school community. While he does mention a few positive experiences at the school and reflects on how the struggles he experienced made him a stronger person, Will ultimately concludes that his educational experience did not strengthen his relationship with God and that the school's focus on religion and the stigma he felt as an outsider were "a distraction from learning." Because he chose not to become fully literate in the community and its rituals, his lack of literacy held him back in his high school career.

Another student, Gabriela, came to see through the literacy narrative assignment that she possesses a literacy not sanctioned by the academy: softball. In her narrative, she describes her initial struggles with the sport and how she became literate by learning the "unofficial" rules, strategies, and plays needed to be successful. Her narrative frames her softball team as a community whose rules and norms she had to learn. When she later struggled with an academic literacy—her college calculus course—her knowledge of alternative literacies gave her confidence. Because she struggled to learn the literacy of softball and eventually overcame her difficulty, she began to understand that she could do the same with calculus. In her interview, she speculates about how writing her literacy narrative will give her confidence in the future, as she works toward medical school:

> I think as I struggle in futures or struggle, like, in the career itself, that I can look back on this and really remember the thing that fired me up about being a doctor as the same as firing me up about being a softball player and to really push it ... I think that my career and education and softball actually lines up pretty well because I was told that I didn't have a good understanding of algebra and understanding math, and that I wouldn't be able to continue. And it was the same thing with softball junior year when I was trying to be on varsity when my coach told me that I just didn't have enough experience or I just wasn't at the level of being a varsity player with the others. And so that set me back, just like in math, but you know you have to come back from it and keep going. And that's when I did varsity senior year ... So I can really connect it and look back. So I'm really happy I wrote [the literacy narrative].

Aside from the inherent benefits of acquiring a clearer and more just worldview, the process of critically analyzing the meaning of literacy can build students' confidence in their own diverse literacies.

Moreover, I believe this unit validates multiliteracies in a way that is mindful of Bruce Horner's critique of the academy's treatment of alternative literacies:

> But in [defending the validity of multiliteracies], we need ... to find ways to focus on the labor of these groups as they continuously rework, and thereby renew, literacy, texts, practices, and contexts—whether deemed "academic" or otherwise ... we should not resort to seeing ourselves as givers of the honorific of "literacy" to a broader range of forms and practices. Instead we can join these others in the

active work with literacy in which they have always already been engaged. (6)

In allowing students to select the topics of their narratives and define literacy for themselves, students are given the opportunity to decide what literacy means to them. This project can therefore be viewed as one step toward creating a classroom that nurtures students' perspectives, experience, and agency. Giving students the power to define their own literacies challenges the traditional power dynamics associated with literacy and helps them move through literacy's context-dependence as a threshold concept.

While the students in this study are, of course, at various stages of moving through the threshold concept of literacy's context-dependence, their work demonstrates that many of them developed a greater understanding of literacy and of composition as a discipline. The diversity of their topic selection also indicates a developing understanding of multiliteracies and how their own lives have been impacted by alternative literacies. As students continue their education and their lives beyond the academy, they can carry with them the knowledge that literacy is dynamic, multivalent, and contextual. While this knowledge may not be enough to rescue us from the perpetual "literacy crisis," individuals' transformed thinking can contribute to a fuller, more inclusive, more just understanding of literacy today.

Acknowledgments

Thank you to Mary Jo Reiff, Peter Grund, Amy Devitt, Megan Hartman, Annarose Steinke, Michelle Beissel Heath, and my reviewers at *Composition Studies* for their feedback at various stages of this project.

Notes

1. All participants provided written consent for their work to be used. They are referred to by pseudonyms. All components of this study have been approved by the University's IRB and the English Department.

2. The instructional materials from this unit, including the literacy narrative project prompt, can be accessed at https://literacynarrativeunit.weebly.com/.

3. While I contacted 55 randomly selected students to be interviewed (five from each section), only five completed an interview.

4. I use passages from student interviews to supplement and illustrate my findings; for the purposes of this article, interview transcripts were not included in the study corpus.

5. I did this by creating "nodes" for each potential category. Nodes allow the researcher to tag entire sources or discrete passages according to common themes.

6. Several papers defined literacy multiple times.

7. In direct quotes, I preserved students' spelling, usage, etc. to accurately portray their voices (except in cases where doing so would impede understanding). In this case, I don't know whether the student is from an area where the construction "an universal" would be common.

Works Cited

Adler-Kassner, Linda, and Elizabeth Wardle, editors. *Naming What We Know: Threshold Concepts of Writing Studies*. Utah State UP, 2015.

Alexander, Kara Poe. "From Story to Analysis: Reflection and Uptake in the Literacy Narrative Assignment." *Composition Studies*, vol. 43, no. 2, 2015, pp. 43-71.

—. "Successes, Victims, and Prodigies: 'Master' and 'Little' Cultural Narratives in the Literacy Narrative Genre." *College Composition and Communication*, vol. 62, no. 4, 2011, pp. 608-33.

Anzaldúa, Gloria. "How to Tame a Wild Tongue." *Borderlands/La Frontera: The New Mestiza*, Spinsters/Aunt Lute, 1987, pp. 53-64.

Beaufort, Anne. *College Writing and Beyond: A New Framework for University Writing Instruction*. Utah State UP, 2007.

Chandler, Sally, and Scenters-Zapico, John. "New Literacy Narratives: Stories about Reading and Writing in a Digital Age." *Computers and Composition*, vol. 29, no. 3, 2012, pp. 185-90, doi:10.1016/j.compcom.2012.07.002.

DeRosa, Susan. "Literacy Narratives as Genres of Possibility: Students' Voices, Reflective Writing, and Rhetorical Awareness." *ResearchGate*, 2008, https://www.researchgate.net/publication/237307101_LITERACY_NARRATIVES_AS_GENRES_OF_POSSIBILITY_STUDENTS'_VOICES_REFLECTIVE_WRITING_AND_RHETORICAL_AWARENESS.

Flesch, Rudolph. *Why Johnny Can't Read and What You Can Do About It*. 1985. Harper & Row, 1955.

Fry, Stephen, writer and performer. *Stephen Fry in America*. Sprout Pictures and West Park Pictures, 2008.

Gee, James Paul. "Literacy, Discourse, and Linguistics: Introduction." *The Journal of Education*, vol. 171, no. 1, 1989, pp. 5-17. doi:10.1177/002205748917100101.

Gere, Anne Ruggles. *Writing Groups: History, Theory, and Implications*. Southern Illinois UP, 1987.

Gingrich, Newt, and Gerard Robinson. "No Literacy, No Liberty: We are Condemning our Children to a Future Without Hope." *Newsweek*, 26 June 2018, http://www.newsweek.com/no-literacy-no-liberty-opinion-993641.

Graff, Harvey J. *The Literacy Myth: Literacy and Social Structure in the Nineteenth-Century City*. Academic Press, 1980.

Heath, Shirley Brice. *Ways with Words: Language, Life, and Work in Communities and Classrooms*. Cambridge UP, 1983.

Horner, Bruce. "Ideologies of Literacy, 'Academic Literacies,' and Composition Studies." *Literacy in Composition Studies*, vol. 1, no. 1, 2013, pp. 1-9, licsjournal.org/OJS/index.php/LiCS/article/view/4.

"Literacy, n." *Dictionary.com*, https://www.dictionary.com/browse/literacy. Accessed 25 Aug. 2019.

Mirabelli, Tony. "Learning to Serve: The Language and Literacy of Food Service Workers." *What They Don't Learn in School: Literacy in the Lives of Urban Youth*, edited by Jabari Mahiri, Peter Lang, 2004, pp. 143-62.

Meyer, Jan H. F., and Ray Land. "Threshold Concepts and Troublesome Knowledge (2): Epistemological Considerations and a Conceptual Framework for Teaching and Learning." *Higher Education,* vol. 49, no. 3, 2005, pp. 373-88. doi:10.1007/s10734-004-6779-5.

"Nvivo 11 Starter for Windows." *QSR International*, QSR International Pty Ltd., 2016, www.qsrinternational.com/product/nvivo11-for-windows/starter.

Rose, Mike. "The Language of Exclusion: Writing Instruction at the University." *College English*, vol. 47, no. 4, 1985, pp. 341-59. doi:10.2307/376957.

Wardle, Elizabeth, and Doug Downs. *Writing About Writing: A College Reader*. 3rd ed., Bedford/St. Martin's, 2017.

Williams, Bronwyn T. "Why Johnny Can Never, Ever Read: The Perpetual Literacy Crisis and Student Identity." *Journal of Adolescent and Adult Literacy,* vol. 51, no. 2, 2007, pp. 178-82. doi:10.1598/JAAL.51.2.8.

Emerging Public Literacies: A Micro-Case Study of Public Writing Pedagogy

Tyler S. Branson

This article conducts an IRB-approved micro-case study of public writing pedagogy by analyzing writing from nine participating college students in a class called "Writing for Public Discourse" at a very high-research institution in California. From a careful analysis of student-writing, coding particularly for the kinds of publics student authors imagine and enact through their writing practices, I offer a brief snapshot of what the public work of rhetoric looks like in one writing classroom. While some definitions of public writing pedagogies stress a *relocation* of writing instruction, I argue that in-class public writing activities like the op-ed can foster *emergent* public literacy skills where students imagine diverse public audiences and "play around" with different authorial roles capable of solving public problems. As writing instructors, we should understand these moves as starting points of public writing pedagogies and consider curricular approaches to this significant invention work that goes on prior to relocating the public writing classroom.

Public Writing and the "Headaches of All Sorts"

This article begins from the premise that teaching public writing is an incredibly fraught area of Writing Studies, despite the fact that field has been calling for its practitioners to "go public" for upwards of 20 years. From Peter Mortenson's call in his landmark *College Composition and Communication (CCC)* article in 1998, to Paula Mathieu's heralding of the "public turn" in Composition in 2005, to other important monographs from Linda Flower, Nancy Welch, Shirley Rose, and Christian R. Weisser—there is no shortage of work dissecting what it means to go public and what specific pedagogical practices encompass the public work of rhetoric. Most recently, Ashley J. Holmes's *Public Pedagogy in Composition Studies* offers case studies of pedagogical and administrative approaches to public writing pedagogy. Holmes notes myriad terms scholars and teachers use to describe public work, from social change to community engagement to real world or even service-learning projects (3). The differences in the terms teachers and scholars use to describe their work, according to Holmes, highlights different institutional values and professional contexts from which practitioners "go public" with their work. In other words, how teachers, scholars, and administrators define going public in their classrooms varies markedly depending on how they understand the word "public" functioning in the context of higher education.

For most, going public means moving the location of writing from the classroom to the outside world. Scholars argue that the benefits to students of such an approach include being able to: assert their own voice in an increasingly privatized world (Welch); influence public ideas (Herzberg); or develop rhetorical capacities to be able to "defend themselves in bureaucratic settings" (Wells 326). For others, this relocation serves a disciplinary purpose, too, as scholars call for practitioners in Writing Studies to be able to articulate its values to outside audiences (Adler-Kassner) or think more deeply about theories of public sphere in their work (Farmer), or even consider the importance of "local publics" and students' "situated public literacies" (Long). In response to these benefits, Weisser has noted that "involving students in 'public writing' is fraught with headaches of all sorts" (xi).

In terms of what public pedagogy actually looks like, though, Holmes has the most cogent definition the field has to offer. According to Holmes, public pedagogy in Composition is:

> An approach to the teaching of writing that values the educative potential for public sites, communities, and persons beyond the boundaries of the traditional classroom and/or campus community; these values initiate moves to go public with composition pedagogies by relocating composition teaching and learning within increasingly public spheres. (4)

In addition, Holmes notes that by relocating the site of public writing from the classroom to the outside world, students engage in exigences with different stakes and different levels of certainty about the outcome, which comes with significant and worthwhile risk:

> I value students going public—physically and spatially—in composition pedagogies, not because I conceive of the classroom as any less real than public spaces beyond, but because the classroom can feel like a somewhat protected environment. Inviting students to go public welcomes riskiness and messiness in the process of composing and community engagement: possibilities that I see as potentially productive for student learning. (23)

For Holmes, the value of public writing pedagogies is not in notions of authenticity of the audiences per se, but in moving from pedagogical spaces that are "low risk" toward "somewhat higher risk pedagogical contexts" (24). In other words, moving students to new spaces in which to encounter learning experiences prioritizes the "messy, complex, and often unexpected" outcomes (24). For example, Holmes describes a class she taught where her students, who served as mentors at a local middle school, were often frustrated when their mentees—deemed "at risk" by administrators—would not show up or were unable to leave class. Holmes describes how she used these unexpected, messy, and complicated moments as opportunities for discussion; as she puts it, the "messiness that came with unexpected challenges in going public represented some of the most valuable lessons students learned in the course" (26). Holmes's idea of "risk" is important for public turn scholarship. Paula Mathieu wrote in her important work *Tactics of Hope* over a decade prior about the ways public writing can be a "mysterious process" and a "risk that requires hope" (47). Though public turn scholarship provides valuable definitions for and benefits of relocating writing pedagogies, supplies authentic audiences, and cultivates more high-stakes writing activities, I often wonder if we have insufficiently interrogated this idea of "risk."

For example, while it is valuable to prioritize a certain amount of "risk" as we shift the exigencies in which students compose, traditional classrooms are still *risky enough* for public writing. As I will show in this article, certain activities may not necessarily leave the classroom yet still have students engage in a kind of "risk that requires hope." Moreover, there is value in classroom assignments modeled on public-facing contexts, even if the writing students produce does not actually circulate in the world beyond the classroom. In fact, from my analysis, I found that classroom-based public writing activities are useful for invention work that can help students define public problems. These activities also serve as a way to make visible the kinds of publics students imagine being impacted by their writing and echo the kinds of activities public rhetors pursue in the world outside the classroom. This kind of work is an *emergent public literacy* where students play around with writerly authority, and it is vital, I argue, for designing more situated public engagement activities that come with relocating the classroom to "higher risk" exigencies.

Rosa Eberly has made a similar point in her famous essay "From Writers, Audiences, and Communities to Publics: Writing Classrooms as Protopublic Spaces." Eberly posited that since writing classrooms have their own unique "institutional supports and constraints," they can "never be public spaces" (172). However, writing classrooms can function as *protopublic* spaces where students "practice public discourse in a writing classroom by thinking, talking, and writing about and for different publics" (172). This is valuable, she writes, because it allows students to take on public subjectivities where writers "invent and present themselves—in different publics or at different points in a public's process of forming, acting, disintegrating" (169). Whereas Eberly's goal with *protopublics* is to move the field away from having students imagine "always-fictional" or "prefabricated, homological audiences" (175), this microcase study understands protopublic work as an emergent literacy skill that can help teachers scaffold assignments toward more purposeful and engaged public writing assignments.

It is also important to understand that all of these discussions of the public turn in Composition draw on a long and complex history of the public sphere. The term "public sphere" was first popularized by historian Jürgen Habermas to describe a domain of society in which citizens unrelated to the nation state came together under a banner of common interests to deliberate political matters. In this idealized democratic space, Habermas writes, the public bracketed their differences and came together as equals to engage in rational-critical debate. Other scholars, chief among them Nancy Fraser and Michael Warner, have critiqued Habermas's vision, questioning if the democratic potential of the public sphere was ever even possible. In his oft-quoted "Publics and Counterpublics," for example, Michael Warner describes the public as spaces organized "by nothing other than discourse itself...only as the end for which books are published, shows broadcast, Web sites posted, speeches delivered, opinions produced. It exists *by virtue of being addressed*" (50). In other words, a public is merely the circulation of texts, or the "concatenation of texts through time" (62). Warner's notion that publics are constituted through the circulation of discourse underscores the open-ended, shifting, and contingent movement of discourse as well as the multiplicity of publics. Warner's theories are important for this study because the student writing I analyzed demonstrated similar kinds of gestures of address into their op-eds. As I will show, these gestures are key starting point for emergent public literacies.

The critiques of Habermas mentioned above also reveal a more situated and dynamic understanding of public discourse, which underscores the value of public writing assignments: they can function as a path for teachers to help students to relocate into the public sphere. This is potentially the kind of risk Holmes is talking about when she suggests that public writing involves relocating the college classroom to higher risk contexts. When writers work in the world to circulate what Warner calls counterpublic discourse, for instance, they are in a *conflictual* relationship to the status quo (85), discursively envisioning how the world should be. As Fraser has shown us, those moves carry very real risk for vulnerable and marginalized communities (66).

Certainly, though, students in a public writing classroom composing op-eds for the school newspaper (op-eds that are not even submitted for publication) are not taking those kinds of risks. There is no authentic circulation, either, at least by Warner's definition (62). Moreover, from the student writing I collected, there is very little evidence of the kind of circulation and counterpublic orientation that public sphere theories tell us "count" as public discourse at all. Instead, the student writers I observed were mostly playing around with language, imagining themselves as authority figures informing some kind of Habermasian public about a pressing need in the world.

And while my analysis of student writing does not necessarily show students taking the same kinds of risks that they might in public engagement partnerships or other kinds of relocation and discourse-circulation, it does show them taking risks of a sort. By posing as authority figures and attempting a variety of rhetorical strategies to address publics they imagine being influenced by their writing outside of the classroom, students are taking rhetorical risks. Indeed, I argue that we need to take more seriously this playing around with language as starting points of public writing. There is still significant intellectual work going on here, particularly when we look at reflective essays students composed that describe their rhetorical choices in their op-eds. In other words, while I do think it is important—as do many others in the field of public rhetoric—that students go outside the classroom into public contexts, this study shows that classroom writing can nevertheless foster what Gogin calls activities of publicity (539). Specifically, while the classroom does mitigate a substantial amount of risk, it still encourages the writer, as Deborah Brandt observes, to appropriate public-facing genres and imagine themselves as agents of change by taking on "the routines, social responsibilities, and epistemologies" associated with them (112).

Writing researchers and teachers, moreover, can build writing curriculum around these initial moments of risk-taking, public imagining, and authorposing as students anticipate readers and orient their writing toward public problems. In what follows, I first discuss my methodology of micro-case study; then, I analyze op-eds and reflective memos from nine student writers. Next, I interpret the intellectual work that students put into their essays, suggesting that rather than being misguided or mistaken, these students were critically grappling with the complexities of public writing. Finally, I suggest ways writing studies practitioners can use public writing activities like the op-ed as invention work for emerging public literacies before we relocate the composition classroom.

Snapshot: A Micro-Case Study of Public Writing Pedagogy

This study developed out of the so-called headaches of the public turn and a desire to look into the thick of it to see how students and teachers are wading through these issues day-to-day. The aim of this study was to analyze how one classroom, in one university, was grappling with these issues in their writing, and to consider how their literate experiences come to matter in the broader constellation of scholarship on the public turn in composition.[1] This article conducts what I am calling a micro-case study of public writing pedagogy by analyzing writing from nine participating college students in a class called "Writing for Public Discourse" at a very high-research activity institution in California. The term micro-case study is borrowed from Bruce McComiskey's edited collection *Microhistories of Composition,* in which he defines the methodology of microhistory as "shifting back and forth among scopic levels (or levels of abstraction), or by beginning with microscopic analysis and spinning its effects out toward larger contexts" (18). This kind of historical interpretation, he argues, creates knowledge "deeper than any knowledge gained through analysis at one level" (18). In a similar way, I am calling this project a micro-case study. By focusing on a tiny data-point in the broader constellation of public writing pedagogy, the goal is not so much to generalize about best practices from this one set of student experiences but rather, to question dominant narratives of public writing—primarily the notion that public writing is best understood in terms of relocation from the classroom to the "real world"—by showcasing how students' individual experiences with public writing in a classroom context can be seen as generative. From a careful analysis of student writing from public-facing writing assignments and reflective essays, a micro-case study offers a brief snapshot of how student writing comes to matter in one public writing classroom and what the public work of rhetoric looks like on the ground floor.

The catalogue description for "Writing for Public Discourse" states that the course is:

> An introduction to writing and public discourse in local, regional, national, and global contexts through analysis of writing in civic contexts, political activism, and public policy. Students reflect on and produce written research in a related area of inquiry.

In this particular section of the course, the instructor asked students to choose one specific issue or problem about which to write and research throughout the quarter and to produce written assignments related to this issue in a variety of genres. For the purposes of this micro-case study, I analyzed two distinct forms of student writing from that course: op-eds that students were asked to compose with the school newspaper as an intended audience, and a metacognitive essay that accompanied the op-ed in which students reflected on their rhetorical choices.

The question I used to approach the data was: what kinds of rhetorical strategies are at play when students compose for public audiences? As I analyzed students' editorials and reflective memos, I found several ways they thought about the audiences of their writing. For example, when analyzing the reasoning students gave in their metacognitive essays, I saw evidence of students addressing an audience, or what Ede and Lunsford describe as "audience addressed," an understanding of audience as a "concrete reality" (156). Thus, I marked any time students explicitly referred to an audience in their writing (even if it was simply "the audience" or "the reader"). I also found evidence of students describing amorphous publics and/or making appeals to specific *kinds* of readers (often, these invocations occurred in reflective memos *and* editorials). Ede and Lunsford call this "audience invoked," or rather, using "semantic and syntactic resources of language to provide cues for the reader—cues which help to define the role or roles the writer wishes the reader to adopt in responding to the text" (160). Students in this study used both of these rhetorical strategies simultaneously to imagine what Ede and Lunsford describe as a "complex series of obligations, resources, needs, and constraints embodied in the writer's concept of audience" (165). As they composed their essays and reflections, in other words, students played around with language and imagined a public readership for their work in unique and generative ways.

Of the nine student editorials and accompanying reflective memos analyzed, the topics students chose to write about were not all that surprising: most of them resembled student papers like those we have all likely read at one time or another when teaching similar assignments. As the chart below indicates, one student wrote in support of a recent piece of legislation, three students wrote editorials highlighting important social issues, two students wrote editorials urging a specific policy reform, and three students wrote editorials having to do with marijuana legalization. Of note in each of these topics is the scope of the issues they investigated. Five students, for example, wrote about widespread social issues impacting broad swaths of the country—a mass, Habermasian-public. Others, like Student A, however, chose issues specific to their local communities. Moreover, the editorials having to do with marijuana legislation were also relegated specifically to local issues, using the recent passage of Proposition 64 in California as exigence to argue about marijuana policy in the state. That some students focused nationally, and others locally, as they addressed/invoked public audiences shows emergent public literacy skills at work: students were playing around with language and imagining "a range of potential roles an audience may play" (Ede and Lunsford 166) as they wrote their work.

Table 1.
Student Editorial Topics

Student	Topic
A	Editorial in support of a California law raising the minimum age to buy tobacco from 18 to 21
B	Editorial calling attention to the nation's opioid epidemic
C	Editorial calling for improvements to the Family and Medical Leave Act (FMLA)
D	Editorial arguing in favor of the recent legalization of marijuana
E	Editorial arguing in favor of the recent legalization of marijuana
F	Editorial urging government investment in rural education
G	Editorial decrying the rising cost of higher education
H	Editorial decrying the prevalence of sexual assault on college campuses
I	Editorial arguing for better defined laws regarding DUI infractions and marijuana-use

Reading through student editorials and their accompanying reflective memos, I was most focused on how students conceptualized the rhetorical task of public-making. Interestingly, there was diversity in terms of the ways students worked rhetorically to create the publics they were imagining, even though—ostensibly—the audience should have been relatively consistent throughout each piece: local readership of the college newspaper. However, students conceptualized this reading public in very different terms, from those in their specific county back home, to wider audiences, to parents, to the American public in general. What is most significant, though, is that all students did incorporate various gestures of address for some kind of reading public.

Imagining Public Audiences and Public Needs: Students' Op-Eds

Student A's op-ed "Stopping Addiction at the Start: A New Hope for Future Generations" and its accompanying reflective memo are in praise of a recently passed California law raising the minimum required age to buy tobacco from 18 to 21. The beginning reads:

> Imagine yourself at 18 years old. You probably think you know it all, and no one can tell you differently. Easily convinced, incredibly impressionable, and dying to be cool, if your friends are smoking cigarettes, you probably are too. There's no reason not to smoke, especially if you legally can, right?

The move here, a direct call to the readers to imagine themselves at a younger age, immediately implies a readership significantly older than the student body potentially reading the college newspaper. The next paragraph reads:

> Fast-forward to now. You're older, wiser, and in hindsight, you probably wish you never picked up that first cigarette. Well the people of California and governor Jerry Brown wish you didn't either. This year, the state of California took the first step toward protecting future generations from the mistakes of the past. On June 6th, the tobacco purchasing age was changed from 18 to 21.[2]

Student A's move—to ask readers to think back to a younger time and then to come forward to the present and rejoice in the benefit of hindsight—constructs a reading public comprised of older smokers in need of guidance and leadership from a civic authority figure. In their reflective memo, Student A made a reference to "the reader" twelve times. Clearly, Student A saw themselves—even if momentarily here for this assignment—as an authoritative author, one capable of providing moral guidance and leadership in this area. Student A also wrote in their metacognitive essay about how their "readers" were persuaded. For example, Student A wrote that the use of this imagery "places the reader in a scene," and their rhetorical strategy "draws the reader in with a few interesting lines while not yet giving away the main argument."

The constant invocation of "the reader" also shows that Student A, however briefly, was imagining a reading public. By positioning themselves as a public figure capable of providing guidance and leadership, they were also assuming the role of a public expert and using the genre of the op-ed as a vehicle for social change. Their authorial voice has a distinct obligation to place the audience "in a scene" and "force a nostalgic feeling for one's youth." For example, in Student A's reflective memo, they want to "remind the reader how they too were once young and impressionable making them realize in some cases they may have been better off if the law upheld what was best for them at that time in their development." Furthermore, by asking "personal and morality" questions in their editorial, Student A was attempting to "question the type of legislation they want protecting their youngest family members when they are most vulnerable." Student A's imagining of a particularly older and misguided audience created the need for rhetorical strategies of "forcing nostalgia" and allowed Student A briefly to write as an authority figure. These kinds of scene-setting strategies are interesting because they represent basic genre conventions associated with various kinds of public writing, particularly in their efforts to effectively engage a public audience. While certainly not circulating counter-public discourse, at least not in the *poetic* way that Warner describes (81), I was struck here by Student A's boldness in their choice to claim ethical authority, their willingness to imagine a public markedly different from the assignment directions, and their attempt to engage in the genres of public writing by posing as an author capable of influencing a public audience from this positionality.

In Brian Gogin's *College Composition and Communication* essay on the op-ed assignment, he describes the different layers of publicness implicit in most op-ed assignments. There is "conditional publicity" when writing assignments assume that publicity is a condition of the assignment or that their rhetorical products are supposed to "interface with an amorphous public" (539). Gogin prefers another kind of publicity, though, that he calls activities of publicity. From this perspective, writers actively seek to engage or widen the attention of publics and see publics "as called into existence by rhetoric" (539). Gogin writes that from this perspective of publicity, students, rather than writing in a priori public genres (as in the case of conditional publicity), are instead able to emphasize and reflect on the various processes by which they "make publics and public knowledge" (539). Student A, in this sense, was not acquiescing to some amorphous public, but was actually engaging in a variety of activities of publicity, seeking to engage or widen the attention of a public they imagined in need of moral guidance and civic leadership.

Similarly, Student B, writing about the nation's crippling opioid epidemic, described in their reflective memo that their audience was "most likely oblivious to the issue," which allowed them to spend their editorial describing how the opioid crisis has "affected society." Student B began the editorial with the following:

> Policy makers and the media have focused on the threat illicit drugs pose on American society since longer than many people today can remember. However, since the late 90s there has been an unsettling rise in addictions to legal pain killers.
>
> Though it may be invisible to the media and the federal government, the opioid epidemic has inflicted terrible damage to millions of Americans and their loved ones. A federal investigation in 2011 reported that since 1999 over 650,000 consumers of opioid medica-

tions died of an overdose, all of which were prescribed by medical professionals. Averaging at around 55,000 deaths per year, the situation we find ourselves in is dire to say the least, yet only recently have we seen any major efforts to curb the problem.

In their reflective memo, after describing their audience as "oblivious," Student B situated the entire editorial as an education, rendering what was previously "invisible" visible again to the public:

> [The editorial's] purpose was to grab the reader's attention and ignite their curiosity on the topic. Following the title, a brief summary of the issue was written to provide the reader a rough idea of the topic, again to draw their attention. By listing the time frame and number of people effected, my first attempt to appeal to the reader's emotions was purposed to ensure the reader was interested in the topic.

While not directly addressing the audience like Student A did, Student B still understood their role as an authority figure and thus imagined an audience completely oblivious to opioid addiction. Then, in an effort to "ignite" the reader's curiosity, the author revealed the startling statistics of the true dangers readers face. Student B, in other words, had to imagine a completely uninformed audience as a prerequisite for positioning themselves as an author. Though some may read that as a lack of confidence (it is much easier to argue with an uninformed audience, for example), we might also see it as a kind of *playing around* with different kinds of audiences capable of being influenced, or a way of adopting a persona empowered to address a public audience about an issue of common concern in a public venue.

Student C, writing about the Family and Medical Leave Act (FMLA), consistently made appeals to a "college-aged reader" in their reflective writing, imagining a public potentially aligned with the college newspaper but also one more attuned to the needs of working families. "Despite the difficulty of attempting to compel college students to be concerned about a social and political issue that won't directly affect them until their procreating stage of life," Student C wrote in their reflective memo, "the author attempts to keep the explanation of the topic fairly simplistic throughout the essay in order to keep students interested." In other words, Student C saw their audience as close in age but nevertheless reluctant to care about FMLA. Student C began their editorial in the following way:

> Imagine walking out of the hospital—holding a newborn, exhausted, and ready to head home.

While driving home, a buzz from your cellphone informs you and your partner that you have received an email containing pertinent information regarding your family leave time. You excitedly read this long-anticipated email in hopes that you meet the qualifications of the 1993 Family and Medical Leave Act (FMLA) that entitles you to twelve weeks of unpaid leave to care for your new child. Unfortunately, as your newborn starts to cry, you and your partner read that your company does not fit the current FMLA qualifications and you must return to work tomorrow.

While most people consider their company's leave policy months before their child is born, the above vignette unfortunately illustrates the United States' inadequate paid leave policy.

As Student C wrote in their reflective memo, the audience they saw for this piece were folks "college-aged" (which to them means childless) who may not yet need FMLA, but an audience that nonetheless has the potential to be persuaded to empathize with FMLA. Student C described these rhetorical moves as "drawing the reader in because he/she is able to imagine the difficulty of being a parent, even from the car ride home from the hospital." So here, Student C pictured a reluctant, college-aged audience, and then took on the role of a public figure whose task was to create empathy through vivid storytelling. What is happening here is an emergent public literacy where this student is addressing an issue of common concern to an audience beyond the classroom and playing around with rhetorical strategies to engage with that audience.

Students D and E, two of the marijuana editorials, invoked the pronouns "we," "our," and "us" to refer to the local communities Proposition 64 impacts. "We must use the states of Colorado and Washington as models of success... Let's have our state embrace those who rely on and benefit from the plant," Student D wrote in their editorial. "We can decide to continue poisoning our society with old vices," Student E wrote about alcohol, "or take a stand for the betterment of future generations." Student I, the third marijuana editorial, maintained a distant stance, never using personal pronouns. In their reflective memo, they write that their assumption was that "the reader will be familiar with the cultural acceptance and 'casual' use of marijuana in California. With this in mind, I knew that I would have to make a logistical approach."

In contrast to Student I's logical prose and distant stance toward the audience, Student D and E wrote in their reflective memos about a different kind of reading public. In Student D's reflective memo, for example, they describe how they wanted to "appeal to the readers' sense of justice in convincing them to do the right thing in legalizing weed," which is why they chose phrases such as "we must" to convince their readers. And Student E wrote in their reflective memo that "most people fail to recognize the importance of marijuana legalization," hence their consistent use of personal pronouns. So even with three fairly similar topics—arguments that in some way support marijuana legalization—these students each imagined different reading publics. Student D saw a public confined to the state of California, one particularly susceptible to populist calls for justice; Student E, while adopting a similar populist style, saw their audience as having failed to recognize how important Proposition 64 actually was; and Student I imagined an entirely different reading public, one already amenable to the idea but lacking in some basic facts and statistics.

Other students, like Student F, who wrote about the topic of rural education reform, described their audience as "familiar" with the issue of rural education. Thus, their editorial is highly technical. They wrote, "Inner city schools especially are prioritized by the government, and while they do desperately need to be reformed, rural education has been put on the backburner," and continued, "the highly-qualified teachers and Adequate Yearly Progress (AYP) provisions of No Child Left Behind (NCLB) have made it difficult for low income, underfunded rural school districts to keep up." In their reflection, Student F wrote that they were attempting to appeal to their readers' "emotion and national pride." Student F also assumed that issues like education legislation and education statistics are "fairly familiar to most people." Student F's audience already understood this complicated issue being addressed (as opposed to Student B's "oblivious" audience), and this informed how Student F took on the role of author.

Other students imagined public audiences with varying degrees of interest in the material at hand. Student G's editorial, for example, constructed an audience with an active "interest on the topic of decreasing the cost of higher education." Their editorial, titled "What is the Cost of Education," argued that "the extreme costs of higher education is putting tens of millions of students in debt and causing students to abandon their degree before it is completed." Student G praised initiatives that provided graduating high school seniors with community college scholarships as "genius," because "making higher education more affordable is not only a want by the students, but it is a need by the nation." In their reflection, Student G noted that they visualized an audience that was multifaceted. Readers might potentially be unaware of the millions of students in debt, however, "for those in the audience that are students, they will hopefully begin to understand" the depth of the problem. So here, Student G saw an audience comprised of potentially everybody—though most with an "active interest" in student debt. This potentiality of audiences informed the rhetorical choices Student G made to help everyone "understand."

And despite the assignment description, which asked students to write for the local school newspaper, Student H nevertheless described their goal as attracting "a wide range of audiences, whether it be my peer students or parents of students." Their editorial, "Students in Danger: Why the Existing Laws on Sexual Assault on College Campuses are Not Enough" wrote, eloquently, that sexual assault laws "are only as effective as the school's noncompliance, as they are largely left to their own devices when creating student conduct codes." In other words, Student H's editorial was, as they described in their reflective memo, "directly addressing universities," but it was also an "informal" piece designed to impact anyone "interested in this issue." Student H imagined specific *and* broad audiences reading this piece at the same time.

Table 2.
Student Editorial Audiences

Student	Kind of Reading Public	Public Needs
A	Older reading public that smokes	Moral guidance
B	"Oblivious" reading public	Information and facts to "ignite curiosity"
C	College-aged reading public, potentially ambivalent	Empathy and facts
D	State of California	Unification, solidarity on an issue
E	State of California	Education on the importance of an issue
F	Public audience familiar with rural education reform	Logical, technical arguments to persuade about an issue
G	Reading public with an active interest the cost of education, from college-aged and up	Emotional arguments to increase understanding
H	Everybody, but especially universities, college students, and their parents	Technical arguments informing of a problem
I	College-aged reading public accepting of marijuana legalization	Facts and statistics

As Table 2 illustrates, the public audiences each student imagined in their editorial ranged from a specific state, California, to the broadest possible understanding of publics, society as a whole. Considering how the assignment asked students to compose an editorial for publication in the student newspaper, the wide-ranging audiences in this one class were perplexing at first. Why weren't the audiences more or less consistent? Why wouldn't the audience students address primarily be peers in the campus community? Why did each student imagine a different kind of potential audience for their piece? And what did they implicitly understand or theorize about publicity that allowed for such a diverse range of potential rhetorical impacts? It appears that each student, in order to engage with a public audience outside of the classroom, played around with various rhetorical strategies to take on the role of authority figures. At first, it seemed like their sense of audience was disjointed from the rhetorical task, a kind of audience dissociation, or maybe students were getting confused about their audiences in the genre of the op-ed. Some of the students who imagined broad swaths of the American readership clicking on their op-ed were perhaps playing it safe so as not to engage in the riskiness of addressing actual people or specific groups. However, as I will outline below, I think audience dissociation or student confusion are misdiagnoses of their writing. Instead, it might be beneficial to ask how these student editorials exhibit evidence of authors critically grappling with the complexity of writing for public-facing audiences—especially in a world where public writing comes with significant risks as well as potential rewards. Whether disqualifying job candidates for their social media posts (Elejalde-Ruiz), or facing extreme consequences when acerbic tweets go viral—as in the case of Justine Sacco, a 30-year-old communications director who was publicly shamed and ridiculed for a poorly worded tweet while traveling to South Africa (Ronson)—writing for public audiences today is incredibly fraught. And for the students in this study, I see in these editorials and their supplemental reflective memos emerging public authors working within the realm of activities of *publicity,* playing around with notions of a reading public as a way to take on the role of an expert author capable of enacting change in a fraught world.

Conclusion: Risk-Taking, Public Imagining, and Author-Posing

Deborah Brandt's *The Rise of Writing,* an interview-based study of what she calls "workaday" writers—or folks for whom writing makes up most of their day-to-day labor—is helpful for reflecting on the students from this study and their emergent public literacies. Brandt shows that by appropriating public-facing genres, even for private use, authors from her interviews were able to cultivate a rich set of rhetorical practices and mindsets. Whether they wrote about protests or composed hip hop lyrics that nobody would read—Brandt's interviewees were pursuing writing-based literacies, trying on "occupation: author" not necessarily because they wanted to become writers for a living, but "for the purposes of trading on its socially recognized forms and resources in order to carry out a project of self-edification" (112). In popular public genres, like news photography, hip hop lyrics, or perhaps even the op-ed, these genres

> often come to be filled up with the routines, social responsibilities, and epistemologies of their best-known public pliers. Taking over

>these genres—seizing them not as means of reception but as means of production—commits unaffiliated writers to these well recognized stances and responsibilities, and they become grounds of self-development. (112)

As I read Brandt's description of workaday writers, civil servant writers, and young writers composing in popular genres, I think of the student writing I analyzed in this study. Though my participants do not align squarely with the participants in Brandt's study, if she is correct that "so-called humdrum, ownerless, authorless writing" is "nevertheless embodied in and emanates from the experiences, personalities, knowledge, and histories of the people who create it" (48), then we can re-read their op-eds and reflective memos differently.

For one, I do not think that the students in this study were misguided or that they misunderstood the assignment. Rather, I see in their writing attempts to engage in activities of publicity, particularly by imagining different public audiences, and then embodying, as authors, what Brandt calls the "social responsibilities and epistemologies" of the op-ed in order to solve public problems. For example, Student A uses their op-ed almost as a public service announcement against smoking; Student C's op-ed functioned as a vehicle to convince college students to care about paid family leave. These students were not so much misunderstanding their audience but imagining themselves as writers in relationship to public problems and then creating what Brandt calls "publicly responsible texts," and using the op-ed to intervene rhetorically. The student writing from "Writing for Public Discourse" seems to be engaging in a kind of emergent public literacy that played around with language to try and embody the "authorial status and social reach and accountability" of the op-ed (Brandt 114). This is a kind of risk-taking. For one, these students are neither experts or authority figures, nor are they professional writers. There is necessarily a kind of vulnerability and/or fear when one takes on unfamiliar roles or postures as someone else. Also, by addressing significant public problems—like opioid abuse, paid family leave, or education reform—there is still an element of risk, because the questions asked and the solutions posed are emotionally charged. The kind of invention work that went into imagining those publics and posing as authors capable of solving those public problems is significant. And the kind of risk-taking I am describing here seems different from the kind in public turn scholarship that stresses the relocation of learning from the classroom to somewhere else.

One potential problem with this analysis is that, at the end of the day, building real connections is still one of the most important goals of public writing pedagogy. That is why Holmes' definition of relocation is the gold standard of public writing. And, as Jeff Grabill has shown, the "knowledge work" that goes on in communities and the inherently collaborative and deliberative ways those communities work together across differences to solve problems cannot be fostered solely by posturing as experts or pontificating on ways certain publics should behave. As Gogin has shown, that is where the op-ed assignment inevitably comes up short. However, the public imagining and author-posing that students do as part of the op-ed assignment should not be overlooked. As Jonathan Alexander and Susan Jarratt show in their interviews with students from the UC Irvine Muslim Student Union (MSU) about an organized protest against a conservative speaker on campus, each student understood their audiences in very different ways, which revealed to them how "profoundly performative" public rhetoric can be (536). The students in their study, they argue, complicate a traditional understanding of how writing is taught: first, students analyze an audience, then they construct an argument to address that audience, and finally they anticipate a specific kind of effect. Instead, the student activists all saw their rhetorical work differently. "When we asked our participants about the intended effects of their protest," Alexander and Jarratt write, "they answered variously, underscoring the complexity of the protest as an event that could—and would—be interpreted in multiple ways by different publics" (537). In this micro-case study, we similarly see students imagining different publics and positioning themselves as authors to solve public problems in different ways. The difference, obviously, is that the public rhetoric of Alexander and Jarratt's students was embedded in a specific context in an event outside of the classroom, which is different from facilitating student experiences with activities of publicity in an op-ed assignment.

Nevertheless, we can consider the op-ed assignment, and others like it, as opportunities to ask students to reflect on the publics they are imagining *prior* to public engagement. For example: what are some audiences that have the potential to impacted by students' rhetorical acts? What risks might students have to take on and/or avoid through these imaginations, and what connections would they need to build in order to be more effective? In some of my own public writing assignments, for example—whether an op-ed or an art installation or an information campaign—I also ask students to produce reflective documents where they answer questions like: what connections do you already have, and what kinds of connections would you need to build with stakeholders in order for your work to make more of an impact? In this way, students can hopefully take the invention work of risk-taking, public-imagining, and author-posing and eventually connect it to the real people and real stakeholders they would need to engage for their public rhetoric to work effectively outside of the classroom.

In the public writing classroom, assignments like the op-ed are potentially useful for teasing out the worldviews attached to particular public problems and for asking students to reflect on how they can orient themselves to those problems. Imagining these new orientations requires a certain amount of risk-taking, public imagining, and author-posing. These early moves of public rhetoric are crucial for moving students toward more complex public rhetoric projects like writing *for* and *with* community partners, as scholars like Thomas Deans have suggested. In order to get students to, as Phyllis Ryder writes, "seek out new opportunities to employ public discourses that capture the vision they wish to promote" (which I think is ultimately the main goal of public writing pedagogy), there is still messy work to be done prior to relocating the classroom. Using this micro-case study, the field can consider the potential of assignments like the op-ed for developing students' emergent public literacies prior to relocating to more "high-risk" pedagogical contexts.

Notes

1. The data-collection for this project was approved by the UCSB Human Subject Committee in September, 2016.

2. I have faithfully reproduced student writing as it appeared in their essays, some of which includes errors. For a variety of reasons, I prefer not to use [sic] to point this out each time, but rather to take each piece of writing on its own terms and look beyond superficial elements of the prose.

Acknowledgments

I would like to thank my former colleagues and students at the University of California Santa Barbara for the initial inspiration for this essay. I would also like to thank Joshua Daniel, Terry Peterman, and James Chase Sanchez for reading early drafts and providing useful feedback. And finally, I would also like to thank the two anonymous reviewers who provided extensive feedback and fair criticism during the revision process. My work would not be able to exist without the generosity of my colleagues all across the country. Thank you.

Works Cited

Adler-Kassner, Linda, and Elizabeth Wardle. *Naming What We Know: Threshold Concepts of Writing Studies*. Utah State UP, 2015.

Alexander, Jonathan, and Susan J. Jarratt. "Rhetorical Education and Student Activism." *College English*, vol. 76, no. 6, 2014, pp. 525–44.

Brandt, Deborah. *The Rise of Writing: Redefining Mass Literacy*. Cambridge UP, 2015.

Deans, Thomas. *Writing Partnerships: Service-Learning in Composition*. NCTE, 2000.

Eberly, Rosa A. "From Writers, Audiences, and Communities to Publics: Writing Classrooms as Protopublic Spaces." *Rhetoric Review*, vol. 18, no. 1, 1999 pp. 165–78, DOI: https://doi.org/10.1080/07350199909359262.

Elajaldo-Ruiz, Alexia. "Using Social Media to Disqualify Job Candidates Is Risky." *Chicago Tribune*, 11 Jan. 2016, http://www.chicagotribune.com/business/ct-social-media-job-candidates-0113-biz-20160111-story.html.

Ede, Lisa and Andrea Lunsford. "Audience Addressed/Audience Invoked: The Role of Audience in Composition Theory and Pedagogy." *College Composition and Communication,* vol. 35, no. 2, 1984, pp. 155-171, DOI: 10.2307/358093.

Farmer, Frank. *After the Public Turn: Composition, Counterpublics, and the Citizen Bricoleur.* Utah State UP, 2013.

Flower, Linda. *Community Literacy and the Rhetoric of Public Engagement.* Southern Illinois UP, 2008.

Fraser, Nancy. "Rethinking the Public Sphere: A Contribution to the Critique of Actually Existing Democracy" *Social Text* no. 25/26, 1990, pp. 56-80, DOI: 10.2307/466240.

Gogin, Brian. "Expanding the Aims of Public Rhetoric and Writing Pedagogy: Writing Letters to Editors." *College Composition and Communication*, vol. 65, no. 4, 2014, pp. 534–59.

Grabill, Jeff. *Writing Community Change: Designing Technologies for Citizen Action.* Hampton Press, 2007.

Herzberg, Bruce. "Service Learning and Public Discourse." *JAC,* vol. 20, no. 2. pp. 391-404.

Holmes, Ashley. *Public Pedagogy in Composition Studies.* NCTE, 2016.

Long, Elenore. *Community Literacy and the Rhetoric of Local Publics.* The WAC Clearinghouse, 2008.

Mathieu, Paula. *Tactics of Hope: The Public Turn in English Composition.* Boynton/Cook Publishers, 2005.

McComiskey, Bruce, editor. *Microhistories of Composition.* Utah State UP, 2016.

Mortensen, Peter. "Going Public." *College Composition and Communication*, vol. 50, no. 2, 1998, pp. 182–205, DOI: 10.2307/358513.

Ronson, Jon. "How One Stupid Tweet Blew Up Justine Sacco's Life." *New York Times,* 12 Feb. 2015, https://www.nytimes.com/2015/02/15/magazine/how-one-stupid-tweet-ruined-justine-saccos-life.html.

Rose, Shirley K., and Irwin Weiser. *Going Public: What Writing Programs Learn from Engagement.* Utah State UP, 2010.

Ryder, Phyllis Mentzell. "Rhetorical Publics: Beyond Clarity and Efficiency." *enculturation,* vol. 6, no. 1, 2008.

Warner, Michael. "Publics and Counterpublics." *Public Culture*, vol. 14, no. 1, 2002, pp. 49–90.

Weisser, Christian R. *Moving beyond Academic Discourse: Composition Studies and the Public Sphere.* Southern Illinois UP, 2002.

Welch, Nancy. *Living Room: Teaching Public Writing in a Privatized World.* Heinemann, 2008.

Wells, Susan. "Rogue Cops and Health Care: What Do We Want from Public Writing?" *College Composition and Communication*, vol. 47, no. 3, 1996, pp. 325–41, DOI: 10.2307/358292.

Improving Instructor Ethos through Document Design

Joanna Wolfe, Ryan Roderick, and Andrea Francioni Rooney

Despite much attention given to visual rhetoric in Composition, there is evidence that most first-year writing instructors overlook document design, both in their instruction and in the documents they produce for their students. These instructors may be underestimating the role that visually informative prose (that uses document design features such as chunking and visual hierarchy) can play both in helping students understand assignment objectives and in establishing a student-centered ethos in their classrooms. To illustrate how visually informative prose helps shape student perceptions of instructors, 166 first-year undergraduates responded to two assignment prompts: a visually informative and a minimally designed prompt. Students perceived the instructor who wrote the visually informative prompt as more experienced, enthusiastic, and caring than the instructor who wrote the minimally designed prompt, and they found the task more interesting when it was presented in the visually informative prompt. These findings suggest that creating visually informative classroom materials is a relatively low-cost/high-payoff strategy that can positively shape students' perceptions of the instructor and assignments.

Introduction

In 1986, Stephen Bernhardt issued one of the first major calls for composition classrooms to pay attention to "visually informative prose" (68). Visually informative prose structures texts into highly visible divisions through the use of design features such as headings, whitespace, and bulleted lists. When implemented well, such design features attract readers and enable them to access information selectively. Since Bernhardt's call to attend to visual rhetoric, we have seen many developments in the ways that visual communication can play a role in the first-year writing (FYW) classroom. Scholars such as Diana George, Dennis Lynch and Anne Wysocki, and Jody Shipka argue for the importance of teaching students to analyze and compose a range of visual texts, and our field now has several textbooks that foreground visual communication, including Donald & Christine McQuade's *Seeing Writing* and Lester Faigley et al.'s *Picturing Texts*. In fact, visual rhetoric has been encoded into the WPA Outcomes Statements, which advocates that students demonstrate an ability to attend to "the interplay verbal and nonverbal elements" in texts and learn common "design features for different kinds of texts" among other visual competencies.

If recent scholarship is any guide, many first-year writing (FYW) instructors tend to interpret the WPA guidelines for visual competencies as calling for the analysis or production of visual artifacts such as photo essays or videos, but perhaps pay less attention to using document design principles to produce the "visually informative prose" that Bernhardt describes. For instance, in a 2005 article on visual design in FYW, Margaret Graham and colleagues state in a footnote that they do not address document design in their essay because it has "received robust consideration in advanced composition and professional communication courses" (38). Similarly, in a 2010 article titled "Teaching Visual Rhetoric in the First-Year Composition Course," Kristen Welch and colleagues mention document design in a historical overview of the topic of visual rhetoric and then move on to discuss two assignments focused on analyzing visual artifacts. Lending further evidence to the interpretation that document design is of little interest to most FYW instructors, a 2007 study found that over half of the composition instructors at one major university "never" or "rarely" addressed document design in their classrooms (Nelms and Dively 220).

One exception to this trend can be found in Rebekka Andersen's recent call to teach document design as a close reading strategy. Andersen encourages her students to consider how the design of a text affects their interpretations and argues that such close reading can make students more adept readers of a range of texts. She first became attuned to the importance of document design when she noted her students struggled to follow "prose-heavy assignment prompts that rely on verbal rather than visual cues to guide reading" (15). When Andersen reformatted her assignment to use visual cues, such as a numbered list calling attention to the three main parts of the assignment, her students were much more successful in completing all parts of the assignment.

Although this visually informative prompt appears to be successful, Andersen worries both that a visually informative design could position her FYW students as passive readers and that her visual redesign might counterproductively inhibit the range of student responses to the assignment. She writes:

> When we design visually informative assignment prompts, we are guiding students to read the prompts in particular ways. We may be persuading them to value some tasks and expectations over others and, through imposing levels of subordination, limiting what might otherwise be creative readings and interpretations of the prompt—interpretations that may lead to more interesting or even appropriate responses to the prompt. (25)

At the end of her essay, Andersen reiterates these concerns. After noting that visually informative prompts have the benefits of reducing student intimidation and increasing motivation, she asks:

> But what kinds of readers are we asking students to be when we design prompts that do the work of comprehension for them? What kinds of responses can we expect when visual cues make assertions as to which aspects of a text students should value? (34)

Andersen advocates for visual rhetoric instruction for students so that they can learn to interpret texts that are both visually informative and non-visually informative. Her goal is to help students become more active and creative readers of a prompt's visual cues by teaching FYW students the core principles of visual rhetoric, and she proposes several activities that engage students in close readings of assignment prompts with differing levels of design.

While we agree that knowledge about visual rhetoric can be a helpful aid for close reading visual elements of assignment prompts, we are more interested in the effects that visually informative prompts might have on students' perceptions and attitudes related to the writing task and the instructor. We ask: how does an instructor's use of document design on an assignment prompt affect how students relate to the task and the instructor?

When we originally embarked on the research described below, we were motivated by the minimally designed assignment prompts that we perceived as common in our discipline. These minimally designed prompts—such as that in figure 1—run counter to the visual design we find in most textbooks and other professionally produced educational materials. Because there is substantial evidence suggesting that visual design can improve reader comprehension (Lorch and Lorch; McCabe et al.; Schriver), we assumed that the major obstacles to producing visually informative assignment prompts centered around effort: instructors lacked the time and the knowledge needed to produce well-designed documents. We thought, then, that we merely needed to provide evidence that document design is worth the investment in time and effort and they would be persuaded.

However, we suspect that Karen Schriver's 1989 characterization of non-academic writing as the "ugly stepsister of academic discourse" (323) might still hold sway today, making instructors inculcated in the rhetoric and values of academic writing reluctant to use strategies associated with non-academic texts. This ideological stance may help explain why even instructors asking students to produce or analyze visual and multimodal texts often use little document design in their assignment prompts. These instructors may associate visually informative text with the rhetoric of bureaucracies and institutions—an association that is at odds with the freedom and creativity they want to prioritize.

In what follows, we first make a case for why assignment prompts could benefit from increased document design. We then present data from a small study that shows increased document design can not only help writers communicate their message (logos) but can also foster a caring relationship with the audience.[1] Instructors may have good reasons for minimal design in their course materials, although they should be able to articulate why they are not using a rhetorical device that, as Charles Kostelnick suggests, "can radically transform the [text's] message" (112). We conclude by suggesting ways that writing program administrators can encourage increased attention to document design while not noticeably increasing the demands made upon already overburdened FYW instructors.

Why Assignment Prompts Can Benefit from Thoughtful Document Design

To illustrate what we mean by visually informative document design, consider figures 1 and 2. The two prompts in these figures have nearly identical content; the only content differences lie in minor changes to the wording (the visually informative design of figure 2 allows us to cut some words because it visually communicates relationships that figure 1 has to explicitly articulate in words). What is different is that figure 2 uses multiple document design features—including bold headings, indentation, different fonts, and shaded boxes—to call attention to the different types of information it contains.

Argument Synthesis Essay
Instructor: Anne Anonymous

In the Argument Analysis, you explained how an individual argument "hangs together" to create agreement between a writer and a reader. For this next major writing assignment you will need to analyze how a field of arguments might "hang together" along particular lines of argument or sets of assumptions. In some fields this kind of task is called a Research Summary, while in other fields, this task is called a Synthesis of Research or a Literature Review. Researchers use a synthesis to create "exigency" for their own research and to interpret a series of arguments that have been made about the issue they are researching.

Your task is to synthesize a field of arguments around an issue from our readings. In the past, some students have thought of this assignment in different analogies: Proposing new research to a group of researchers with a common interest; Telling a story of how prior research has responded to a problem; Constructing a "conversation" among researchers concerned with a common problem
All of these analogies suggest a need for particular rhetorical moves. The next section describes some of the rhetorical moves that will help you get started.

1) Pose a Research Question A **research question** will allow you to explore an issue raised by the essays we have been reading. One good way to generate ideas is to think of a question that one author would want to ask another author. For example, if you are focusing on the role of amateurs in participatory media, your first priority might be to work out what issues are at stake in this topic, and what questions come up around it that your essay will attempt to work out, and answer. A good research question might ask, "how do economic pressures relate to the rise of citizen journalism?" A poor research question might ask "What role does the Internet play in society?"

2) Incorporate a Paradigm Case—a case that, for you, sums up or epitomizes the issue. A case can be an effective way to begin integrating perspectives that answer your question and to grab your reader's attention. Referring to it throughout your paper can strengthen your evaluation of positions on the issue. For example, A specific political event such as Occupy Wall Street, or a specific public incident (such as the Boston Bombings) might help you talk about problems or questions that arise when we think about the role social media plays for journalism.

3) Analyze Major Approaches to Your Question An approach is "a belief, goal, or method that a large group of authors adopts for handling similar problems" (Charney & Neuwirth, 349). You'll need to analyze the 2-3 major approaches to handling the problem, using a minimum of 5 sources from the syllabus. For example, one approach to understanding the role of participatory media in political change is to focus on causes of political change, and such complex events can have multiple significant factors that affect them.

Figure 1. The original assignment document (attributed to "Anne Anonymous")

> **Argument Synthesis Essay**
> **Instructor: Debra Doe**
>
> **Background**
> In the Argument Analysis, you explained how an individual argument "hangs together" to create agreement between a writer and a reader. For this next major writing assignment you will need to analyze how a field of arguments might "hang together" along particular lines of argument or sets of assumptions. In some fields this kind of task is called a Research Summary, while in other fields this task is called a Synthesis of Research or a Literature Review. Researchers use a synthesis to create "exigency" for their own research and to interpret a series of arguments that have been made about the issue they are researching.
>
> **Overview of Goals**
> Your task is to synthesize a field of arguments around an issue from our readings. In the past, some students have thought of this assignment in terms of:
> - Proposing new research to a group of researchers with a common interest
> - Telling a story of how prior research has responded to a problem
> - Constructing a "conversation" among researchers concerned with a common problem
>
> All of these analogies suggest a need for particular rhetorical moves. The next section describes some of the rhetorical moves that will help you get started.
>
> **Rhetorical Moves to help you get started:**
> 1) **Pose a research question**: A research question will allow you to explore an issue raised by the essays we have been reading. One good way to generate ideas is to think of a question that one author would want to ask another author.
>
> > **EXAMPLE:** If you are focusing on the role of amateurs in participatory media, your first priority might be to work out what issues are at stake in this topic, and what questions come up around it that your essay will attempt to work out, and answer.
> >
> > | <u>Good</u> | <u>Poor</u> |
> > |---|---|
> > | "How do economic pressures relate to the rise of citizen journalism?" | "What role does the Internet play in society?" |
>
> 2) **Incorporate a paradigm case**: This is a case that, for you, sums up or epitomizes the issue. A case can be an effective way to begin integrating perspectives that answer your question and to grab your reader's attention. Referring to it throughout your paper can strengthen your evaluation of positions on the issue.
>
> > **EXAMPLE:** A specific political event such as Occupy Wall Street, or a specific public incident (such as the Boston Bombings) might help you talk about problems or questions that arise when we think about the role social media plays for journalism.

Figure 2. A more visually informative version that calls attention to the different types of information (attributed to "Debra Doe").[2]

Scholars investigating assignment prompts—including Irene Clark, Anis Bawarshi, and Melanie Burdick—have found these documents to contain a wealth of implicit and explicit information. This information includes the skills teachers want students to acquire; the values and assumptions of the academic discourse community students are invited to join; and the steps and procedures students are encouraged to take. Clark describes writing prompts as invitations for students to play a particular role that leads to the production of a new genre—the college essay (8-10). To help students understand their roles, Clark advocates that instructors make their expectations and assumptions explicit.

Both versions of the assignment in figure 1 attempt to follow Clark's advice to make explicit the roles students are invited to play. However, we argue that the visual design of figure 2 does a better job of calling attention to the multi-faceted nature of the assignment context by foregrounding the different kinds of cues the instructor has embedded in the prompt. In particular, the visual design of figure 2 encourages students to read the document at different levels and for different purposes. The design frees the reader from the linear reading strategies that are most common when we process text-heavy documents.

Figure 2 uses multiple document design strategies to facilitate different reading strategies. First, the headings encourage readers to first form a mental structure—or "skeleton" (Kumpf)—of the text that identifies its main working parts. Such a skeletal view helps with comprehension and recall by providing a structure for readers to encode and retrieve information in memory (Hyönä and Lorch; Lorch and Lorch; Sanchez, Lorch, and Lorch). Research indicates that such skeletal views are particularly beneficial when readers are unsophisticated or documents are complex (Hyönä and Lorch; McCabe et al.). Likewise, the fine-grained chunking—or breaking of information into short, meaningful units—aids with comprehension by allowing readers to process the document in parts rather than as a continuous flow of text (Murphy; Redish). This chunking invites readers to pause frequently and absorb what they have read. Thus, both chunking and headings encourage students to take in the complex, multi-faceted nature of the writing prompt.

In addition, the visual design of figure 2 invites rereading. As any experienced instructor knows, many students choose not to reread the prompts we give them, simply working off their first impressions of the assignment. A major benefit of visual design is that it enables the reader to scan a document for specific information they have already encountered (Ganier). By designing prompts that facilitate rereading, we send students a message that they should revisit these documents as they compose.

So far, the benefits we have discussed are mainly cognitive: visual design can help readers make sense of the complex requirements and cues embedded in assignment prompts and can assist in rereading. But, as we hope to show in the study discussed below, the benefits of well-designed assignment prompts can also be social. Our classroom documents establish a relationship between us and our students. Increasingly, as many universities require instructors to post syllabi and other materials online in advance of class start dates, our classroom documents are the first encounter students have with us as instructors. Students use these documents not only to determine our policies and requirements, but also to figure out who we might be as people and who we are as writers. For instance, researchers have found that minor changes in the wording of a syllabus can influence how likely students are to approach an instructor or how effective or caring students perceive an instructor to be (Ishyama and Hartlaub; Perrine, Lisle, and Tucker). Likewise, changes to a document's design have the potential to affect how students perceive their instructor.

Positive instructor perceptions are correlated with higher levels of student learning and in-class participation. Teven and McCroskey's survey of 273 undergraduate students showed that students who perceived an instructor to be more caring also believed that they would achieve higher levels of learning and engagement with the course. Other studies reinforce this finding by showing that students who perceive instructors to be more credible are more willing to talk in class (Myers) and more likely to engage in out of class communication with an instructor (Nadler and Nadler). Furthermore, positive instructor ethos is constructed through classroom communication. Some studies have shown how this positive ethos emerges from an instructor's verbal and nonverbal communication style. In one study, an instructor's tendency to use humor in the classroom was correlated with an increase in the amount of content students felt they learned (Wanzer and Frymeir). A separate study showed an instructors' verbal argumentativeness—a communication style characterized by attacking issues and advocating for a position—correlates with students' perceptions of instructor credibility (Schrodt).

However, the verbal and interactive communication styles discussed above are not the only areas where instructors construct their ethos. Instructor-authored documents (e.g assignment prompts, syllabi, course schedules) also factor into students' perception of instructors. Yet, to our knowledge, there is little research investigating how the visual design of assignment prompts influences student perceptions of their instructor.

Our Study

This study began as a class project in which we asked students to think aloud as they read classroom documents with and without visual design. We expected to find differences in what information students attended to and comprehended. However, what took us by surprise was how often students made inferences about the personality of the instructor based on the design. Students found instructors of visually informative documents to be younger, more enthusiastic, and all-around someone from whom they would be more likely to want to take a class. This seemed to us to be an important finding. If a change as seemingly small as using visual design in our classroom materials could not only help students understand our assignments but also motivate them and pave the way for more productive student-teacher rapport, wouldn't instructors want to know about it?

While research on teaching evaluations has called student perceptions into question—finding, for instance, that such evaluations are biased against female instructors (MacNell, Driscoll, and Hunt)—it is still the case that perceptions matter in some substantive ways. Researchers have consistently found that perceptions of instructor enthusiasm are strongly correlated with student interest and motivation in a course (Frenzel et al.; Patrick et al.; Scott; Stronge, Ward, and Grant; Zhang), which in turn can lead to higher student achievement (Stronge, Ward, and Grant). Other teacher-related factors strongly linked to student motivation include knowledge of subject (Patrick et al.; Scott), clarity of presentation or expectations (Patrick et al.; Stronge, Ward, and Grant), and having a caring attitude towards students (Scott; Stronge, Ward, and Grant). Thus, there is strong evidence that perceptions of an instructor can affect student motivation and performance.

Only one study we found has systematically looked at the effect of visual rhetoric on student impressions of their instructor. Harrington and Gabert-Quillan found that adding images to a syllabus had no effect on student perceptions. These authors note that both syllabi that they examined were already visually informative, making effective use of white space, headings, and tables. They conclude that the addition of images and graphs may not have added value and that the overall design and layout of a classroom document are more important than more graphic images. These results are consistent with Moys' finding that there is a happy medium when it comes to document design: too little variation suggests a writer who is distant and unengaged while too much variation can suggest a writer who is clamoring for attention (7-13).

Given that a teacher's ethos—which we define here to include an instructor's perceived competence, enthusiasm, and concern for students—affects the learning environment, our research question is: what impact does the increased use of document design in an assignment prompt have on student perceptions of an instructor's ethos?

Methods

To pursue our research question, we designed a survey that asked students to read two assignment prompts that presented similar content in different visual designs. Incoming first-year students received the survey via email. For one prompt, we applied visual cues to present assignment instructions (figure 1), and for the second prompt we relied on verbal cues to present instructions (figure 2). Students read both the original prompt that appears in figure 1 (attributed to Anne Anonymous) and the visually informative prompt in figure 2 (attributed to Debra Doe). Both prompts are two pages long and are identical aside from some rewording—mostly deletion—to accommodate the visually informative document. The visually informative prompt was slightly shorter than the original (841 words vs. 915) because the visual redesign allowed us to eliminate words introducing different types of information (e.g., the phrases "a good research question might ask…" and "a poor research question might ask…" were replaced with the headings "good" and "poor").

The prompts ask students to write a synthesis essay of 1250-2100 words that poses a research question, describes a case illustrating this question, and then defines how different authors the class has read respond to this question. We chose this prompt because both students and instructors routinely identify the synthesis essay as the most difficult assignment of the semester, and students generally struggle to understand what the assignment requires. The original and visually informative prompts appear in figures 1 and 2. The students were not told that one of the prompts was original and the other redesigned, nor were they given any information characterizing the prompts.

The order in which students encountered the prompts was randomized: 87 freshmen read the original prompt followed by the visually informative prompt, and 79 read the visually informative prompt first. The only substantial content difference between the two prompts was in the instructor's name: Anne Anonymous (minimally designed prompts) vs. Debra Doe (visually informative prompt). We chose a female instructor's name for both prompts both because the majority of first-year writing instructors at our institution are female and because recent research suggests that student perceptions of teacher effectiveness are biased against women (MacNell, Driscoll, and Hunt). Because of this bias, we reasoned that we would see a larger effect size if students believed the instructor was female, and we could also be more confident that any improvements in student perceptions would accrue to our largely female instructor population.

On a 4-point Likert scale, students answered a series of questions addressing their impressions of the assignment, course, and instructor for each prompt. The order of these questions was randomized. We then asked students which prompt they preferred and invited them to provide open-ended comments.

Participants

Participants included a random sample of 500 members of the incoming freshmen class at a private, research I university. Of these original 500, we received responses from 166 students, a response rate of 33%. The students completing the survey were evenly split by gender. In terms of major, their areas of study roughly reflect campus demographics, with 41% of survey respondents from Engineering or Computer Science, 20% from Fine Arts, 19% from Humanities and Social Sciences, and the rest from Business or Science. All participants were over 18 years of age. We limited our participants to U.S. citizens to limit cultural differences in how students relate to and talk about an instructor's character (Maitra and Goswami).

Findings

Students Strongly Preferred the Visually Informative Prompt

Figure 3 indicates that incoming freshman preferred the visually informative prompt. Overall, 65% of our participants indicated that they somewhat or completely preferred the visually informative prompt whereas only 18.7% of participants somewhat or completely preferred the original. This difference is highly statistically significant, χ^2 (4) = 34.07, p < .0001. As will be seen below, student comments leave no doubt that their preferences were based on the visual design.

Students' preference for the visually informative prompt was consistent regardless of their gender, major, or self-proclaimed interest in writing. There was a slight effect for the order in which students saw the prompts: those who saw the original prompt first were even more strongly in favor of the visually informative prompt than those who saw the visually informative prompt first.

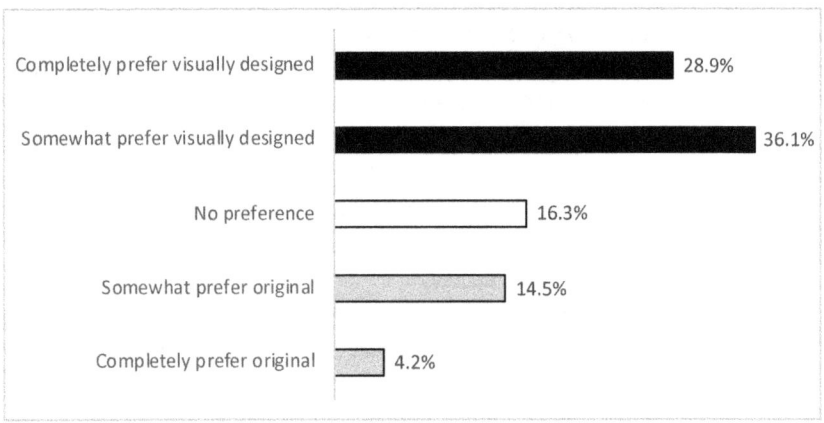

Figure 3. Student preference for the two assignment prompts

In open-ended comments, students noted that the formatting of the visually informative prompt helped them better comprehend the task. They claimed that the distinctions among different types of information helped them "mentally compartmentalize" different aspects of the project, gave them a better idea of the task and where to start, and made for generally "less boring" reading than the original prompt.

Students Made Inferences about Instructor Ethos from the Design

Not only did students prefer the visually designed prompt and find it easier to read, but table 1 below shows these preferences translated into a more favorable impression of the instructor who created the prompt. Students were more likely to indicate that the instructor behind the visually designed prompt was knowledgeable, caring, and enthusiastic—all factors that prior research indicates are strongly associated with student motivation. While the differences between the two versions is not major, students consistently inferred more positive impressions of the instructor from the visually designed prompt.

Table 1.
Student impressions of instructors who wrote the prompts on a 4-point Likert scale (1=not at all; 4=very much). * $p < .05$, ** $p < .01$

Survey questions	Anne (Original)	Debra (Visually informative)
How knowledgeable do you think this instructor is about academic writing?	3.58	3.70*
How experienced do you think this instructor is?	3.45	3.68**
How much do you think this instructor cares about her students?	3.16	3.39**
How enthusiastic do you think this instructor is about the course?	3.13	3.33**
How comfortable would you feel asking this instructor questions about this assignment?	3.17	3.27

Several students elaborated on these perceptions in their comments, noting the additional effort and care the visually designed prompt required. Students wrote that they perceived the instructor of the visually designed prompt as more knowledgeable, more caring, and more attentive to student needs:

> Debra Doe seems more likely to be able to answer questions and definitely more willing to, as she spent the time to try and clarify the assignment
> —Completely preferred visually informative prompt

> Her instructions are clearly and consistently formatted. This makes it seem like she really cares about her students: she seems to have put time and thought into the preparation of this assignment so that her students understand it and learn from it. It lends credibility to the instructor and makes her seem knowledgeable.
> —Completely preferred visually informative prompt

It is more engaging and gives me a sense that Debra is more willing to work for her students (which I'm sure both would do but just given that sheet)

—Completely preferred visually informative prompt

Debra Doe's instructions makes her seem more attentive to students' comprehension of the task.

—Somewhat preferred visually informative prompt

She generally seems kind even if demanding of the same expectations as Anne Anonymous.

—Somewhat preferred visually informative prompt

These comments indicate that at least some students perceived the document design as evidence that the instructor was dedicated to her students and concerned about their understanding, evident in students who described Debra Doe with labels like "attentive," "willing to work for her students," and "kind." These students believed that the instructor of the visually informative prompt perceived the assignment from her students' perspective, trying to imagine how students might use the document. They perceived this effort as evidence of pedagogical competence and investment.

The Prompt Design Affected Students' Perceptions of the Task

Table 2 indicates that the visually informative prompt also influenced students' perceptions of the assignment. Students were more confident in their ability to complete—and more interested in completing—the task described in the visually informative prompt. While this effect is not strong, it does resemble other studies that suggest a change in the tone of course documents affects students' beliefs in how difficult the class will be (Babad et al.; Harnish and Bridges).

Table 2.
Student impressions of the task on a 4-point Likert scale (1=not at all; 4=very much) *p < .05, ** p < .01

Survey questions	Anne (Original)	Debra (Visually informative)
How well do you understand what the instructor is asking you to do?	3.08	3.16
How challenging do you think this assignment will be?	3.18	3.06*
How much do you expect to learn from this assignment?	2.97	3.02
How interesting is this assignment?	2.41	2.57**

In open-ended comments, students elaborated on how the formatting affected their interest, comprehension, and confidence in their ability to complete the assignment:

> Debra Doe's instruction were more structured in their presentation, allowing me to begin addressing the assignment in a more analytic and cohesive manner.
> —Completely preferred visually informative prompt

> The aesthetic quality made the project seem more interesting.
> —Completely preferred visually informative prompt

> Her assignment was more interesting to me, so I feel that I would already be more prepared when I started it.
> —Completely preferred visually informative prompt

These students felt that the visually informative prompt gave them a clearer entry point into the assignment. Other students noted that the visually informative prompt would help them review the instructions during the writing process:

> I felt like it would be easier to refer back to the Doe instructions while writing the paper.
> —Somewhat preferred visually informative prompt

Such students indicated that the design of the prompt would help them locate particular information needed at a particular point in time.

However, not all students liked the redesign and some seemed to share Andersen's concerns that visual rhetoric can limit creativity:

> Anne Anonymous' instructions left more open to interpretation…I feel like I would get more out of her assignment because it feels more like actual writing rather than plugging information into a predetermined mold.
> —Somewhat preferred original prompt

Other students stated that they preferred the more linear presentation of the original instructions, which they perceived to flow more like a traditional academic essay:

> The instructions were written out in a linear, paragraph form. It seemed more conversational…My eyes were also less inclined to wander over the page.
> —Somewhat preferred original prompt

> The instructions flow more naturally because there are fewer breaks between points
> —Completely preferred original prompt

> I thought the layout was less disjointed in Anne Anonymous' instructions
> —Somewhat preferred original prompt

These students perceived the formatting of the visually informative prompt as restricting freedom and suggesting a "plug-and-chug" model of writing. For these students, the essayistic conventions of the original prompt better adhered to what they expected in a writing classroom.

Discussion

There is a wealth of research about inventing effective assignments that promote a variety of writing, reading, and thinking skills that has resulted in a number of respected guidebooks on assignment construction (e.g. Bean; Gardner). These guidebooks demonstrate careful thinking about what tasks students should perform and how those tasks might be structured to facilitate learning. However, most guidebooks dedicate little or no attention to how the visual design of assignment prompts might affect students' experiences.

Our study suggests that these guidebooks should be updated to discuss the visual design of assignment prompts. We found that visual design positively influences students' impressions of the instructor and assignment. Consistent with research suggesting that well-designed documents can enhance perceptions of the author (Moys; Townsend and Shu) and with research suggesting that small changes to a course syllabus can influence how effective, caring, or helpful students perceive the instructor to be (Harrington and Gabert-Quillan; Jenkins, Bugeja, and Barber; Perrine, Lisle, and Tucker), our students perceived the ethos of the instructor who wrote the visually informative prompt as more experienced, caring, knowledgeable, and enthusiastic than the instructor who wrote the original version. They also perceived the assignment as more interesting and less daunting when the visually informative design was employed. While these differences were not always major, they were consistent, and the visual redesign seemed to raise student responses across what psychologists agree are two primary dimensions on which we judge others: warmth and competence (Fiske, Cuddy, and Glick).

This study also complicates Andersen's concerns that increased document design can encourage passivity (by doing too much work for the reader) and limit creativity (by inhibiting readers from drawing connections across document sections). While Andersen is correct that ineffective use of document design can backfire, our survey results suggest that document design can also increase students' interest in the task and willingness to engage with the instructor. If an instructor feels that students are interpreting an assignment too rigidly, it may be unfair to blame document design in general, just as it may be unfair to blame any rhetorical device for its ineffective use. If we avoid visual rhetoric because it makes an assignment too easy to understand—but continue to use transitions, parallelism, and other forms of verbal rhetoric that can add clarity to a text—we are simply privileging the verbal over the visual.

Although our study focuses on visual rhetoric in traditional print documents, it also has implications for instructors who attempt to push the boundaries of composition with multimodal or non-traditional texts. As we experiment with new modes of delivery, we should evaluate the effects our texts have on our student readers. Our assignments, syllabi, handouts, and other materials serve many functions, including communicating a relationship with our students. As instructors experiment with what is possible, they should attend to how new modes of delivery impact the student-teacher relationship. Does an instructor who designs a prompt as an infographic or a video appear more enthusiastic, competent, or interesting? Do our materials and their design encourage a positive relationship that motivates students or do we convey an ethos that is detached and unconcerned with our readers' needs? Research suggests that there is reason for caution: Moys and colleagues found that visual design can lead to negative impressions if it is seen as cluttered or sensationalistic, and Harrington and Gabert-Quillan found that adding images to a syllabus had no effect on student perceptions. Thus, more may not always be better.

One clear drawback of our study is that it only looks at how design affects students' first impressions of instructors and has little to tell us about how these perceptions might take shape within the extended interaction of a classroom setting. Yet, research suggests that first impressions—particularly impressions of teaching style and personality—are lasting (Ambady and Rosenthal; Babad et al.). Moreover, there is logic behind these first impressions: it is reasonable to assume that an instructor who invests time and effort to visually design classroom documents for her students might also be willing to invest time and effort in other aspects of her instruction. As Ambady and Rosenthal suggest, it may be possible to predict factors such as enthusiasm, likeability, and competence from small samples of behavior (438).

Our study did not address how different groups of students might respond differently to the redesigned prompt. Most particularly, we did not specifically examine whether neurological differences (such as ADHD) or cultural differences might influence student perceptions. Prior research indicates that culture influences readers' reactions to visual rhetoric (Maitra and Goswami), so it is highly possible that a class of international students would respond differently to our redesigned prompt. Additional research could tease out some of these group differences.

Implications for Teaching and Instructor Training

We recognize that designing texts takes time and effort and many instructors may not have the background knowledge needed to design documents effectively. Yet preparing instructors to design classroom documents need not be time-consuming. Program administrators can provide their new instructors with examples of syllabi and assignments that are effectively designed and encourage new instructors to use these sample documents as templates. In addition, in forums for training new instructors, program administrators might follow Andersen's suggestion and show instructors multiple versions of an assignment, syllabus, or handout that uses different levels of visual rhetoric and ask instructors to hypothesize how students might respond to these variations. Such an activity might be followed by sharing the results of the study reported here, providing instructors with evidence illustrating how document design can influence student impressions of their teachers. Such activities should raise instructors' appreciation of document design as a valuable rhetorical tool. This appreciation could then be reinforced in myriad small ways. For instance, when administrators give instructors feedback on assignments, they might also mention how redesigning the document might help students unpack the expectations, requirements, helpful hints, and other types of information contained in the prompt.

Finally, guidebooks that provide advice on assignment design—such as John Bean's well-regarded *Engaging Ideas* or Traci Gardner's *Designing Writing Assignments*—should be updated to provide advice on visual rhetoric and assignment design. Such advice should not only discuss how document design can facilitate comprehension of an assignment's goals and requirements, but also how it can help foster a positive teacher-student relationship. By giving time to document design, instructors can show that they care about their audience and that they value multiple manifestations of rhetoric in their own writing: the visual and the verbal.

Notes

1. IRB approval was obtained. Protocol #: HS15-363

2. To transform the prompt in figure 1 to the one in figure 2, we applied two main design concepts: chunking and visual hierarchy. Chunking involves breaking information into short, meaningful pieces that readers can digest without overtaxing their working memory (Murphy; Redish). Effective chunking provides readers with "visual relief" (Kumpf) by allowing them to process the document in parts rather than as a continuous flow of text. In figure 2, the text has been chunked into information units averaging 40 words per text block whereas figure 1 averages 95 words per text block. Visual hierarchy adds order to chunking by presenting information on the page in a way that implies importance and signals the relationships of various elements to one another. Where chunking identifies basic units of information, visual hierarchy provides organization to those units, grouping them into larger blocks of similar content. Figure 2 uses visual hierarchy to help readers see that there are three main blocks of information: Background, Goals, and "Rhetorical Moves to Help you get Started" and that the last of these has several steps, each of which has an associated example. This visual hierarchy is achieved through the following elements:

- *Contrast and size* in the form of headings and subheadings that are visually distinct from the main text
- *Spacing and proximity*, in the form of indentation, to distinguish the hierarchal relationships of the headings, subheadings and examples
- *Contrast* in the form of text boxes that visually distinguish different types of information.

These various elements work together to help readers quickly visualize the different types of information and how these types are related to one another.

Works Cited

Ambady, Nalini, and Robert Rosenthal. "Half a Minute: Predicting Teacher Evaluations from Thin Slices of Nonverbal Behavior and Physical Attractiveness." *Journal of Personality and Social Psychology*, vol. 64, no. 3, 1993, p. 431.

Andersen, Rebekka. "Teaching Visual Rhetoric as a Close Reading Strategy." *Composition Studies*, vol. 44, no. 2, 2016, pp.15–38.

Babad, Elisha, et al. "Prediction of Students' Evaluations from Brief Instances of Professors' Nonverbal Behavior in Defined Instructional Situations." *Social Psychology of Education*, vol. 7, no. 1, 2004, pp. 3-33.

Babad, Elisha, et al. "A "Classic" Revisited: Students' Immediate and Delayed Evaluations of a Warm/Cold Instructor." *Social Psychology of Education*. vol.3, no. 1-2, 1999, pp. 81-102.

Bawarshi, Anis. *Genre and the Invention of the Writer: Reconstructing the Place of Invention in Composition*. Utah State UP, 2003.

Bean, John C. *Engaging Ideas: The Professor's Guide to Integrating Writing, Critical Thinking, and Active Learning in the Classroom*. John Wiley & Sons, 2011.

Bernhardt, Stephen A. "Seeing the Text." *College Composition and Communication*, vol. 37, no. 1, 1986, p. 66.

Burdick, Melanie N. "Teacher Negotiation and Embedded Process: A Study of High School Writing Assignments." *Journal of Teaching Writing*, vol. 26, no. 2, 2011, pp. 21–44.

Clark, Irene. "A Genre Approach to Writing Assignments" *Composition Forum*, vol. 14, no. 2, 2005.

Faigley, Lester, et al. *Picturing Texts*. W.W. Norton & Co., 2004.

Fiske, Susan T., Amy JC Cuddy, and Peter Glick. "Universal Dimensions of Social Cognition: Warmth and Competence." *Trends in Cognitive Sciences*, vol. 11, no.2, 2007, pp. 77-83.

Frenzel, Anne C., et al. "Emotional Transmission in the Classroom: Exploring the Relationship Between Teacher and Student Enjoyment." *Journal of Educational Psychology*, vol. 101, no.3, 2009, p.705-716.

Ganier, Franck. "Factors Affecting the Processing of Procedural Instructions: Implications for Document Design." *IEEE Transactions on Professional Communication*, vol. 47, no. 1, 2004, pp. 15–26.

Gardner, Traci. *Designing Writing Assignments*. Urbana, Illinois: NCTE, 2008.

George, Diana. "From Analysis to Design: Visual Communication in the Teaching of Writing." *Cross-talk in Comp Theory: A Reader*, vol. 54, no. 1, 2011, pp. 765–790.

Graham, Margaret, Katherine Hannigan, and Paula Curran. "Imagine: Visual Design in First-Year Composition." *Journal of Visual Literacy*, vol. 25, no. 1, 2005, pp. 21-40.

Harnish, Richard J., and K. Robert Bridges. "Effect of Syllabus Tone: Students' Perceptions of Instructor and Course." *Social Psychology of Education*, vol. 14, no. 3, 2011, pp. 319-330.

Harrington, Christine M., and Crystal A. Gabert-Quillen. "Syllabus Length and Use of Images: An Empirical Investigation of Student Perceptions." *Scholarship of Teaching and Learning in Psychology*, vol. 1, no. 3, 2015, p. 235-243.

Hyönä, Jukka, and Robert F. Lorch. "Effects of Topic Headings on Text Processing: Evidence from Adult Readers' Eye Fixation Patterns." *Learning and Instruction*, vol. 14, no. 2, 2004, pp. 131–152.

Ishiyama, John T., and Stephen Hartlaub. "Does the Wording of Syllabi Affect Student Course Assessment in Introductory Political Science Classes?" *PS: Political Science & Politics*, vol. 35, no. 3, 2002, pp. 567-570.

Jenkins, Jade S., Ashley D. Bugeja, and Larissa K. Barber. "More Content or More Policy? a Closer Look at Syllabus Detail, Instructor Gender, and Perceptions of Instructor Effectiveness." *College Teaching*, vol. 62, no. 4, 2014, pp. 129-135.

Kostelnick, Charles. "From pen to print: The New Visual Landscape of Professional Communication." *Journal of Business and Technical Communication*, vol. 8, no. 1, 1994, pp. 91-117.

Kumpf, Eric. "Visual Metadiscourse: Designing the Considerate Text." *Technical Communication Quarterly*, vol. 9, no. 4, 2000, pp. 401–424.

Lorch, R. F., Jr., & Lorch, E. P. Effects of Organizational Signals on Text-Processing Strategies. *Journal of Educational Psychology*, vol. 87, no. 4, 1995, pp. 537-544.

Lynch, Dennis, and Anne Frances Wysocki. "From First-Year Composition to Second-Year Multiliteracies: Integrating Instruction in Oral, Written, and Visual Communication at a Technological University." *WPA: Writing Program Administration*, vol. 26, no. 3, 2003, pp. 149–170.

MacNell, Lillian, Adam Driscoll, and Andrea N. Hunt. "What's in a Name: Exposing Gender Bias in Student Ratings of Teaching." *Innovative Higher Education*, vol. 40, no. 4, 2015, pp. 291-303.

Maitra, Kaushiki, and Dixie Goswami. "Responses of American Readers to Visual Aspects of a Mid-Sized Japanese Company's Annual Report: A Case Study." *IEEE Transactions on Professional Communication*, vol. 38, no. 4, 1995, pp. 197-203.

McCabe, Patrick P., et al. "The Effect of Text Format Upon Underachieving First Year College Students' Self-Efficacy for Reading and Subsequent Reading Comprehension." *Journal of College Reading and Learning*, vol. 37, no. 1, 2006, pp. 19-42.

McQuade, Donald and Christine McQuade. *Seeing and Writing*. Bedford/St. Martin's. 1994.

Moys, Jeanne-Louise. "Visual Rhetoric in Information Design." in *Information Design: Research and Practice*, edited by Alison Black, Paul Luna, Ole Lund, Sue Walker New York: Routledge, 2017, pp. 205-220.

Murphy, Stephen. "The Paragraph: The Weak Link in Technical Communication?" *Proceedings of 2000 Joint IEEE International and 18th Annual Conference on Computer Documentation*, 2000, pp. 477–482.

Myers, Scott A. "The Relationship between Perceived Instructor Credibility and College Student In-class and Out-of-class Communication." *Communication Reports*, vol. 17, no. 2, June 2004, pp. 129–37.

Nadler, Marjorie Keeshan, and Lawrence B. Nadler. "The Roles of Sex, Empathy, and Credibility in Out-of-Class Communication Between Faculty and Students." *Women's Studies in Communication*, vol. 24, no. 2, 2001, pp. 241–61.

Nelms, Gerald, and Ronda Leathers Dively. "Perceived Roadblocks to Transferring Knowledge from First-Year Composition to Writing-Intensive Major Courses: A Pilot Study." *WPA: Writing Program Administration*, vol. 31, no. 1-2, 2007, pp. 214-240.

Patrick, Brian C., et al. "'What's Everybody So Excited About?': The Effects of Teacher Enthusiasm on Student Intrinsic Motivation and Vitality." *The Journal of Experimental Education*, vol. 68, no.3, 2000, pp. 217-236.

Perrine, Rose M., James Lisle, and Debbie L. Tucker. "Effects of a Syllabus Offer of Help, Student Age, and Class Size on College Students' Willingness to Seek Support from Faculty." *The Journal of Experimental Education*, vol. 64, no. 1, 1995, pp. 41-52.

Redish, Janice C. "Understanding Readers." *Techniques for Technical Communicators*, 1993, pp. 13-41.

Sanchez, Rebecca Polley, Elizabeth Pugzles Lorch, and Robert F. Lorch. "Effects of Headings on Text Processing Strategies." *Contemporary Educational Psychology*, vol. 26, no. 3, 2001, pp. 418–428.

Schriver, Karen A. "Document Design From 1980 To 1989: Challenges That Remain." *Technical Communication*, vol. 36, no. 4, 1989, pp. 316-33.

Schrodt, Paul. "Students' Appraisals of Instructors as a Function of Students' Perceptions of Instructors' Aggressive Communication." *Communication Education*, vol. 52, no. 2, Jan. 2003, pp. 106–21.

Scott, Patricia A. "Attributes of High-Quality Intensive Courses." *New Directions for Adult and Continuing Education*, vol. 2003, no. 97, 2003, 29-38.

Shipka, Jody. "A Multimodal Framework for Task-Based Composing." *College Composition and Communication*, vol. 57, no. 2, 2010, pp. 277–306.

Stronge, James H., Thomas J. Ward, and Leslie W. Grant. "What Makes Good Teachers Good? a Cross-Case Analysis of the Connection Between Teacher Effectiveness and Student Achievement." *Journal of Teacher Education*, vol. 62, no. 4, 2011, pp. 339-355.

Teven, Jason J., and James C. McCroskey. "The Relationship of Perceived Teacher Caring with Student Learning and Teacher Evaluation." *Communication Education*, vol. 46, no. 1, Jan. 1997, pp. 1–9. *Crossref*, doi:10.1080/03634529709379069.

Townsend, Claudia, and Suzanne B. Shu. "When and How Aesthetics Influences Financial Decisions." *Journal of Consumer Psychology*, vol. 20, no. 4, 2010, pp. 452-458.

Wanzer, Melissa Bekelja, and Ann Bainbridge Frymier. "The Relationship between Student Perceptions of Instructor Humor and Students' Reports of Learning." *Communication Education*, vol. 48, no. 1, Jan. 1999, pp. 48–62.

WPA Outcomes Statement for First-Year Composition (v. 3.0), 2014. http://wpacouncil.org/files/WPA%20Outcomes%20Statement%20Adopted%20Revisions%5B1%5D_0.pdf

Zhang, Qin. "Assessing the Effects of Instructor Enthusiasm on Classroom Engagement, Learning Goal Orientation, and Academic Self-Efficacy." *Communication Teacher*, vol. 28, no. 1, 2014, pp. 44-56.

Course Design

English 3374: Writing, Rhetoric, and Multimedia Authoring

Estee Beck

English 3374: Writing, Rhetoric, and Multimodal Authoring, an introduction to multimodal composition rooted in the subfield of computers & writing, thrives in the literary studies focused English BA undergraduate program at The University of Texas at Arlington.[1] UT-Arlington is a Carnegie classified "very high research activity", HSI-designated, comprehensive university with a global enrollment of approximately 49,000 undergraduate and graduate students.

The English BA degree program offers undergraduate students some flexibility in degree progress. In addition to meeting state of Texas common core requirements, English BA students must enroll and complete three foundational courses (ENGL 2350: Introduction to Analysis and Interpretation, ENGL 2384: Structure of Modern English, and ENGL 3333: Dynamic Traditions in Literature) and meet credit requirements in "Early English Literature and Language" (3-credit hours), "Rhetoric and Theory" (6-credit hours), "Digital Writing and Authoring" (3-credit hours), and complete the 3-credit hour Senior Seminar. Students may also take four electives in any subfield course of English studies offered by faculty in the department.

An underlying assumption of the course reflects a long-standing position in Rhetoric and Composition—students do not compose in the alphabetic mode only and need exposure to and practice with the many modes of communication. Thus, the major goals of the course include development of the five multiliteracies (Arola, Sheppard, & Ball; New London Group; Selber)—with an introduction to an implicit sixth multiliteracy: tactility—through hybrid pedagogies of collaboration, feminism, and technological approaches.

The department describes the course in the undergraduate catalog as an "Introduction to the rhetorical structure of multimodality. An emphasis on composing writing-intensive and research-oriented projects for academic, business, and/or creative audiences. May be repeated for credit as topic changes. Prerequisite: ENGL 1301, ENGL 1302."

---

1. You can find the syllabi and course calendars for each Course Design essay on the *Composition Studies* website at https://compstudiesjournal.com/.

Institutional Context

The design of Writing, Rhetoric, and Multimodal Composition intersects with two local histories and personal experiences. The first history, located within computers and writing scholarship, continues the tradition of multimodal composition of teaching web design/development and in-class crafting and adds a new component: use of a university makerspace, a FabLab, developed in 2013 (with significant expansion in 2017).

Background and Observation of a University FabLab

Prior to my faculty arrival in 2015, a librarian—now director of the FabLab—sought funding for a small FabLab space through an internal university grant. The university granted seed money to purchase the required equipment needed for a space to be designated as a FabLab.

My path intersected when I joined UT-Arlington, prepared to teach this course with the composing practices common to what I conceived of as multimodal composition. Such projects included a digital literacy video biography and a made-from-scratch website using HTML and CSS, as well as activities with blogs, social media, and in-class crafting of objects that engaged with visual, spatial, linguistic modes though not necessarily through computing technology. When I toured the university during faculty orientation, the guide walked us through the FabLab located on the first-floor of the main library. Buzzing machines fabricating objects whirled. Bodies camped out. Hunched over computer screens, students sat, while the contents of backpacks littered the linoleum. On occasion, a FabLab worker offered assistance. Students engaged politely but firmly—just waiting. For these makers, crafting meant investing time. Near covetous of the technologies and the dedication to making, I visualized how to integrate the FabLab in Writing, Rhetoric, and Multimodal Authoring. I desired to inspire students to make things through rapid prototyping and iterative design.

The second history and experience occurred during the first offering of my course design and through the second and third iterations the course. A former faculty member, trained in computers & writing, proposed this and other courses (like ENGL 3372: Computers & Writing) during the 2000s, to expand undergraduate multimodal and electronic curricular offerings. Given this history, I assumed student exposure to multimodal composition in the curriculum when I joined faculty in 2015.

When students encountered the course, backlash to non-alphabetic essayistic writing ensued—fast. I learned, from enrolled students, that many courses in the English undergraduate program privileged "textual" work—with a strict definition of text as words on a page. This definition is quite different than how computers & writing specialists define "text" as a body of work with linguistic, visual, and aural modes in multiple mediums (cf. Arola, Sheppard, & Ball, 2014). I also learned, from students, that faculty usually assigned projects with emphasis on alphabetic essays of literary analysis with little to no deviation except for some rhetorical analyses (conducted in essay form) and creative writing projects. Time has borne out some evidence to the contrary, and a couple of colleagues have shared student multimodal projects with faculty. However, student reports led me to conclude that the prevailing view of composition in the undergraduate curriculum assumed alphabetic essays.

Risky Reflection

Given this tension between the integration of the FabLab and English majors reporting experience with (and reliance on) essays, an alchemy transforming students' knowledge and practice from essayistic composition to multimodal composition occurred in spectacular fashion. I share here these two issues as points of professional vulnerability: 1) a feeling of being so out-of-bounds within an English studies program that I wondered—for some time—what I had to offer to the students and if my training fit with the overall culture of the department; and 2) a feeling of student uncertainty about moving outside of the intellectual comfort zone of essay writing—honed over years of practice—to use technology in the FabLab for projects that did not quite fit their conception of what English studies did or was. I discuss this strange mixture further in the critical reflection.

Theoretical Rationale

This course draws on the teacher/scholar history of multimodal theories and practices and uses hybrid pedagogies to train students for rhetorical production and distribution of the many modes and media available. Because students do not compose strictly essays in other courses or in their personal and professional lives, I see it as my job to prepare them for the multimodal and literate realities they inhabit; thus, the course design and scaffolded course learning outcomes, which I discuss in this section, reflect this position.

In contrast to the essayistic tradition of English studies, the NCTE 1996 statement, "On Viewing and Visually Representing as Forms of Literacy" posits educators need to introduce students to print and non-print texts. I use this statement to open discussion with students on the theoretical underpinnings of the course, which argue multimodality is not a new concept; rather, teacher/scholars in Rhetoric and Composition and English studies writ-large have advocated for writing with multiple modes of communication for decades. As Cynthia Selfe repeatedly argued, multimodality opens up all available means of communication and persuasion. As such, teachers must integrate these modes in instruction unless they want to make English studies irrelevant for students who participate in a landscape saturated with multimodality across media.

Because of the complexity of multimodality and the need to convince students in ENGL 3374 of its relevance in English studies, the NCTE statement—in combination with two lectures, activities, and small- and large-group discussions about these many modes—forms a foundation for students. Additionally, this intellectual work prepares students to engage with one of the course learning outcomes, "Discuss how traditional forms of writing, i.e., the college essay, have changed in response to multimedia forms of authoring." I intend that students exit the course conversant in multimodality and are able to articulate, through personal advocacy and theoretical justification, the importance of the use of multimodal composition alongside (or in lieu of) the essayistic tradition in English studies.

Building upon this foundation, the course lectures, directed discussions, small-group work, and scaffolded activities include works by New London Group (1996) on multiliteracies in combination with *Writer/Designer*. I find that the authors of *Writer/Designer* expertly unpack the scholarly writing by New London Group to make terms accessible for an undergraduate audience. I use the multiliteracies article (1996) in two ways: first, to expand on definitions and terms given by *Writer/Designer*, and second, to show how Arola, Sheppard, and Ball explained complex scholarly work in a textbook for an undergraduate audience.

The two goals of these points intersect with another course learning outcome: "define key course terms (such as digital rhetoric/humanities, multimodality, multiliteracies, HTML/CSS) and be versed in the theories and practices of digital rhetoric & digital humanities." This outcome prepares students to speak conversationally to non-academic and academic audiences on these terms after course concludes.

The dual preparation of learning how to address varying primary and secondary audiences connects to another learning outcome of the course: "represent information ethically for diverse audience/stakeholders/clients." To meet this goal, students conduct audience analyses with each course project. By practicing audience analysis, students attend to the rhetorical situation, exigency, and 'difference zone' (Biesecker) when writing texts in varying contexts. Coverage of the Bitzer/Vatz debate—with Jenny Rice's (née Edbauer) and Biesecker's elaborations to draw attention to the complex and dynamic iterative process of audience and exigence (re)formation—informs lecture and discussion on the rhetorical situation. In bridging theory and practice, I provide students with an audience analysis heuristic to help orient them toward imagining audience. When course projects have real audiences, students use heuristics to observe and record audience characteristics gleaned from visual and aural clues.

For every course project, students defined and used terms and developed audience analyses to meet another course learning outcome endemic to a multimodal composition course: "define, examine, and create different discourse modes (aural, visual, spatial, verbal, & linguistic) under rhetorical dimensions (audience, purpose, context)." It is not enough to lecture and teach students concepts and assess learning through quizzes, tests, or essays. Rather, the thrust of this outcome is that students gain proficiency with the internal logics and structures of both electronic and non-electronic composing and can define, evaluate, analyze, and create multimodally with attention to tactility.

When students begin the FabLab course project, lectures and discussions about the place of rhetoric, its connection with tactility, and culturally-situated practices of making objects with symbolic meaning emerge. Connecting theories of rhetoric with making objects in a FabLab requires readings, appropriate for an upper-level undergraduate audience, that specifically address how objects exert suasive forces upon other objects and people.

Thus, I found David Sheridan's "Fabricating Consent" an appropriate entry for students. Sheridan's thesis makes scholarly room to theorize how three-dimensional fabricated objects afford rhetors with four new types of rhetorical arguments arising from certain modes of communication. Specifically, in the literature review, Sheridan builds a case for teacher/scholars to consider how objects function rhetorically with, "... their own distinctive rhetorical power" (255). This savvy argument provides fertile ground for discussions with students about: a) the nature and being of rhetoric; and b) how objects operate in the spatial and gestural modes through interaction with other bodies and objects; and c) what forces objects bring to bear in environments.

While his work does not explicitly address the tactile nature of making, in my reading of his work an implicit stance emerges that the tactile mode is integral to making in his discussion of objects and their rhetorical affordances. In order to gain entry to the five modes of communication, one needs to use the sixth mode—the tactile mode—to interact with or create and form materials and objects. In conversation with Sheridan's work, I introduce students via lecture to Angela Haas' article, "Wampum as Hypertext," where she argues American Indians—in their use of wampum shells and other weaving materials to record alliances, ceremonies, treaties, and wars—were the first hypertext theorists and practitioners. American Indians create wampum hypertexts, according to Haas, through digital rhetoric, which she defines as "...refer[ring] to our fingers, our digits, one of the primary ways (along with our ears and eyes) through which we make sense of the world and with which we write into the world" (84).

While she does not explicitly name 'tactililty,' she makes a link through the definition with how people use fingers to 'make sense' (i.e. to receive and make tactile signals and memories). If the five modes communication—linguistic, visual, aural, gesture, and spatial—lead to what the New London Group called "...significant modes of meaning-making," (64) and the tactile sense leads to making meaning for people, then there are six modes of multimodality—not five. Teasing this nuance out for students also helps them experience how knowledge is co-constructed through conversation with scholarly work.

At the same time, this outcome is not the only reason I use Haas' scholarly work with students. There are two additional motives: 1) the recent history of makerspaces has been coded as cis-white-male, which excludes the centuries of practices of women homemakers and indigenous peoples; and 2) the racially and ethnically diverse student population of UT-Arlington calls upon me to integrate the constellation of methods and practices by many cultures. I also want to honor students own culturally-situated practices and encourage them to bring these practices with them into their coursework.

The design of this course, with an assignment that uses the university's FabLab, allows for students to make things that honor and respect their cultures and lifeworlds. Central to the theoretical design of this course, then, is a series of readings and discussions of counterpoints that synthesize several course goals. This synthesis allows students to intellectually and culturally engage with multiple viewpoints throughout the remaining semester.

Self-Assessment, Reflection, and Revision

The final two course goals help students learn revision, self-reflection, assessment, and collaboration—key practices for multimodal composition, especially if a student is new to creating multiple modes. For these practices, I rely upon the work in the edited textbook, *Multimodal Composition*. This resource provides multiple heuristics for students to use when they first design and prototype projects with unfamiliar hardware and software. Specifically, I select tables from the textbook, depending upon the nature of the assignment, to guide students toward self-reflection with their own technology use. These tables are especially helpful for those teachers who, like me, want students to build meta-awareness and critical thought from the failures and successes that emerge during multiple iterations of designing and re-designing a project. I also find that many of the tables can be modified and built upon for local contexts.

Guiding students along this path of meta-awareness and critical thought also serves a larger purpose in the course: assessment via grading. In teaching multimodal composition, I take Cheryl Ball's editorial pedagogy to heart, believing that students who do the work will perform exceedingly well in terms of grading. I do this in the service of a larger belief that students need to know it is okay to fail in a classroom—and to fail often—especially when learning how to compose in new modes. It is often the multiple failures that teach the most valuable lessons.

Supporting this belief is assessment that rewards labor not the product of the labor. The labor-based assessment takes into account the labor performed on projects via weekly progress reports, weekly check-in discussions with students, and students' accounts of the work performed for each stage of each assignment. This may remind some readers of Asao Inoue's labor-based grading contacts; however, at the time I ran ENGL 3374, in Summer 2015, Fall 2015, and Fall 2016, I was unaware of Inoue's teaching practices with labor-based grading. That said, in reviewing his 2019 publication on the topic, a full integration of the theories and practices he espouses would fit well within the scope of this course design. I think so for two reasons: first, I find merit in his argument that single dominant standard assessment grading leads to White language supremacy; second, I believe, with Inoue, that measuring labor benefits students, because students take responsibility for articulating their own labor practices and account for—in an empowering manner—how their labor meets the learning goals of the course. The assessment via grading learning outcome of the course thus asks students to develop and maintain meta-awareness and reflective accounts of their progress on projects and to document their own learning progress. This includes successes, failures, and their labor in process.

The design of the course weaves together theory with practice to situate students' learning, regardless of what knowledge of multimodal composition with which they begin. It also promotes multimodal creation, development, and distribution as a valued form of representation of thoughts alongside essayistic traditions. The structure of the course introduces students to multimodality across a range of learning outcomes; the guiding philosophy urges students to see the instructor as a guide or mentor who has specialized knowledge and respects students' personal ways of coming to knowledge. The tables from *Multimodal Composition* show this philosophy in practice, as does Haas' comparison of wampum to hypertext.

In putting the theory into practice, my assumptions was that students would have experience encountering and interacting with multimodal composition but would also need explicit assurance feeling comfortable with failure when designing and prototyping projects. Thus, building in activities help students practice meta-awareness and self-reflection of learning are key to this course design.

Critical Reflection

Each iteration of the course resulted in varied feedback from students—with the second run of the course tending toward more positive reactions and feedback, and the third tending toward more teaching failures and students' expressions of feeling overwhelmed and uncomfortable with failure. It is this third run of the course which invites opportunity to discuss teaching failures and gives significance to the field of writing studies.

The first few weeks of the 15-week semester proved challenging in terms of student buy-in to theories and practices to which the literary-studies focused English undergraduate curriculum had not previously exposed them. Despite the careful introduction of readings and lectures on multimodal composition, during one particularly memorable class session, five students experienced dissonance toward material and lectures learned in other courses.

Defining Text: Rhetoric and Composition Versus Literary Studies

During one lecture, I introduced the term "text" and defined it through Arola, Sheppard, and Ball's expanded definition in *Writer/Designer*. One student immediately responded with a reference to a literature colleague's definition of text as, "printed words on a page only" and followed-up with other remarks about the wrongness of the definition to which I introduced the class. Four other students chimed in with support for text being printed words only. This moment brought lecture to a halt. I explained that, perhaps the colleague in Literature—whose training in literary studies—probably held this definition of text, those in Rhetoric and Composition (and in the sub-field of Computers and Writing) tended toward the more expansive definition. I explained that this was due to research on multimodality emerging from the New London Group, with subsequent scholars building upon this work to open writing studies toward many modes of communication. Interestingly, as another student shared during discussion, some students read this as a progressive movement in English studies, one that the "conservative curriculum" of the English program at UT-Arlington did not integrate in other courses. Since this iteration of the course held class once a week for 2 hours and 50 minutes, and I began class with lecture (and was only able to progress in for ten minutes before this moment), I elected to spend the next hour and a half with students discussing their experiences with the curriculum and their thoughts about text and multimodality.

While I would like to report that I found this discussion enriching, I left course that day with the following questions: "Why did I get hired here? What do I have to contribute? What do I have to offer students?" I also felt like I did not have adequate exposure to the culture of the undergraduate program to prepare me for how to integrate multimodality with students enrolled in this course.

This feeling of alienation from my turf left me professionally bruised. I had not read the culture of the BA curriculum. Nor did I complete my homework on previous course offerings through the undergraduate course descriptions posted each semester, where I could have gleaned important information on how to frame multimodal composition to students whose primary production relied upon years of a well-honed craft: the alphabetic essay.

If I had done my homework, I would have seen that my course design, however innovative, clashed with student expectations of a course in a literary-studies focused general English education curriculum. While I would not have changed the course assignments, I would have delivered lectures and activities with different strategies, including discussing the role of a multimodal composition course in a literary studies focused BA English curriculum and how the projects in the course compared and contrasted with projects in other courses. While dusting off my disaffection for my teaching approach in the course, I had to forge ahead with the course projects and remind students of the time and labor involved in creating multimodal works; I had to assure them that it is okay to fail, while I felt I failed the students.

I noticed during the first project of the course that some students tended to work up against the deadline for projects, which left them fatigued about the unexpected labor needed to complete the assignment. Thus, with the second, larger project, I redesigned deadlines to allow for five smaller deadlines so that when students neared the major deadline for the project, smaller portions of the work—abstract, prototypes, reflection, photographs with captions—were completed and needed to be reassembled and revised for a coherent and polished final submission. During the second course project, students reported greater sensitivity toward failure: some believed that failure to design or compose their project as imagined (especially given the products of their labors) correlated to a poor assignment grade. On a weekly basis, I disabused them of this destructive notion through sharing stories and images of my failures first learning how to compose multimodally as a graduate student. In my mind, I thought I was promoting a non-shame based culture in the classroom by showing my early attempts—and then my later polished and published projects—to illustrate how developing the literacies for multimodality takes time, patience, practice—and most importantly humility.

The weekly stories and sharing of failures did seem to help students feel more comfortable and less overwhelmed about developing their projects. Some students reported relief in seeing that even professors sometimes fail to produce intended results. The same students also shared seeing the quality and number of attempts to produce a multimodal project helped them realize expectations for their own work. I began to perceive that tangled in the anxiety of learning multiliteracies and new hardware and software were imaginings of highly polished compositions—the kind of quality that an advertising agency might produce in a digital campaign. Once students understood my expectations for production were far from a professional production, most seemed relaxed and more willing to dive into uncharted composition territory.

At the same time, an interesting observation emerged with a focus on composing both in-class and out-of-class on a near weekly basis. On the class meetings where we discussed course readings, especially ones where students could connect theoretical texts from other courses into ENGL 3374, students became animated and rather lively during discussion. However, on the class meetings where in-class composition with new software and techniques occurred, the room seemed less spirited. Of course, large-class discussion presents rather unique benefits and constraints for those who participate in the ways they choose. In my broad experiences outside of this course, it seems that (on average) three or four students tend to speak more often with others remaining silent observers. This was not the case in ENGL 3374. It was common to have approximately 50 to 75% of students speak with aplomb during class discussion. When students focused on composition individually or in pairs, however, the same energy receded. I suspect this occurred because of two motivations. First, students had practiced and performed in class discussion in their other English courses with faculty expectation that students would engage verbally during discussion of the concepts or themes from the books assigned in courses. Because this practice emerged as a featured cultural habit of the undergraduate program, students participated with gusto. Second, as students learned how to compose with new modes and new software and hardware with which they were not readily familiar, the cognitive load for entering a new composition space required greater demand with new neuro-pathway development. Thus, the barrier to entry was higher and required a good deal of effort and labor and new type of intellectual work. My observation, while anecdotal, does support Pamela Takayoshi and Cynthia Selfe's acknowledgement that composing with multimodal elements requires an intellectual demand unlike composing in one mode only (2008).

Students also drew on familiar, already developed skills when working with the sixth mode of multimodality, tactility. For some students, sketching ideas and thinking through the spatial environments their projects would inhabit provided focus, because these traits had previously been developed in other areas of their life domains (e.g. through personal hobbies or art classes). Once students realized that previously acquired skills could be useful for this course and that multimodality was not such a foreign concept—only a term and definitions for things they've already known— some of them relaxed and seemed to enjoy working on the projects more. When we discussed putting the theory of multimodality into practice with each project, students commented on how the focus on tactility helped them to make sense of the world around them, and they saw tactility as an integral part of multimodal composition.

When students began working with multiple modes for the FabLab project—the second assignment of the course that asked students to create an object using the hardware and software of the university's FabLab to solve a problem on campus—time management became an issue for some students, regardless of my attempts to make smaller deadlines. A couple of students working full-time and a part-time jobs alongside schoolwork, designed their schedules for attending classes—even being on campus—with great care to maximize time. Additionally, since UT-Arlington's campus is within the 4th largest metropolitan area in the United States and the majority of students live off-campus, it is common to have student commute times exceed one hour each way. What I did not anticipate in asking students to use the FabLab was the extreme burden this would place upon one student, in particular, whose commute time each way was approximately 45-50 minutes; for this one student, time on campus was only for classes, with the rest of this student's time allocated for their full-time job and personal life.

While some class time was allocated to work on the FabLab project, it was not enough time to complete a project; the number of hours involved with iterative design meant that much of the designing and prototyping had to occur outside class time. A few other students did not anticipate how much time would be needed not only to learn new hardware and software but also how much time it would take some hardware—like a 3D printing device—to manufacture the object. No matter how much class time I allocated for students to work on their projects or mini-deadlines I set or weekly verbal and email reminders I made about completing work early due to the number of hours needed, a few students experienced barriers that delayed their work—and admitted as much during the reflective writing process. Lest readers think students were procrastinating, I assure you that stalling did not happen. Rather, these three students understood how to organize their work and time for an alphabetic essay; but multimodal composition was uncharted territory in terms of organization.

Assumptions I held about transferable skills from alphabetic essay production bubbled toward the surface of my thoughts, fast. I realized a grave error in my thinking—skills learned in alphabetic essay production may not transfer when learning multimodal composition because the cognitive load of organizing, arranging, and designing many modes can be overwhelming. Effectively teaching multimodal composition, I have learned, requires teaching all of the base skills for multimodal composition with no room for assumptions of transferable skills for some students, because students' own time management strategies may not account for the layered, distributed, and dynamic iterative design of multimodality.

Final Thoughts

Since the last course offering, in Fall 2017, I have yet to teach ENGL 3374 again. I would like to say that I stopped offering the course because the department required me to teach other courses, but that is only partially true. I could have offered this course again. Really, I needed a break. I needed time to assess the intellectual culture of the curriculum. The pivotal lesson I learned as a new faculty member, eager to offer a course steeped in theories and practices of multimodality I had read about for years as both a masters and doctoral student, included reading the local conditions of a curriculum before offering innovative courses. I learned that I needed to talk to colleagues, read syllabi, learn colleagues' pedagogical approaches in the classroom, and most importantly, talk to undergraduate and graduate students about their experiences with coursework.

Given the many valuable lessons learned from this course, I remain convinced that the FabLab project provides value to writing studies writ large by focusing our attention on the theory/practice of the sixth mode of multimodality—tactility. Tactility focuses attention on the immediate sensations of feeling different textures of objects and thus works for electronic and non-electronic multimodal compositions. It is especially effective when engaging with non-electronic texts. I know of many excellent teacher/scholars who integrate non-electronic multimodal composition in their classes, including Kristin Arola, Lisa Blansett, Regina Duthley, and Krystin Gollihue (just to name a few), and I suspect that, in addition, to the design thinking and theory/praxis they each integrate, tactility is implicit in their instruction. Future teaching and research into tactility, however, could locate a sixth mode of multimodality by embracing both the logics and the emotions that govern tactile experiences. Possible avenues for theory building may include transdisciplinary research available from several fields and disciplines, including health sciences (how the body processes touch), anthropology (how bodies use felt senses in cultures), sociology (how bodies address felt senses socially), and rhetorical studies (how bodies interact and commune with felt sense) as starting points. A robust theory/practice for tacility, however, might include a course design themed on the sixth mode with students enrolled researching, defining, and theorizing this integral mode for composing. It is my hope that a reader of this course design, perhaps one of the next generation of scholars and teachers, picks up on this thread and develops a robust course and research trajectory in this area.

Works Cited

Arola, Kristin L, Jennifer Sheppard, and Cheryl E. Ball. *Writer/Designer: A Guide to Making Multimodal Projects*, Bedford/St. Martin's, 2014.

Ball, Cheryl. "Editorial Pedagogy, Pt. 1: A Professional Philosophy." *Hybrid Pedagogy*, 2012. http://hybridpedagogy.org/editorial-pedagogy-pt-1-a-professional-philosophy/

Biesecker, Barbara A. "Rethinking the Rhetorical Situation from within the Thematic of 'Différence.'" *Philosophy & Rhetoric*, vol. 22, no. 2, 1989, pp. 110–130.

Bitzer, Lloyd F. "The Rhetorical Situation." *Philosophy & Rhetoric*, vol. 1, 1968, pp 1–14.

Edbauer, Jenny. "Unframing Models of Public Distribution: From Rhetorical Situation to Rhetorical Ecologies." *Rhetoric Society Quarterly*, vol. 35, no. 4, 2005, pp. 5–24.

Haas, Angela M. "Wampum as Hypertext: An American Indian Intellectual Tradition of Multimedia Theory and Practice." *Studies in American Indian Literatures*, vol. 19, no. 4, 2007, pp. 77–100.

Inoue, Asao B. *Labor-Based Grading Contracts: Building Equity and Inclusion in the Compassionate Writing Classroom*. Perspectives on Writing/The WAC Clearinghouse and UP of Colorado, 2019.

New London Group. "A Pedagogy of Multiliteracies: Designing Social Futures." *Harvard Educational Review*, vol. 66, no. 1, 1996, pp. 60–92

"Resolution on Viewing and Visually Representing as Forms of Literacy." *NCTE*, 30 Nov. 1996. http://www2.ncte.org/statement/visualformofliteracy/

Selber, Stuart A. *Multiliteracies for a Digital Age*. Carbondale: Southern Illinois University Press, 2010.

Selfe, Cynthia L. (Ed). *Multimodal Composition: Resources for Teachers*. Cresskill, NJ: Hampton Press, 2008.

Sheridan, David. "Fabricating Consent: Three-Dimensional Objects as Rhetorical Compositions." *Computers and Composition: An International Journal of Teachers of Writing*, vol. 27, no. 4, 2010, pp. 249–265.

Takayoshi, Pamela and Cynthia L. Selfe. "Chapter 1: Thinking about Multimodality." *Multimodal Composition: Resources for Teachers*, edited by Cynthia L. Selfe, Hampton Press, 2008, pp. 1–12.

Vatz, Richard E. "The Myth of the Rhetorical Situation." *Philosophy & Rhetoric*, vol. 6, no. 3, 1973, pp. 154–161.

Syllabus Works Cited

Arola, Kristin L, Jennifer Sheppard, and Cheryl E. Ball. *Writer/Designer: A Guide to Making Multimodal Projects*, Bedford/St. Martin's, 2014.

Anton, Kelly Kordes and John Cruise. *Adobe InDesign CC Classroom in a Book (2015 Release)*, Indianapolis: Adobe Press, 2015.

"Digital Composition, Storytelling & Multimodal Literacy: What is Digital Composition & Digital Literacy?" Stony Brook University Libraries, 3 Jul. 2018. http://guides.library.stonybrook.edu/digital-storytelling/home

Faden, Eric. "A Fair(y) Use Tale." *Media Education Foundation.* https://www.youtube.com/watch?v=igtwv1067oM

Farnham, Jason. "Site-Specificity, Pervasive Computing, and the Reading Interface." *The Mobile Story,* 2013. http://themobilestory.com/sample-chapters/chapter-1/

"Honor Code" *UTA,* n.d. https://www.uta.edu/conduct/

"How to Give Attribution." *Creative Commons,* n.d. https://creativecommons.org/use-remix/get-permission/

Saranow, Jennifer. "The Cut-and-Paste Personality." *Wall Street Journal,* 15 May 2008.

"Share Your Work." Creative Commons, n.d. https://creativecommons.org/share-your-work/

Sheridan, David. "Fabricating Consent: Three-Dimensional Objects as Rhetorical Compositions." *Computers and Composition: An International Journal of Teachers of Writing,* vol. 27, no. 4, 2010, pp. 249–265.

"Teaching Copyright." *EFF,* n.d. https://www.teachingcopyright.org

"Use & Remix." Creative Commons, n.d. https://creativecommons.org/use-remix/

English 382: Special Topics in Multimodal Composition

Jaclyn Fiscus-Cannaday and Sophia Watson

English 382 is a multimodal composition course that counts as a "C" credit, a composition course that fulfills one of the courses mandated as general education requirements.[1] The writing program administration at the university created this course as one in a series of four new multimodal composition courses in response to increasing scholarship on the connections between transfer and multimodality (DePalma). English 382 is described in the University of Washington's course catalogue as a course whose "topics vary" because each iteration "focuses on emerging questions, debates, genres, and methods of multimodal analysis and production." This iteration of English 382 considered the multimodal nature of feminist research methodologies, writing practices, and design strategies through a class-wide simulation of a feminist grassroots organization.

Institutional Context

English 382 was taught in Fall 2017 at the University of Washington, a large, public university whose undergraduate students most often are STEM-focused.[2] English 382, like all courses, functioned within institutional affordances and constraints: our classroom layout, technology available in class, and course requirements shaped the trajectory of the course. Capped at 23, our course had fifteen students enrolled. This allowed for a smaller class community, which aided in community building and dialogue. Further aiding in class community-building, the class met twice a week for two hours, once in a computer classroom with desks arranged in three-person pods and the other in a traditional classroom with desks and attached chairs that rolled to create mini-groups easily. The material conditions in each space promoted collaboration, both because of the materials within the classrooms and the frequent in-class use of collaborative digital mediums. However, there were some drawbacks within the institutional context that affected collaboration and overall

---

1. You can find the syllabi and course calendars for each Course Design essay on the *Composition Studies* website at https://compstudiesjournal.com/.

2. The most popular majors, according to the Office of the Registrar, are science, technology, engineering, or math related in the last five years. For example, in Autumn 2017—the quarter this version of English 382 course was taught—the five most popular undergrad majors were (in order of most to least popular) Computer Science, Psychology, Business Administration, Biochemistry, Electrical Engineering, and Business Administration (Finance).

course success. The course had no pre-requisites, which meant there was no shared knowledge, and the institution was on the quarter system, and thus, we had ten weeks for the course. This expedited time frame made it challenging to cultivate a class community, set up the theoretical framework necessary, select and become familiar with a social justice issue, brainstorm rhetorical responses to that issue within the university community, and provide enough time for students to execute those responses successfully. This was particularly complicated given that English 382 was marked as "writing intensive," meaning students were tasked with completing a minimum word count by the end of the course that averaged "three to four pages per week." [3]

To capitalize on affordances and work within limitations, the course instructor—Jaclyn Fiscus-Cannaday—designed course assignments that helped simulate feminist grassroots organizing, which the course broadly defined as working with local community to address feminist social issues. All quarter, students were working toward a final project, which required students communicate with a public of their choice about a class-selected social justice issue. This assignment gave the class an opportunity to showcase their work, as well as practice in-person activism. In order to scaffold for this final project, there were four shorter assignments throughout the semester, which consisted of:

1. Reflections: Students created a biweekly reflection to a common prompt in a medium of their choosing and shared them with a partner. These reflection prompts were designed to promote transfer of knowledge, foster the feminist value of reflexivity, build community, and receive feedback on ideas for other assignments.
2. An ideation assignment: Students began brainstorming for the cause of the class's feminist grassroots organization by authoring a children's book about a feminist issue of each student's choice. This assignment served as a practical application of the multimodal and feminist theory taught in the first weeks of the course, as well as a way for students to explore ideas for what would become the class's overall social issue of choice.
3. An assignment that invited them to share expertise with each other: Students selected one of three choices, emulating how labor might be divided amongst teams or individuals within a grassroots campaign outside of the classroom:
    a. A pitch of what the social justice topic should be for the

---

3. Though there is not an official policy listed on the registrar website, the student guidelines for the Expository Writing Program explain, "The minimum writing requirement for our "C" classes is 7,500 words submitted, of which at least 3,600 must be graded."

       final project,
    b. Three annotations for the class annotated bibliography, which was used as a collective research archive to help students with their final project, or
    c. A design worksheet that could be used to help students with their final projects.
 4. An assignment that required them to know themselves as learners and coordinate with others: Students were tasked to create a self-designed project meant to support the class's final project goals. The assignment could be done individually or in groups. This assignment was meant to mimic the kind of collaboration necessary within grassroots organizing, as well as teaching the kind of self-sponsored scaffolding that often occurs in the workplace.

To see the pacing of these assignments and the readings that were assigned in support of them, see the course calendar in the syllabus online on the *Composition Studies* website (https://compstudiesjournal.com/).

In addition to the typical institutional constraints, this course was held in the wake of the 2016 presidential election, amidst the influx of explicitly queer-phobic, racist, sexist, and xenophobic rhetoric both nationally and on University of Washington's campus. One of the most prominent examples of this on campus occurred in early 2017. A Resident Student Organization sponsored Milo Yiannopoulos, a Brietbart news pundit, to hold a talk on campus on inauguration night, January 20, 2017. Leading up to the event, the university's student-run newspaper, *The Daily*, chronicled the debate amongst students about how to distinguish free speech from hate speech (Ross), and tensions grew so high that there was a Change.org petition, signed by over 4,000 people, to ban Yiannopoulos from campus. President Ana Mari Cauce ultimately allowed the event to go forward, emailing all faculty, staff, and students to announce her decision and cautioning them to avoid campus if possible. Protests and counter-protests staged outside the event, and the tensions between them erupted, resulting in Joshua Dukes getting shot as he attempted to break up a conflict. Those charged with his assault, Marc and Elizabeth Hokoana, were there with "intent to provoke altercations with protesters," based on prior messages uncovered during the investigation (Carter). Alan-Michael Weatherford, a graduate student who protested the university's hosting of Yiannopoulos by hosting peaceful teach-ins across from where the event took place, was subsequently doxed, harassed, libeled, and sent death threats by right-wing supporters (Weatherford). Students were outraged with the university's failure to ensure the safety of students—both graduate and undergraduate—amidst the increasingly dangerous campus climate (Ross; Weatherford).

This was the campus-environment that permeated the University of Washington at the time this course was developed and consequently taught: (1) the high political tension; (2) the heated debates over the idea of free speech; and, (3) the fear that many marginalized students carried with them to class that they could be a victim of harassment or violence. English 382 offered students an opportunity to explore and discuss issues related to intersectional feminism in a safe environment that might otherwise remain unavailable to them. Simultaneously, it provided the educational opportunity to practice grassroots advocacy that the University of Washington desperately needed, and continues to need.

Theoretical Rationale

In response to the dangerous rhetoric happening at the university, Fiscus-Cannaday wanted to develop a course that would simulate the kind of feminist grassroots organizing that was happening nationally with The Women's March and social media campaigns like #metoo. Fiscus-Cannaday then began contemplating how feminist pedagogy—combined with influences from transfer studies, rhetorical genre studies, and simulation practice—might work to emulate the kind of feminist grassroots organizing students were watching nationally and provide an opportunity for students to practice this kind of grassroots organizing in their local context. Feminist collections, anthologies, and manuscripts have "come to occupy canonical, yet transformative discussions within our [composition studies] discipline" (Lee and Nickoson), and this course emerged from that rich lineage (e.g. Jarratt and Worsham; Kirsch et al.; Royster and Kirsch; Schell and Rawson). In this iteration of feminist pedagogy, Fiscus-Cannaday was primarily concerned with doing more with less, a pressure many of us face in our writing classes today (Welch and Scott), so she chose to not use the service learning model that other feminist social activism courses have used (Godbee; Williams), nor did she employ a computer mediated system (Russell and Fisher). Rather, Fiscus-Cannaday considered the long history of composition classes to analyze or participate in progressive social action (Adler-Kassner et al.; Fleckenstein) by asking students to engage in a topic of their choosing and then having students work together to create an organization that inspired change within the local community on the university's campus and the surrounding Seattle area called the "university district." The students elected the topic of climate change refugees, and then created an organization called the Movement for Climate Refugee Awareness (MCRA). Assignments and in-class activities prompted students to act as professional colleagues of the MCRA, creating public-facing and professional genres for the MCRA, in the hopes that students would learn things like genre, rhetorical, and audience awareness.

In asking students to create professional and public-facing genres on behalf of the MCRA instead of creating "mutt genres" (Wardle) like writing research papers about climate change, Fiscus-Cannaday hoped that the course would fit into national conversations about facilitating knowledge transfer (Baird and Dilger). Fiscus-Cannaday hoped that students could transfer in knowledge about writing as they understood it from feminist grassroots organizing in their lives; build upon their own academic writerly knowledge as they produced in new genres for new audiences and rhetorical purposes; and then be prepared to transfer the writerly knowledge they gained from doing class work to future situations. To facilitate transfer in these new writing situations and prepare them for future transfer, students were tasked to reflect, or "[recall] writing experiences to reframe the current writing situation" (Taczak 78), through biweekly, multi-genred reflections because reflection is "identified as a key move in the transfer of writing knowledge and practice" (Yancey 303). Students were tasked to select a genre of their choice to reflect through because traditional reflection-in-presentation texts often lead to students putting forth a claim about the rhetorical effectiveness of one's own work (Greene; Sommers; Yancey, Robertson, and Taczak).

Fiscus-Cannaday most wanted students to practice and transfer the threshold concept of writing studies that writing is socially situated (Adler-Kasner and Wardle), so her course design was heavily influenced by rhetorical genre studies (see, for example, Bawarshi; Bawarshi and Reiff). Studying genre uptake explicitly can help illuminate how genres circulate (Bawarshi; Fisher; Emmons; Rounsaville; Roundtree) because it allows students to explore either the complicated process of considering potential genre productions or the cause-and-effect relationship between genre production (Fiscus). Therefore, Fiscus-Cannaday used these qualities of genre-based instruction – how it can help students understand writing as socially situated and see genres as interconnected to the materials, technologies, and people from which they emerge – and connected them to simulation practice, a practice often used for students emulate a situation from a future professional career like doing simulations of patient care to learn nursing charting (Campbell). The kind of pedagogy Fiscus-Cannaday employed hoped to emulate the kind of networked activity within organizations that Clay Spinuzzi has documented so students can be rhetorically effective in similar companies in future workplace situations. In essence, Fiscus-Cannaday hoped her combination of feminist pedagogy, transfer-oriented course design, genre-based instruction, and simulation practice would work together to make the classroom a site of resistance for the institutional context from which this course emerged.

Critical Reflection

For this critical reflection, we begin with a conversation between ourselves as authors—the teacher for the course and a student who took the course—to consider the extent to which English 382 accomplished Fiscus-Cannaday's goals. We hope this conversational style about our own reactions to our course might illuminate our own experiences more clearly. Then, we end with our collective thoughts on how teachers can foster spaces for collective social activism within a formal, academic environment.

Fiscus-Cannaday: Initial Takeaways

I think my biggest takeaway is that writing classrooms can be a space of resistance but that simulating grassroots activism is much more difficult than I anticipated. As a compositionist and feminist, I am so proud that our classroom was used to create real, public-facing texts that were created to inform our local community about the climate refugee crisis. The class's final projects—taken collectively as a co-authored Facebook page, zine, short documentary, and collection of flyers—were all exceptional writing. And, I was most impressed by the way that the class worked together in collective social action: distributing the zine and short documentary on the Facebook page, along with organizing an event through the distribution of flyers to share the documentary and zine. It showed the potential for classrooms to educate a university community about a kairotic social issue and encourage social change. I do believe this course could be done in another context successfully, but I would caution practitioners to keep in mind their own identities, the identities of their students, and the institutional context as they consider the adaptability of this course design.

At UW, I was incredibly nervous about teaching this course because the political climate at our institution was fraught with division and tension. I felt uncomfortable tasking a group of students to work together to resist hateful rhetoric when I was unsure if they themselves espoused or supported it. However, as a white, cis-gender woman, I have the privilege to facilitate resistance work without aspects of my own identity being targeted. I think this position of power, along with the theoretical tools provided early on in the quarter about rhetorical listening, feminist collaboration, and usability in multimodal design, helped mitigate the risks of this kind of pedagogy. But, I do not think it was risk-free. If teachers tried this pedagogy and did not embody the kinds of privilege I hold or had a different collection of students, teachers might experience harmful emotional or even physiological violence when doing this kind of pedagogy, much like the doxing that happened to other instructors on UW's campus. And, I could have unintentionally put students at risk for becoming unofficial spokespeople for a problem, much like students of color are often looked to when in a predominately white classroom talking about race. In this iteration of English 382, for instance, I had to be especially cognizant of that, as climate change refugees are disproportionally international people of color.

In general, I do think the course was successful in providing students with tools for engaging with their community about issues they cared about while enrolled in my course, but my goal of simulating grassroots activism was not all together successful. In evaluations, students reported how the course material decolonized their conceptions of what counts as writing and saw writing as a form of social action, but they did not talk about how this course had inspired them to do social activism outside of class. Moreover, students did not choose to continue our social activist work after the quarter was over, despite agreeing to do so when we discussed next steps at the end of the course.

Watson: Response to Fiscus-Cannaday's Takeaways

I would agree, in part, with your assessment. Yes, writing classrooms can function as resistance to our political environment, and what we produced as a class did that work. However, my lasting impression of this course is how it served as resistance to how we typically understand writing. As a Law, Societies, and Justice major with a background of classes in the University of Washington's Gender, Women, and Sexualities Studies and English department, this course intrigued me. When the syllabus was handed out on the first day, I was sold: a non-traditional approach to both grading and the classic English/Composition class formula was refreshing after years of traditional academia. The idea that English as a subject no longer needed to be bound by the strict formulas drilled into my mind from a young age was new and exciting. Being able to bring my personal love of art and passion for activism to the classroom was a new occurrence. With each assignment, I had the opportunity to express myself and convey my message through new forms. Furthermore, I discovered the importance of using multimodality and breaking down the often classist hierarchy inherent in academic and activist circles. Though, I will introduce a caveat that as a white, cis-gendered woman who identified as a feminist prior to the beginning of the course, the topics we approached were less "risky" for me. This meant that I felt comfortable openly speaking in front of the class in ways other students may not have. Alongside that same vein, I was not afraid of being a personal victim of the oft racially based violence escalating on campus.

Today, I use this feminist take on classic composition for my writing in other classes and internship work. The idea that a "paper" doesn't necessarily have to be argumentative is something I'm particularly taken with; my essays no longer center on trying to "win" a debate, but rather evolve through my analysis of opposing views. Alongside this is my newfound consideration of accessibility in my own work, and that knowledge—especially feminist research—can and should be conveyed in multiple formats to reach the often-ignored groups it centers around.

Therefore, I agree your second goal of simulating grassroots organizing was not entirely successful. We were all too nervous or too polite to choose an idea we were passionate about, and in the end, chose to focus on an issue that was not personally affecting any of us in the classroom. Despite the tense political climate at the time, the University of Washington remains a predominantly liberal campus. As this class was marketed as a feminist approach to multimodal composition, it's unlikely that anyone with strongly held oppositional views to the course's content would admit to holding those opinions within the environment cultivated within the classroom. Instead, we settled on an amalgamation of the proposed subjects in the pitches, which most of us had little-to-no background in, in order to avoid rejecting each other's proposal. We eventually named the amalgamation the "Movement for Climate Refugee Awareness," but there were still at least three separate collaborative projects—a Facebook page, a short documentary, and a zine—and all of these genres allowed people to work outside of class individually. In my opinion, we approached our collaborative campaign as individualized projects due to the fact that we were in a University setting. Everyone had different responsibilities to juggle, and it was far easier to manage our own projects and compile them together, rather than working on a text alongside our classmates. Furthermore, from my perspective, everyone simply put different levels of effort in the work they produced for this class. Combined with the fact that not many people seemed particularly passionate about the topic we chose, it led to our collective action project appearing a bit disjointed – a collection of texts about a similar topic rather than a simulation of a grassroots social activist movement.

Fiscus-Cannaday's Response

Yes, I agree. I saw these things happening and tried to circumvent the challenges you describe in various ways, but my efforts were not successful. I learned that creating a sense of community that goes beyond the classroom is incredibly challenging. The writing and sharing of our children's books before deciding on a topic, for example, was my attempt to foster a community of writers. When I saw the collaborative writing projects splinter into individually written elements, I encouraged the class came to come up with accountability and collaboration measures—and we did with both a Slack channel and a tracking system on our shared Google Drive for visualizing project development—but these measures were hardly ever utilized. The collaborative nature of the campaign often took place because I scheduled it in class with group work and whole class conversations. Next time I teach a course like this, I would use the grading contract again—this seemed to be one of the things that made this course work—while also adding requirements to the contract that incentivizes the use of participating in the accountability measures. And, I would make that group work, whole group class discussion, and assignments function more explicitly as a simulation of grassroots organizing. I would also make it clearer how the writing assignments, especially the pitch, the shared research, the one-page design worksheet, and the scaffolding assignments map onto realistic practices in a grassroots activism movement. Because our collaborative work was framed as group check-in time and assignments were thought of as academic-only situations, students did not see this course as an opportunity to practice the grassroots activist skills necessary for them to be prepared to do this work on their own outside of class, and therefore they did not learn grassroots activism skills to transfer to their future situations.

Collective Takeaways

As an instructor and student who have used genre-based instruction and classroom as simulation pedagogy to do social activist work within the academy, we can attest that the classroom has the potential to stage resistance against the nationalist, hate-filled rhetoric omnipresent about immigration and other issues as they arise. However, we can equally account for – and warn – that there are inherent limitations of using the classroom as a simulation for grassroots organizing. Classroom dynamics are situated within the discourse archive of the academy, which draws boundaries on who is invited to participate in social action and how that social action might naturally occur. Furthermore, there are no guarantees that the students who elect to take such a class will align with the foundational ideals of the course. Even widely assumed "liberal spaces" like the university setting have faced frequent – and occasionally violent – political clashes, which make it risky but crucial to establish activist environments in academic spaces in this politically tumultuous time. A class like this provides an opportunity for students to practice activism and prepares them for potential activist work outside the academy. Not only that, but it can encourage students to take stock of their role in higher education and question the traditional hierarchy and inaccessibility of academia.

From our experience, we think this course can be adapted for other contexts and we have recommendations for how to best do so. In creating a course like this for your own context, we recommend the following:

1. Consider the identities you have and how they may come under attack in this kind of context. Consider ways of protecting yourself and mitigating those risks. It is possible that the risks outweigh the potential of teaching a similar course.
2. Use contract grading that aligns with the goals of this course. For example, this course required self-sponsored learning and revised assignments for a 4.0 because of its transfer-oriented goals, but could have done better in adding requirements that would have fostered class community because of its feminist goals. Know that contract grading is essential to the course's pedagogy, as it was consistently cited as the main reason that the collaborative nature of this course worked. Students noted that contract grading made it so they were not worried about how their grade would be affected by another's quality of work, nor were they worried to take risks and try new kinds of writing that was required in the course.
3. Create real-life simulations on some class days rather than assigning group work so that the collaborative writing is more enmeshed and transferable for future activist experiences. For example, students could create specific job titles for themselves and host meetings where they enact their professional personas, or each class could start with a "morning stand up" practice that many companies use now. Similarly, frame writing assignments as simulations for activist work rather than responses to prompts.
4. Consider putting a course like this in tandem with an existing knowledge-building framework, like pre-requisites, another disciplinary course, or service learning experience. This, we believe, would allow more time to not only build the foundational knowledge of activism and multimodality, but lead to more investment in the chosen topic if it's discussed and researched together as a class. If this is not possible, we would suggest trying to pick a topic immediately, instead of weeks into the class.

Overall, an organic, grassroots campaign about a collective issue will never be perfectly simulated in a university setting. This does not mean, however, that a class like this cannot be an impactful and worthwhile experience. As both a student and instructor who have experienced this course, we hope you can take from our successes and build from our failures as you design your own courses to stage resistance.

Works Cited

Adler-Kassner, Linda and Elizabeth Wardle. *Naming What We Know: Threshold Concepts of Writing Studies*. Utah State UP, 2015.

Adler-Kassner, Linda, et al. *Writing the Community: Concepts and Models for Service-learning in Composition*. Stylus Publishing, 1997.

Baird, Neil, and Bradley Dilger. "How Students Perceive Transitions: Dispositions and Transfer in Internships." *College Composition and Communication*, vol. 68, no. 4, 2017, pp. 684–712.

Bawarshi, Anis. "Beyond the Genre Fixation: A Translingual Perspective on Genre." *College English*, vol. 78, no. 3, 2016, pp. 243-249.

Bawarshi, Anis. *Genre and The Invention of The Writer*. Utah State UP, 2003.

Bawarshi, Anis, and Mary Jo Reiff. *Genre: An Introduction to History, Theory, Research, andPedagogy*. Parlor Press and WAC Clearinghouse, 2010.

Blair, Kristie and Lee Nickoson. *Composing Feminist Interventions: Activism, Engagement, Praxis*. The WAC Clearinghouse and University Press of Colorado, 2018.

Campbell, Lillian. "The Rhetoric of Health and Medicine as a 'Teaching Subject': Lessons from the Medical Humanities and Simulation Pedagogy." *Technical Communication Quarterly*, vol. 27, no. 1, 2017, pp. 7-20.

Carter, Mike, and Steve Miletich. "Couple Charged with Assault in Shooting, Melee during UW Speech by Milo Yiannopoulos." *The Seattle Times*, The Seattle Times Company, 1 May 2017, https://www.seattletimes.com/seattle-news/crime/couple-charged-with-assault-in-shooting-melee-during-uw-speech-by-milo-yiannopoulos/.

Deans, Thomas. *Writing and Community Action: A Service-learning Rhetoric and Reader*. Longman, 2003.

DePalma, Michael. "Tracing Transfer across Media: Investigating Writers' Perceptions of Cross-Contextual and Rhetorical Reshaping in Processes of Remediation." *College Composition and Communication*, vol. 66, no. 4, 2015, pp. 615-42.

Emmons, Kimberly. "Rethinking Genres of Reflection: Student Portfolio Cover Letters and the Narrative of Progress." *Composition Studies*, vol. 31, no. 1, 2015, pp. 43-62.

Expository Writing Program Policies. "For Students." english.washington.edu/expository-writing-program-policies. Accessed 3 Sept. 2019.

Fiscus, Jaclyn. "Genre, Reflection, and Multimodality: Capturing Uptake in the Making." *Composition Forum*, vol.37, 2017.

Fisher, David. "CMS-based Simulations in the Writing Classroom: Evoking Genre through Game Play." *Computers and Composition*, vol. 24, no. 2, pp 179-197.

Fleckenstein, Kristie. *Vision, Rhetoric, and Social Action in the Composition Classroom*. Southern Illinois UP, 2010.

Godbee, Beth. "Pedagogical Too-Muchness: A Feminist Approach to Community-Based Learning, Multi-Modal Composition, Social Justice Education, and More." *Composing Feminist Interventions: Activism, Engagement, Praxis*, edited by Kristine Blair and Lee Nickoson, The WAC Clearinghouse and University Press of Colorado, 2018.

Greene, Ken. "Research for the Classroom: The Power of Reflective Writing." *English Journal*, vol. 100, no. 4, 2010, pp. 90-93.
Jarratt, Susan, and Lynn Worsham. *Feminism and Composition Studies: In Other Words*.Modern Language Association of America, 2008.
Kirsch, Gesa, et al. *Feminism and Composition: A Critical Sourcebook*. Bedford/St. Martin's, 2003.
Roundtree, Aimee. *Computer Simulation, Rhetoric, and Scientific Imagination*. Lexington Books, 2014.
Rounsaville, Angela. "Worlding Genres through Lifeworld Analysis: New Directions for Genre Pedagogy and Uptake Awareness." *Composition Forum*. vol. 37, 2017.
Ross, Jakob. "Ban Milo Yiannopoulos' Punk Ass from Speaking on Campus." *The Daily of the University of Washington*, The Daily, 5 Dec. 2016, http://www.dailyuw.com/opinion/article_234ac85c-ba93-11e6-b556-f3d880223f37.html.
Royster, Jacqueline J. and Kirsch, Gesa. *Feminist Rhetorical Practices: New Horizons for Rhetoric, Composition, and Literacy Studies*. Southern Illinois UP, 2012.
Russell, David, and David Fisher. "Online, Multimedia Case Studies for Professional Education: Revisioning Concepts of Genre Recognition" *Genres in the Internet: Issues in the Theory of Genre*, edited by Janet Giltrow and Dieter Stein, Benjamins, 2009.
Schell, Eileen, and K.J. Rawson. *Rhetorica in Motion: Feminist Rhetorical Methods and Methodologies*. University of Pittsburgh Press, 2010.
Sommers, Jeff. "Problematizing Reflection: Conflicted Motives in the Writer's Memo." *A Rhetoric of Reflection*, edited by Kathleen Blake Yancey, UP of Colorado. 2016.
Spinuzzi, Clay. *Network: Theorizing Knowledge Work in Telecommunications*. Cambridge UP. 2008.
Taczak, Kara. "Reflection Is Critical for Writers' Development." *Naming What We Know: Threshold Concepts of Writing Studies*, edited by Linda Alder-Kassner and Elizabeth Wardle, Utah State UP, 2016.
Wardle, Elizabeth. "'Mutt Genres' and the Goal of FYC: Can We Help Students Write the Genres of the University?" *College Composition and Communication*, vol. 60, no. 4, 2009, pp. 765–789.
Welch, Nancy, and Tony Scott. *Composition in the Age of Austerity*. Utah State UP, 2016.
Weatherford, Alan-Michael. "Guest Editorial: Being Harassed in the Wake of Milo." *The Daily of the University of Washington*, The Daily, 27 Jan. 2017, http://www.dailyuw.com/opinion/article_586eec3a-e43b-11e6-906e-8389e04a23e6.html.
Williams, Danielle. "The Unheard Voices of Dissatisfied Clients: Listening to Community Partners as Feminist Praxis." *Composing Feminist Interventions: Activism, Engagement, Praxis*, edited by Kristine Blair and Lee Nickoson, The WAC Clearinghouse and UP of Colorado, 2018.
Yancey, Kathleen Blake, et al. *Writing across Contexts: Transfer, Composition, and Sites of Writing*. Logan: Utah State UP. 2014.
Yancey, Kathleen Blake. *A Rhetoric of Reflection*. Utah State UP, 2016.
—. *Reflection in the Writing Classroom*. Utah State UP, 1998.

Engl 101: Writing in Wikipedia

Matthew A. Vetter and Oksana Moroz

Indiana University of Pennsylvania's (IUP) course catalogue describes English 101: Composition I as a first-year writing course in which students use a variety of resources—including but not limited to memory, observation, critical reading and viewing, analysis, and reflection—and a focus on writing process to create projects in a variety of writing genres.[1] The course design presented here, Composition I - Writing in Wikipedia, takes an innovative approach to learning about writing, rhetoric, and research in that the large majority of work revolves around reading, evaluating, and writing in Wikipedia. To frame this engagement with Wikipedia, we rely on Anne Beaufort's writing knowledge domains, which allow students to become familiar with policies and practices for contributing to the encyclopedia.

Description of the Institutional Context

IUP is a mid-sized university, situated in rural Western Pennsylvania. Nearly 12,000 undergraduate and graduate students are enrolled in the university; in fall 2018, the undergraduate student body consisted of 9,215 students ("IUP at a Glance"). The majority of first-year student population is White (71,22%), followed by Black or African American (14,80%), and Hispanic (5,46%) students by ethnicity ("First-year Profile"). Among first-year students, the most popular majors are university college (undeclared), nursing, and criminology. In general, English 101 requires students to engage in different writing genres, create projects, and expand their literacy skills. In particular, students are usually required to submit several writing assignments, such as literacy autobiography, reflective and argumentative essays. This particular English 101: Composition I class met twice per week in a computer lab; with each class session lasting for 75 minutes. IUP's Composition I teaching handbook recommends a genre-based approach to teach for transfer of learning. In particular, students compose multiple diverse genres and adapt their writing to those genres' rhetorical situations, in terms of context, audience, convention, and purpose. The benefit of teaching composition through this approach is its highly contextual nature, which helps students to consider various aspects of a genre's purpose and setting. Moreover, the genre approach promotes learning transfer: students are able to transfer what they learn in Composition I to other courses and beyond the academic setting. Genre knowledge is described by Perkins and Salomon as a "mental gripper"

---

1. You can find the syllabi and course calendars for each Course Design essay on the *Composition Studies* website at https://compstudiesjournal.com/.

(qtd. in Beaufort, *Writing* 5); it is a meaningful, contextual, and situated tool to move writing away from the boundaries of academic rules. This pedagogy enables students to use "resources that assist them in producing genres while also developing long-term rhetorical competence that transfers to other writing situations" (Bawarshi and Reiff 180).

Theoretical Rationale

An increasingly mature and diverse body of work in composition has demonstrated the efficacy of Wikipedia-based pedagogy for writing instruction geared toward both traditional FYC educational outcomes (Cummings; di Lauro and Shetler; Hood; Kuhne and Creel; Vetter, "Archive 2.0"; Vetter, McDowell, and Stewart) and more critical approaches to understanding writing, media, and culture (Kill; Vetter, "Teaching Wikipedia"; Vetter and Pettiway). Our focus here will be on demonstrating an accessible theoretical framing for Wikipedia-based FYC by drawing on the work of Anne Beaufort ("College Writing and Beyond"; *Writing in the Real World*). Beaufort identifies five "overlapping yet distinct domains of situated knowledge entailed in acts of writing: (1) discourse community knowledge; (2) subject matter knowledge; (3) genre knowledge; (4) rhetorical knowledge; and (5) writing process knowledge" (18, *College Writing*, numbers added). In particular, we see Beaufort's knowledge domains as a compelling model because of their influence on and easy integration with other mainstream movements in composition pedagogy and theory, especially, writing about writing (Downs and Wardle), transfer (Driscoll), and declarative and conceptual writing knowledge (Wardle and Adler-Kassner). While we recognize that Wikipedia-based education has been framed in many ways, we draw on Beaufort's scheme in this course design for the sake of accessibility, and with the hope that it will be easily taken up by other teacher-scholars interested in Wikipedia-based education. In the following sections, we work through four[2] of Beaufort's five writing knowledge domains to describe a Wikipedia-based version of FYC. As part of our critical reflection, we provide qualitative feedback from students collected in an IRB-approved focus group on the final day of class. Student experience and feedback, accordingly, contextualizes and extends our own critical reflection, as authors and co-teachers, regarding the course design's value and efficacy.

---

2. While we did not explicitly engage students with Beaufort's subject knowledge domain, we view this course design as enabling students to summarize content knowledge from other sources as they contribute to the encyclopedia. Our focus in this course design is on the remaining four knowledge domains.

Writing Knowledge in Four Domains
Discourse Community Knowledge in Wikipedia-based FYC

While we use a slightly different inflection, the term "social knowledge,"[3] the integration of discourse community knowledge is emphasized throughout the course design. Our inclusion of social and discourse community knowledge as a major knowledge domain is supported by a pedagogical tradition that emphasizes conceptual, declarative knowledge about writing, metacognition, and transfer (Beaufort, *College Writing*; Read and Michaud; Wardle). Social knowledge—including knowledge of discourse community theory (Beaufort; Swales) and an awareness of social contexts as major influences on texts and writing—accomplishes specific pedagogical goals in Composition I: Writing in Wikipedia.

Beaufort identifies four particular aspects of what we call social knowledge particularly useful for first-year writing students: (1) the "values and goals of the [discourse] community;" (2) the "communications process derived from those goals;" (3) the "overarching norms for written texts;" and (4) the "specific writing literacy tasks required to participate in the discourse community" (*College Writing* 186). The Wikipedia community might be understood as a discourse community practicing a type of radical transparency in which many of the processes, policies, and community values of the encyclopedia are visible to individuals who aren't actually involved in the community. Once students begin to dig beneath what is known as the article mainspace they gain access to a number of policies, guidelines, and even philosophies of the encyclopedia in order to learn more about the discourse community's values and goals. Wikipedia's "Five Pillars," introduced to students early in the course, are a great example of this. The fundamental principles of Wikipedia (from which multiple other guidelines and policies emerge) are as follows: (1) "Wikipedia is an encyclopedia; (2) "Wikipedia is written from a neutral point of view" (3) "Wikipedia is free content that anyone can use, edit, and distribute"; (4) "Wikipedia editors should treat each other with respect and civility"; and (5) "Wikipedia has no firm rules" ("Wikipedia: Five Pillars"). When students begin to understand the "neutral point of view" (NPOV) pillar, for example, they can make connections between neutrality and the informative and accessible objectives of an encyclopedia as a genre, and begin to understand how NPOV governs certain communications processes, textual norms, and literacy tasks.[4]

---

3. Our use of the terminology *social knowledge* emerges from the first author's realization that *discourse community* may be less accessible to first-year college students.

4. Wikipedia's NPOV pillar and policy has been usefully critiqued from a feminist perspective as prohibiting the contribution of personal and/or embodied writing and knowledge (Gruwell; Vetter and Pettiway).

Genre Knowledge in Wikipedia-based FYC

In her retrospective article, Beaufort again argues for the importance of teaching genre awareness in FYC, though she does back away somewhat from the argument that students should be exposed to multiple genres—asserting instead the importance of deep engagement with fewer genres over shallow engagement with multiple ("Five Years Later"). Beaufort also stresses the need to help students move away from the rote understanding of "school genres or 'mutt genres'" (Wardle, "Mutt Genres"). "Students," she argues, "need to see these genres as particular to a given course—a temporary discourse community—or as 'owned' by a particular disciplinary discourse community and not as universal genres used in all academic subjects." In our course design, we view genre knowledge as both essential for students' success in writing Wikipedia articles; and helpful in aiding the transfer of knowledge across academic and non-academic texts. Students in this course read Kerry Dirk's "Navigating Genres" and practice genre analysis of specific Wikipedia articles in order to better understand features such as NPOV and the encyclopedic linguistic register, section headings to organize content, form and formatting of references, and lead (introductory) sections. Such formalistic knowledge is important to their own success in the course later on, when they draft new sections and new content to add to their chosen Wikipedia articles. But we also ask that they move beyond formalist understandings of the genre towards a type of genre awareness that will allow for transfer across contexts. For instance, we ask students to consider why certain features of the genre have emerged and how they further certain goals of the Wikipedia community. In this way, students engage social knowledge as we introduce genre and genre analysis. Additionally, as students complete an argumentative essay, required as the final writing project in this course, they are also provided the opportunity to reflect on differences between personal, academic, and encyclopedic genres.

Rhetorical Knowledge in Wikipedia-based FYC

Early on in this course, students are asked to complete a major assignment in which they critically evaluate a Wikipedia article according to quality standards set by the Wikipedia community (see: "Wikipedia: Content Assessment"). These are integrated into the Wiki Education Program and help students understand and engage the standards as criteria for evaluation. This is an especially important assignment in the sequence, because it allows students to begin to find gaps and problems with a Wikipedia article that they are then encouraged, later in the assignment sequence, to improve through further content development. In terms of the knowledge domains, we see the "Article Evaluation" assignment as a useful opportunity for students to practice and engage rhetorical knowledge. In addition to a set of questions designed to engage students in the critical evaluation of an article according to Wikipedia standards for content quality, we also ask students to consider the following, "If the purpose of this article is to inform a general audience on the topic of X, how well has that purpose been accomplished?" Answering this question in a rhetorical, evaluative essay allows students to engage concepts related to purpose, audience, accessibility and style, evidence, and authorship, as well as help them become more familiar with a particular article they work to develop later in the course.

Writing Process Knowledge in Wikipedia-based FYC

A remarkable aspect of this course design is the move towards multiple, scaffolded assignments. Though this particular design feature became a barrier for a number of students—simply because they struggled to meet deadlines for each project—the choice to create multiple assignments, however, was one motivated by a concern for procedural knowledge. We wanted students to think about writing as "a series of problem-solving activities [that] will enable writers to approach unfamiliar genres and rhetorical contexts for composing with a greater confidence" (Beaufort, "Transferring Writing Knowledge" 183). The assignment sequence was also carefully crafted to guide students towards (successfully) publishing their work in Wikipedia. For instance, the "Evaluate Wikipedia" assignment helped students both better understand the basic features of a Wikipedia article and select an article to edit and develop later. The "Copyedit an Article" and "Add to an Article" assignments both allowed students to practice Wikipedia editing by making a small change or revision and writing about their experience. The "Wikipedia Article Proposal & Draft" gave students a chance to create a proposal for how they would improve a particular article in Wikipedia, as well as a bibliography of sources, and a draft of new or revised content to be added to the article. This entire assignment was completed in students' Wikipedia user sandboxes, a practice page that novice editors can use to draft content. Students completed a "Wikipedia Peer Review Response" by reviewing a peer's article draft, and a "Final Article" assignment which consisted of them moving their new or revised article content from their sandbox into the article mainspace. Finally, students completed an "In-class Presentation" on their Wikipedia editing experience, as well as a rough draft, peer review, and final draft of a reflective, argumentative essay which asked them to look back at the course to better understand their learning about Wikipedia and writing. It may be a simple lesson, but it is an important one: students in this course learned that they needed to follow through with all of the assignments in order to be successful. We view this as procedural knowledge: all of the sequential steps were important and significant in terms of the project outcomes, leading students to better understand the importance of process for complex writing tasks.

Critical Reflection

Although most critical reflections published in *Composition Studies* course designs are those of the teacher, we viewed this course as an opportunity to gather feedback from students as well. Accordingly, in order to gather qualitative description of student experience, we conducted an IRB-approved focus group with 8 student participants. The focus group was held on the final day of class, after students had completed all coursework except for a final reflective essay.[5] Moroz, who served as a Teaching Assistant for the course, presented students with four questions for discussion.[6] We present these findings in three categories below in order to provide other instructors with insight into common student experiences with a Wikipedia-based assignment. In particular we view their identification of challenges, benefits, and transferability of writing knowledge as especially valuable contributions alongside our own instructor reflections.

"Getting Over the Stigma" - Challenges Faced by Students

Students discussed several challenges they experienced that instructors should be aware of. First, students mentioned the difficulty they had accepting Wikipedia as a credible source, as many were told in high school not to use it as a reference. One of the participants stated that the major challenge was, "[to get] away from…the norm that Wikipedia is bad and that it's not a credible source." Therefore, at the beginning the majority of them were skeptical about a whole course designed around writing for Wikipedia. In addition, students expressed the feeling of fear of writing for the large community of Wikipedia. For example, one student mentioned, "I [have] never posted anything online for everybody to see." This fear was also fueled by their unfamiliarity with the style of Wikipedia writing that should be objective and factual.

"I Liked How Everything Was Sort of Chunked Up into Sections"—Benefits of the Course

In addition to their focus on the challenges associated with the course, students also expressed positive attitudes towards the course design. In particu-

---

5. As per IRB stipulations, students were not required to participate in the focus group and were ensured that their participation would in no way influence their standing in the course. To further avoid conflict of interests and promote student anonymity, the instructor of record (Vetter) took no part in conducting the focus group and did not have access to the dataset yielded by the focus group until after grades had been submitted for the course.

6. These questions were as follows: How did working with Wikipedia help you understand writing as one of the knowledge domains? What is your overall experience with the class design? What worked well for you? What would you change if you were to teach this class? What sorts of skills and knowledges are transferable from this class to other writing contexts? What were some challenges you have experienced in this class?

lar, they benefited from the structure of the course where "everything was sort of chunked up into sections [...and] it wasn't all just thrown at us as a big project." Students praised the agency they could exercise with the freedom to choose article topics. Several students also mentioned helpful training modules provided on the Wiki Education Dashboard. Another positive outcome of the course was gaining procedural knowledge by completing various tasks. One student commented, "you had to do the drafts, the edits, the peer reviews, get checked through the teacher, makes sure that Wikipedia is okay with it." In addition, a few students mentioned learning what citations are, what they are for, and how to properly use them. Students' interest in Wikipedia beyond the course assignments is a final positive outcome of the course, as evidenced by students' continuing work outside the requirements of the course: "this course did actually get me interested in [the] Wikipedia gender gap, and I have edited another article that was outside of this class."

"Thought Process It Takes to Edit Something" - Transferability of Gained Writing Knowledge

One of the course objectives was encouraging the transfer of learning. This aspect of the course was voiced by all students participating in the focus group. Some mentioned that the course expanded their view on writing and editing processes. Other students focused on specific skills they learned in this course that will help them to become better writers: "[c]itations, proper paraphrasing, plagiarism, all of that's going to be, you know, a necessity." Students in the class reported developing not only writing, but also research skills: "I got a lot of experience in looking for really hard to find research and or making sure that the very few sources I did find were credible."

In addition to students' reflections, we conclude this course design with individual reflections from each of the co-authors. For Vetter, two important lessons came from teaching this specific design. First, while the scaffolding of multiple assignments towards course products and goals was appreciated by some of the students (and referenced in the focus group discussion as a positive), I also witnessed a number of students struggle with multiple deadlines for these smaller assignments. In a future revision of this course, I would consider limiting the number of smaller assignments, and also doing more to emphasize why they are scaffolded to help students understand the process of writing in this unique composing space. Secondly, I am reminded that students struggle with the article selection process in a Wikipedia-based assignment. I encourage students to work on articles within the stub-class to C-class range, which are under-developed according to Wikipedia's internal assessment process. This helps ensure that students will be able to make a tangible contribution to an article in need of development. For some students who chose stub-class

Wikipedia articles to edit, however, this turned out to be a constraint. Stub-class articles are often underdeveloped because there aren't many secondary resources to draw from. This limited how much content students could actually add to a given article. In a future course, I will try to do more to anticipate this particular outcome.

For Moroz, as a novice teacher-scholar, the main takeaway is the fact that students come into a course with diverse expectations and background knowledge. It is difficult at the beginning to get them interested in an atypical writing course on Wikipedia editing. Students' disinterest was especially high when they had to complete numerous training modules provided by Wiki Education. Later, students experienced challenges adhering to various rules of editing, even with the support of training modules. Therefore, instructors engaging Wikipedia-based assignments should provide more explanation and practical tasks prior to the actual editing. One of the major positive outcomes is that students started to view Wikipedia as a credible source that can be referenced. Almost every student shared stereotypes about Wikipedia that were formed in a high-school environment but were positively changed due to the course. Moreover, they experienced what it takes to be an editor for a massive online platform. The course enhanced students understanding of writing as a rhetorical act and increased their experience with various forms of digital writing.

Ultimately, the Wikipedia-based FYC course design offered here represents an accessible curriculum that is consistent with current pedagogical approaches in composition. Furthermore, Wikipedia-based educational approaches offer a number of opportunities for students to engage genuine rhetorical situations and communities, while also improving a public knowledge archive. This course design demonstrates one version of what that might look like. It also provides an opportunity for other scholars to adapt and extend future course designs that are attentive to conceptual knowledge domains in writing pedagogy while engaging students in digital writing practice.

Works Cited

Adler-Kassner, Linda, and Elizabeth Wardle. "Naming What We Know: The Project of This Book." *Naming What We Know: Threshold Concepts of Writing Studies*, edited by Linda Adler-Kassner and Elizabeth Wardle, U P of Colorado, 2015, pp. 1-11.

Bawarshi, Anis and Mary Jo Reiff. *Genre: An Introduction to History, Theory, and Pedagogy*. Parlor Press, 2010.

Bazely, Dawn. "Why Nobel Winner Donna Strickland Didn't Have a Wikipedia Page." *The Washington Post*, WP Company, 8 Oct. 2018, washingtonpost.com/outlook/2018/10/08/why-nobel-winner-donna-strickland-didnt-have-wikipedia-page/?utm_term=.4fbbaf6b55a7. Accessed 6 Apr. 2019.

Beaufort, Anne. *College Writing and Beyond: A New Framework for University Writing Instruction*. Utah State UP, 2007.

Beaufort, Anne. "Transferring Writing Knowledge to the Workplace: Are We on Track?" *Expanding Literacies: English Teaching and the New Workplace*, edited by Mary S. Garay and Stephen A. Bernhardt, SUNY P, 1998, 179–99.

—. *Writing in the Real World: Making the Transition from School to Work*. Teachers College Press, 1999.

—. "College Writing and Beyond: Five Years Later." *Composition Forum*, vol. 26, 2012, compositionforum.com/issue/26/college-writing-beyond.php.

Carroll, Laura Bolin. "Backpacks vs. Briefcases: Steps Toward Rhetorical Analysis." *Writing Spaces*, vol. 1, edited by Charles Lowe and Pavel Zemliansky, Parlor Press, 2010, pp. 45-58.

Cohen, Noam. "Define Gender Gap? Look Up Wikipedia's Contributor List." *The New York Times*, 31 Jan. 2011, nytimes.com/2011/01/31/business/media/31link.html.

Cummings, Robert E. *Lazy Virtues: Teaching Writing in the Age of Wikipedia*. Vanderbilt U P, 2009.

Di Lauro, Frances, and Angela Shetler. "Writing with Wikipedia: Building Ethos through Collaborative Academic Research." *Preparing Teachers to Teach Writing Using Technology*, edited by Kristine E. Pytash, Richard E. Ferdig, and Timothy V. Rasinski. ETC, 2013, pp. 209-226.

Dirk, Kerry. "Navigating Genres." *Writing Spaces*, vol. 1, edited by Charles Lowe and Pavel Zemliansky, Parlor Press, 2010, pp. 249-262.

"Discourse Community." *Wikipedia*, Wikimedia Foundation, 26 July 2019, en.wikipedia.org/wiki/Discourse_community. Accessed 6 Apr. 2019.

Downs, Douglas, and Elizabeth Wardle. "Teaching about Writing, Righting Misconceptions:(Re) Envisioning 'First-Year Composition' as 'Introduction to Writing Studies.'" *College Composition and Communication*, vol. 58, no. 4, 2007, pp. 552-584.

Driscoll, Dana Lynn. "Connected, Disconnected, or Uncertain: Student Attitudes about Future Writing Contexts and Perceptions of Transfer from First Year Writing to the Disciplines." *Across the Disciplines*, vol. 8, no. 2, 2011.

"English Portfolio & Placement Exam Information." *IUP*, iup.edu/orientation/pretesting/english/.

"Enrollment." *IUP*, iup.edu/snapshot/enrollment/. Accessed 6 Apr. 2019.

"First-year Profile." *IUP*, iup.edu/snapshot/firstyearprofile/. Accessed 6 Apr. 2019.

Giles, Sandra L. "Reflective Writing and The Revision Process: What Were You Thinking?" *Writing Spaces*, vol.1, edited by Charles Lowe and Pavel Zemliansky, Parlor Press, 2010, p. 191-204.

Gruwell, Leigh. "Wikipedia's Politics of Exclusion: Gender, Epistemology, and Feminist Rhetorical (In)action." *Computers and Composition*, vol. 37, 2015, pp. 117-31, https://doi.org/10.1016/j.compcom.2015.06.009.

Hood, Carra L. "Editing out Obscenity: Wikipedia and Writing Pedagogy." *Computers and Composition Online*, 2007.

"IUP at a Glance." *IUP*, iup.edu/about/iup/. Accessed 6 Apr. 2019.

Kill, Melanie. "Teaching Digital Rhetoric: Wikipedia, Collaboration, and the Politics of Free Knowledge." *Digital Humanities Pedagogy: Practices, Principles, and Politics*, edited by Brett Hirsch, Open Book, 2011, pp. 389–405.

Kuhne, Michael, and Gill Creel. "Wikipedia, 'The People Formerly Known as the Audience.'" *Teaching English in the Two-Year College*, vol. 40, no. 2, 2012, pp. 177–189.

Lamott, Anne. "Shitty First Drafts." *Language Awareness*, edited by Paul Eschholz, Alfred Rosa, and Virginia Clark. 9th ed. Bedford/St. Martin's, 2005, pp. 93-96.

McClure, Randall. "Googlepedia: Turning Information Behaviors into Research Skills." *Writing Spaces*, vol. 2, edited by Charles Lowe and Pavel Zemliansky, Parlor Press, 2011, pp. 221-241.

Pettigrew, Todd. "The Case against Wikipedia in the Classroom." *Macleans.ca*, 23 Dec. 2011, macleans.ca/education/uniandcollege/the-case-against-wikipedia-in-the-classroom/. Accessed 6 Apr. 2019.

Purdy, James P. "Wikipedia Is Good for You!?" *Writing Spaces*, vol. 1, edited by Charles Lowe and Pavel Zemliansky, Parlor Press, 2010, pp. 205-224.

Read, Sarah, and Michael J. Michaud. "Writing about Writing and the Multimajor Professional Writing Course." *College Composition and Communication*, vol. 66, no. 3, 2015, pp. 427–57.

Singh-Corcoran, Nathalie. "Composition as a Rite of Passage." *Writing Spaces*, vol. 2, edited by Charles Lowe and Pavel Zemliansky, Parlor Press, 2011, pp. 24-36.

Stedman, Kyle D. "Annoying Ways People Use Sources." *Writing Spaces*, vol. 2, edited by Charles Lowe and Pavel Zemliansky, Parlor Press, 2011, p. 242-256.

Swales, John. *Genre Analysis: English in Academic and Research Settings*. Cambridge U P, 1990.

Vetter, Matthew A. "Archive 2.0: What Composition Students and Academic Libraries Can Gain from Digital-collaborative Pedagogies." *Composition Studies*, vol. 42, no. 1, 2014, pp. 35-53.

—. "Teaching Wikipedia: Appalachian Rhetoric and the Encyclopedic Politics of Representation." *College English*, vol. 80, no. 5, 2018, pp. 397-422.

—, and Keon Mandell Pettiway. "Hacking Hetero/Normative Logics: Queer Feminist Media Praxis in Wikipedia." *Technoculture*, vol. 7, 2017. tcjournal.org/vol7/hacking-hetero-normative-logics.

—, et al. "From Opportunities to Outcomes: The Wikipedia-Based Writing Assignment." *Computers and Composition*, vol. 52, 2019, pp. 53-64.

Walker, Janice R. "Everything Changes, or Why MLA Isn't (Always) Right." *Writing Spaces*, vol. 2, edited by Charles Lowe and Pavel Zemliansky, Parlor Press 2011, p. 257-269.

Wardle, Elizabeth. "'Mutt Genres' and the Goal of FYC: Can We Help Students Write the Genres of the University?" *College Composition and Communication*, vol. 60, no. 4, 2009, pp. 765-789.

"Content Assessment." *Wikipedia*, Wikimedia Foundation, 30 Aug. 2019, en.wikipedia.org/wiki/Wikipedia:Content_assessment. Accessed 6 Apr. 2019.

"Wikipedia: Five Pillars." *Wikipedia*, Wikimedia Foundation, 31 July 2019, en.wikipedia.org/wiki/Wikipedia:Five_pillars. Accessed 6 Apr. 2019.

Where We Are

Dialogue and Disciplinary Space

"Where We Are" highlights where we are as a field on matters current and compelling. For this installment, we invited two groups—the WPA-L Reimagining Work Group and the nextGEN Start Up Team—to dialogue about disciplinary spaces. In particular, we invited them to think through the events of the last year in our discipline's public, electronic spaces. We proposed that recent conflicts were rooted in at least two tensions: the first, that writers and rhetors do not feel mutually understood in these spaces. In other words, in many cases the one thing all parties can agree on is that they are not being read carefully and interpreted generously. The second tension is that strong responses to such events often take one of two paths: folks either decide to stay and attempt to reform the spaces into something more hospitable; or, folks leave those spaces to find and found newer, more hospitable spaces. We, borrowing from The Clash, thought of this the "should I stay or should I go?" question. As you will read below, both groups productively pushed back against that frame. In doing so, their responses contextualize recent conflict in (electronic) disciplinary spaces, chart paths of advocacy and support, and extend invitations for collective action and activism. We are thankful that both groups took up the invitation as they did, and in the spirit of equity, we present their dialogue in alternating order.

The WPA-L Reimagining Work Group members are Kyle Bohunicky, Kefaya Diab, Karin Evans, Christine Garcia, Traci Gardner, Mara Lee Grayson, Regina McManigell Grijalva, Holly Hassel, Brian Hendrickson, Adam Hubrig, Barry Maid, Cara Marta Messina, Bernice Olivas, Mike Palmquist, and Iris Ruiz.

The nextGEN contributing start up members are Sweta Baniya, Sara Doan, Gavin P. Johnson, Ashanka Kumari, Kyle Larson, Virginia M. Schwarz.

Opening Statements

WPA-L Working Group

Our WPA-L Working Group formed in response to list discussions on WPA-L in Spring 2019, but we had all been observers and list participants at various points before then when list conflict erupted around discussion of Vershawn Ashanti Young's 2019 CFP for CCCC (in Spring 2018); the "WPA ListServ Feminist Revolution" mansplaining series of discussions; and then most recently, the "Heterodox," Asao Inoue's "CCCC's Chair's Address," and "Grand Scholar Wizard" posts. We saw how these incidents disproportionately harmed marginalized people, including graduate students, and continued to make the list a hostile and combative environment when it—as we understand its history—was intended to serve as a professional support community. To experience such marginalization in a field that claims to do the opposite was (and is) troubling to us.

As academics and activists, we believe that our social justice work cannot be solely limited to teaching and publication: it must start from within.

To reclaim and enhance the WPA-L as a just space, we decided to assist with transitioning the WPA-L to a new listserv platform that allowed for a multi-institutional moderation board. It was serendipitous that Barry Maid, the WPA-L's current administrator, had been looking to rehome the list in advance of his retirement. For some of us, the WPA-L had long served as a unique place that allowed for interactions on professional issues across rank, geography, institution, and specialization; much valuable scholarship in Writing Studies references discussions that started on the WPA-L. Others, like graduate students and rising scholars, have imagined and are advocating for a more equitable, antiracist, and anti-misogynistic field. We all, however, recognized that the list—and the field at large—would not magically transform itself in the absence of specific intervention. We anticipated facing many challenges in our efforts to revise the WPA-L toward what we perceived as its potential. To intervene with an amorphous structure that has been there for a long time, with no specific rules, governing structure, or formal mechanism for resolving conflict beyond rhetorical participation, and to attempt to change people's attitudes and practices with no guarantee that our initiative would be credible in the eyes of the WPA-L audience—these were all challenges for which we aimed to account.

Thus, we approached the revision effort with the intention to energize and engage all WPA-L participants; had we worked solely within our comparatively small working group, we would have been contributing to the culture of exclusion we sought to revise. Assembling a group comprising individuals with diverse positions in the field, career stages, and identities was also critical to effective intervention.

While these efforts are in progress, we agree that marginalized and vulnerable groups benefit from having their own spaces to guarantee academic growth in a relaxed and motivating space. For this reason, two-year college faculty whose priorities were rarely addressed on WPA-L (though first-year writing instruction is core to their work) started the TYCA Listserv in 2016. Thus, we do not see the situation as either/or. Both the WPA-L and the next-GEN are needed in our field, and each serves a unique role that we believe complements the other.

nextGEN

nextGEN is a networked advocacy space for graduate students and those who actively support graduate students to build a social justice-oriented community. nextGEN's emergence in the field offers a new discursive space for the cultivation of a horizontal-mentoring culture of mutual respect and upliftment. Members of the list, nevertheless, remain committed to multi-pronged organizing efforts by continuously working to make all disciplinary spaces (listservs and beyond) radically open and safe. The question of when to stay, leave, and/or renegotiate the relationship with a space is not new or simple: many graduate students invested in social and institutional change perpetually face these dilemmas in the context of their programs, communities, and families.

Why, then, did graduate students and one faculty accomplice decide to create a new space, nextGEN? A long-overlooked need for a disciplinary community space became visible and pressing when those needing that space did not have it. Namely, graduate students challenged complicity in white language supremacy during a March 23, 2018, discussion on WPA-L, introducing their perspectives and supporting them with insights from well-respected linguistic diversity scholars. The listserv quickly became dismissive of, inhospitable to, and aggressive towards these contributions in both public comments and even private comments to graduate students' directors, professors, and mentors. From these experiences and numerous discussions, both good and bad, it became clear that, for graduate students, reforming an entrenched disciplinary space (that was not built for us) through a single-pronged approach—that is, through staying only on WPA-L and advocating from a disadvantaged position of power as individuals—would be a commendable effort but a deeply flawed organizing strategy. An open call was then circulated seeking volunteers to join the "Startup Team" and form a new listserv that centered graduate students and their networking, learning, and advocacy needs.

As a collective, the Startup Team organized quickly, worked diligently, and announced the launch of the nextGEN listserv on April 5, 2018—less than two weeks after its exigence. The community work of building nextGEN and the subsequent overwhelming response from graduate students and faculty accomplices demonstrate the potential for collective power inherent in communicative, kairotic spaces like disciplinary listservs. Since its launch, nextGEN has attracted 586 subscribers, held conference meetups, enjoyed an official presence at CCCC, received recognition from *Inside Higher Ed*, won the 2019 Kairos Service Award, and been invited to three publications and three interviews. But more importantly, nextGEN has given space to graduate students and accomplices to build discussions around honoring colleagues' academic and personal achievements, practicing self-care, building disciplinary resources, compiling a list of graduate student scholarship, celebrating Juneteenth, and committing ourselves to the observance of and continued resistance against tragedies and injustices inflicted upon each other's communities. Furthermore, while primarily used as a listserv to facilitate dialogue between graduate students, nextGEN also moves beyond institutionalized genres by taking on a social-movement orientation when necessary. This orientation afforded us a genre-inventing method of communication that we did not have before as individuals; this genre materialized in nextGEN's 'listserv to listserv' response, which provided an avenue for nextGEN subscribers to voice their concerns about the (recurrence of) ongoing WPA-L crisis.

Long-standing institutions are not infallible and often need to be rethought, redefined, and re-established, which should be commonplace in a field that claims to value revision and metacognitive reflection. As we grow, we hope to continue looking for shortcomings in our practices, in our genres, and in our institutions. We need the field to learn that whatever the context, our commitment should be to a simple, consistent, and hopeful praxis: we rise together.

Responding

nextGEN

As we consider and respond to the WPA-L Working Group's opening statement, we, representatives of nextGEN's Startup Team, keep returning to thoughts about who asserts power in disciplinary spaces and how power relates to those whom these listservs are meant to benefit. While we agree that social justice work starts from within, this point raises a question: how can we create socially just spaces when some participants are not committed to—or even hostile to—doing this kind of work for themselves? In some cases, those who do not treat others with dignity on the WPA-L have doubled-down on their offensive and toxic views after being challenged or made aware.

To further this conversation, we raise a series of questions:

1. When toxic views are expressed openly and without caution, who should stand up against those espousing such toxicity?
2. When dangerous effects spill over into "non-digital" spaces, how can our collectives counteract professional, emotional, and psychological violence?
3. What roles do those in precarious employment positions, particularly graduate students, have in reforming and contributing to disciplinary spaces designed by those with stable positions?

4. How might we discuss the creation of new spaces and collectives that prioritize the well-being and safety of members without resorting to rhetorics of exclusion?
5. In what ways can our two collectives, and perhaps a host of other collectives and organizations, form coalitions to better address issues of power, marginalization, and democratic discourse that currently animate discussions within and beyond our discipline?

WPA-L Working Group

Since the WPA-L crises of 2018 and 2019, we have been impressed with the thoughtfulness, dedication, and courage of the nextGEN members who have challenged the entrenched white supremacy and misogyny of the WPA-L and created an alternative disciplinary space tailored to the needs of graduate students. The Reimagining WPA-L Working Group is much smaller than nextGEN, and, unlike nextGEN, we have limited our work to the purpose for which we were formed: the revision of the WPA-L. Though we are a diverse group of established and young scholars, many of our members are active within various professional organizations, caucuses, and special interest groups (see: note 1). We aimed to draw from some of our experiences with our other professional spaces to help with the reimagining work.

We see our efforts working in tandem with nextGEN's: nextGEN is creating a space that has a more defined audience, purpose, and mission, as well as a set of guidelines for participation that WPA-L has lacked. By contrast, our Reimagining WPA-L Group's work toward reforming WPA-L from within, while challenging and imperfect, aims to learn from the work of nextGEN and other online communities in order to do better in the existing spaces—and expect community members to be better. One important example of us learning from nextGEN is our use of nextGEN's 'listserv to listserv' response in proposing participation guidelines for the new WPA-L.

This suggests to us that, despite the marginalization that occurs on WPA-L and in many of our disciplinary spaces, there is reason to hope that we can collectively rearticulate the values and practices of these spaces so long as we're willing to learn from the experiences and contributions of emerging scholars such as those who led efforts to create a more social justice-oriented community in nextGEN.

Note

1. Our members are also part of the following professional organizations and affinity groups: CCCC Feminist Caucus; CCCC Intersectional Approaches to FYC SIG; Coalition for Community Writing; Coalition of Feminist Scholars in the History of

Rhetoric and Composition (CFSHRC); Coalition on Community Writing (CCW); Council of Writing Program Administrators; NCTE/CCCC Jewish Caucus; NCTE/CCCC Latinx Caucus; National Writing Project (NWP); Society for Disability Studies (SDS); and the Two-Year College English Association, among others.

Continuing the Conversation

WPA-L Working Group

As you—our nextGEN peers—identify through your questions, this conversation is about more than the specific platforms that house our disciplinary discourses: it is a conversation about the power, vulnerabilities, and privilege baked into the structures of academia. The harmful WPA-L discussions are only symptomatic of more deeply entrenched inequalities in Composition and Rhetoric.

Because of these asymmetries in power and privilege, it is vital to recognize that any platform feigning neutrality supports structural inequalities and creates space for professional, emotional, and psychological violence. As such, we think multiple spaces—like the space provided for graduate students by nextGEN—are necessary for those most vulnerable among us to have (often difficult) conversations. Simultaneously, we hesitated to leave the WPA-L precisely because we worry that not challenging the harmful ideologies expressed there would allow these discourses to proliferate. The WPA-L Working Group is committed to building ecologies that make a more equitable, more socially just vision of the field possible. That commitment requires constant and consistent effort, and yet must be sustainable.

We acknowledge that this effort—and risks of this effort—all-too-often fall to those who are already vulnerable because of the structural inequalities we are trying to challenge. We hope that by adopting policies and appointing moderators to ensure those policies are followed, this labor on the WPA-L will fall to the most vulnerable among us less often, as was the case in responding to misogyny and racism in recent months. But we acknowledge that is not enough.

So what can we do and who should do it?

We can work to demand more from scholars in positions of power. We can recognize that policy changing needs activists, and activists need policy changes. We can continue to build professional relationships that have both compassion and accountability. We can acknowledge that working within the inequitable system will never be enough to fully change its inequity, but knowing how systems function can facilitate change.

We can demonstrate the power of policy creation: it might not rid us of all the harmful behaviors, but it makes explicit that there are consequences for hurting others.

We look forward to collaborating with nextGEN and other groups who seek to create new spaces for more equitable discourses as well as to challenge inequalities in existing spaces.

nextGEN

Members of the Startup Team established nextGEN to answer growing, kairotic calls for a graduate-centered space oriented towards social justice and community uplift. Working on and against entrenched systems of power is as daunting as it is necessary. What makes it even more daunting is the extent to which toxic individualism remains a structural barrier to wide-scale, coalitional action and accountability in the field, in academia, and in culture writ large.

After using this brief exchange to reflect on the work done in the last year, we continue to be energized in our commitments moving forward. The authors of this response—the "we" here—are particularly excited by the coalitional possibilities resulting from this exchange with the WPA-L Working Group. In closing, then, we want to suggest paths for thinking and moving forward while the field continues to invent, reform, and imagine disciplinary spaces.

1. The question is never "should we stay or should we go," but rather "what are the series of actions made more possible or likely through staying and/or going?" This shifts the question from a single decision to a framework for unfolding and ongoing inquiry and emergent interactions rooted in invention, fluidity, and persistence. No space is perfect; utopia does not exist. But we should be determined to find ways in which spaces are made and maintained as livable, accessible, and possible for all who want to join and contribute.

2. As these conversations continue, we need to remember that reform is happening in small pockets and moments. In our organizations and at our institutions, justice work is often compartmentalized, and collaboration can be contingent upon having overlapping members. Relationships might also be mediated through friendship and dialogue at an individual level. While important, these methods are not reliable, sustainable, or fair. We need to be attentive to the whole of our communities. We believe Rhetoric and Composition scholars should foster more sustainable practices at the structural level that strengthen communication and enhance the likelihood of collaboration. This kind of praxis would benefit from a networked, genre-blending and -bending structure that recognizes and values spaces and collectives like nextGEN. It's a structure that—in contrast to traditional, hierarchical organizations—embraces a more

tactical orientation for responsive fluidity, kairotic movement, and justice advocacy.

In the spirit of rising together, we would like to extend two invitations to the WPA-L Working Group:

1. We invite members of the WPA-L Working Group to collaborate with nextGEN and interested others on a position statement and subsequent rhetorical, material, institutional actions about how the job market marginalizes international graduate students. The field should be against border walls in all forms.
2. We, the nextGEN Start Up Team invite members of the WPA-L Working Group to help nextGEN and interested others build a public spreadsheet detailing disciplinary graduate programs' stipends and benefits. Collective knowledge inspires collective action. WPA-GO has begun this work in their Labor Census published last spring, and we hope to build from their important labor.

As representatives of an advocacy space, we end this dialogue where we began: We rise together. Justice is never achieved in isolation, and we hope this dialogue continues and extends beyond these participants and spaces allowing various emerging and established scholars to work together in moving the field forward.

Book Reviews

Teaching Readers in Post-Truth America, by Ellen Carillo, Logan: Utah State UP, 2018, 144 pp.

What Is College Reading?, edited by Alice S. Horning, Deborah-Lee Gollnitz, and Cynthia R. Haller. The WAC Clearinghouse, 2017, 304 pp.

Reviewed by Meghan A. Sweeney, Saint Mary's College of California

In 2006, I earned a graduate certificate in teaching post-secondary reading at San Francisco State University by taking courses on theories of reading and integrated reading and writing. Notably, only a few of our texts included post-secondary reading research because, quite simply, not much research had been conducted. Instead, we read research from education about readers in K-12 environments. Those readings we were assigned with a post-secondary emphasis tended to align with reading theories in education, but mostly focused on literature, such as Louise Rosenblatt's transactional theory of reading, which posits the act of reading involves a transaction between reader and text, both being changed by the act. Similarly, one of the most influential texts for my own teaching was Glynda Hull and Mike Rose's 1990 "'This Wooden Shack Place': The Logic of an Unconventional Reading" that described how the schema, or background knowledge, of a basic writing student can result in an interpretation of a poem that is different than the teacher's interpretation, the teacher having a different (and more socio-economically privileged) schema, background, experience from which to pull.

Within this generally literature-focused research on K-12 reading, a few scholars, such as Charles Bazerman, Christina Haas, and Linda Flower, were researching *rhetorical* reading practices. These researchers used methodologies common in education research, like think aloud protocols, and education-based theories, like schema theory. This reading research in composition and rhetoric from the 1980s and 90s integrated seamlessly with education, which worked well to prepare teachers for the integrated reading and writing classrooms that were becoming more and more common in community colleges and four-year universities. Unfortunately, this promising work did not result in much sustained research beyond the 1990s.

In 2005, Patricia Harkin traced the historical and theoretical explanations for this dearth of post-secondary reading research. The short of it: as rhetoric and composition professionalized into a discipline, reading research was deemphasized in favor of writing (Harkin). Writing became the discrete area of study (Salvatori and Donahue). The divide can perhaps best be seen in the Gary Tate and Erika Lindemann debate of 1993 about the role of literary texts in composition classrooms. The debate did not open the conversation to how students read, but instead on what they should or should not read. The word "reading," according to Salvatori and Donahue, became invisible for 17 years, even disappearing as a category for presentation proposals at CCCCs, until recently.

Seven years ago, reflective of the resurgent interest in reading, Mike Bunn, Ellen Carillo, and Debrah Huffman began a special interest group on reading, and reading can now be found as a presentation proposal option at CCCCs. Salvatori and Donahue have described this revival as "baffling," but now current post-secondary reading researchers have begun to build a good understanding of the diverse contexts of readers and reading, moving us past the Tate-Lindemann debate and into questions of *how* students read and *how* reading affects their writing (199). Several studies add to Hull and Rose's early work by examining reading in the basic writing classroom (Goen and Gillotte-Tropp; Smith; Sweeney and McBride); other research adds to early work by Haas and Flower who use research to describe how students read in first-year writing classrooms, whether it be reading like a writer (Bunn), reading reflectively (Carillo), or reading rhetorically (Downs). Some recent post-secondary reading research has also taken up growing trends in writing research, like transfer (Lockhart and Soliday) and threshold concepts of reading (Sweeney). Collectively, these studies bring us, as teacher-scholars, toward a better understanding of post-secondary readers. These researchers recognize that we benefit by looking beyond our theoretical and methodological frameworks to ask new questions or challenge previous ways of thinking. For example, the interest in learning transfer, from educational psychology, has transformed reading pedagogies to include metacognition to support movement to other disciplines.

A reconnection of education and composition and rhetoric is vital to post-secondary reading research as it allows us to deepen the complexity of our studies but more importantly move past the deficit model thinking of reading (i.e., why students don't or can't read). While this is an understandable and well-documented concern, composition and rhetoric has more to gain from understanding how students read in different contexts. Two new books--Ellen Carillo's *Teaching Readers in Post-Truth America* and Alice Horning, Deborah-Lee Gollnitz, and Cynthia Haller's edited collection *What is College Reading?*—help us do just that, as they reflect the connection between education-based K-12 reading research and composition- and rhetoric-based reading research from the 80s and 90s. By embracing that stance, these books allow us to map several trends in post-secondary reading research that intersect with current research trends in education: rejection of the deficit model, expansion of interdisciplinary potentials, and acknowledgement of disciplinary literacy.

The primary way these texts connect post-secondary reading research to K-12 education is by addressing how that K-12 education affects how students read in college. In chapter two, "Theoretical First Principles," Carillo argues that students taught under the confines of the Common Core State Standards (CCSS) are less equipped for reading in an information-rich society, especially one with a rise in political divisiveness and post-truth culture, a culture in which an opinion often seems to be worth more than facts. To make reading assessment-friendly, CCSS encourages text-centered analysis, minimizing the importance of the meaning that a reader brings to the act of reading, thereby rejecting Rosenblatt's transactional theory. In other words, Hull and Rose's student would not have been successful under this curriculum. To prepare students to participate in an information-rich democratic society, Carillo teaches empathic reading, which she describes in chapter three, "Cultivating Empathic Reading, Readers, and Researchers." For Carillo, empathy is not just asking students to open themselves to others' perspectives but also to identify with and mirror those perspectives as a comprehension strategy. While I have reservations about Carillo's argument that reading fewer literary texts in favor of more explicitly rhetorical texts creates less empathetic readers, I do find merit in her arguments that the way reading is taught in the CCSS curriculum makes students less prepared to read with empathy. In chapter four, "Modeling Reading through Annotation," Carillo demonstrates how she uses annotation to guide students toward empathy. She recommends teachers use public annotations now available as models, for example journalists annotating political speeches online, or tools that allow multiple students to annotate one text. These activities highlight for students that reading is a social act. Along with making reading processes visible with annotations, Carillo chooses texts for shared annotations that allow students to see what it looks like to open up a question and linger, rather than rushing to judgment. I found this chapter especially helpful as it gives concrete tools for helping students read with empathy and openness.

In *What is College Reading?* Justin Young and Charlie Potter's "Reading about Reading" further strengthens our understanding of the K-12 context and how it might affect college readers. They argue that higher education faculty and administrators "must proceed with a clear understanding of the wide range of P-12 pedagogical approaches to literacy" so they can build a bridge from those literacy practices to college practices (118). These pedagogical practices include phonics, direct instruction, whole language, constructivism, and balanced literacy. Young and Potter claim that material differences between high school and college contexts, with No Child Left Behind demanding approaches that have been scientifically verified and CCSS promoting close reading, make it difficult for students transitioning to college. Typically, the reading instruction promoted in high school is the type that produces short-term, measured results: direct instruction, or explicit demonstration and practice of skills. However, constructivism, an approach that values the meaning the reader constructed and that we embrace in composition and rhetoric, is dismissed in high school environments. In response, Young and Potter provide strategies for post-secondary reading teachers to bridge the gap from high school's direct instruction focus to college reading that demands deeper, rhetorical reading across the disciplines. These strategies include a balanced literacy approach that teaches students to analyze, retain, and apply complex academic material, while also engaging students' personal experiences, or schema, with literacy and classroom learning. Young and Potter close their essay with a key point: "communication between the two groups [P-12 and post-secondary educators] is not common or easy" (132). However, both Carillo and Horning et al.'s collection do an effective job of establishing the context that often remains invisible to better strengthen those connections.

The most prominent trend in these books is the sound rejection of the deficit model of reading. Composition and rhetoric scholarship has done, I suggest, an effective job of rejecting the deficit model of writing; however, these efforts seem to be more difficult with reading. Carillo offers an intriguing perspective on this point. In chapter three, "Cultivating Empathic Reading, Readers, and Researchers," Carillo argues that teachers need to consider how students' emotions, when reading, affect the meaning students construct. Therefore, teachers should consider both triggers when choosing texts and also the potential violence in asking students to play Peter Elbow's believing game with hateful texts. Beyond that main argument, Carillo also reflects on empathic reading practices in composition and rhetoric, such as the empathic reading that Mina Shaughnessy modeled of student error in writing or that Hull and Rose modeled in their reading of a student's unconventional interpretation of poetry. Carillo celebrates the history of empathic reading in composition and rhetoric research. In doing so, Carillo offers an interesting lens to consider post-secondary reading research, suggesting we might see it as falling on an empathic continuum. This chapter left me wondering, as researchers, are we recognizing the range of ways we construct meaning and knowledge through our studies?

Some of the studies in the Horning et al. collection are examples of empathic research or empathic approaches to teaching reading. My favorite study was Martha Townsend's "High-Profile Football Players' Reading at a Research University" because it challenges the deficit model of reading by using in depth interviews and data triangulation to paint a detailed picture of student readers. In a qualitative case study that relied on interviews and standardized tests, Townsend finds that student-athletes have a rich reading life. She details their preferences and passions as they relate to reading, describing students who do excel at and enjoy reading (though science and math were more difficult for the students). Townsend argues that reading and writing instructors may want to reconsider overwhelmingly negative stereotypes they have about athletes, but I would extend that to stereotypes about reading and readers more generally.

Townsend also recommends that WAC practitioners "delve more deeply into the excellent literacy research" in education to understand how context mediates readers and texts, thereby strengthening those connections between composition and rhetoric and education (112). Similarly, many of the studies focus on helping teachers create opportunities for more empathic reading across the curriculum. In "The Un-Common Read," Jennifer Maloy et al. demonstrate how a Common Read program can foster a reading community for community college students. While most Common Read programs are used for a pre-fall orientation, Maloy et al. integrate the texts into faculty development and year long cross-disciplinary events and assignments. Through this approach, they find that students make more and stronger connections between the text and their courses. In their description of how the reading is discussed, how it moves across disciplines and contexts, and how it is used to pull community college students into the community of college, I was struck by how effectively the program supported the empathic reading for which Carillo advocates.

There are several more examples of approaches to teaching empathic reading and helping students move beyond CCSS ways of reading in Horning et al.'s collection. In "Multiliteracies and Meaning-Making," Mary Lou Odom demonstrates how digital reading can aid student development of new practices that will help them with college reading—just as composition teachers have adjusted college writing for digital genres, like blogs and wikis, so too can they adjust college reading. Odom notes what Carillo and Young and Potter highlighted with the K-12 context: students read a lot, but they may come to school with inaccurate views of what reading in college means. However, Odom finds that when teachers adjust their writing prompts for reading assignments, they get different results. She advocates that teachers change from using writing to check for completion of reading and instead focus on engagement (e.g. write a blog to react to a part of the reading). For example, a professor of conflict management asked students to respond to a reading by critiquing one of their past negotiations in a memo to themselves. This teacher's adjusted assignment helped students use technology to make text-to-world connections but also highlighted how students are ready to do the reading expected in college.

While moving beyond the deficit model is one trend these books embrace, they also signal an expansion of our current theoretical frames to education, psychology, educational psychology, and disciplinary literacy as a way to better understand reading. In chapter five, "Moving Forward," Carillo suggests composition and rhetoric look to psychology to deepen our understanding of reading. Psychologists have shown that emotion and beliefs are bound up with one another. Therefore, Carillo says, if we teach critical reading, we must teach students about cognitive emotion theory to expand their, and our, understanding of how people are persuaded: through logos *and* pathos. Second, Carillo advocates we look to education psychology as it supports argument writing that includes listening, empathy, and reflection—all practices that can deepen argument writing and challenge the post-truth culture. Third, Carillo continues the argument that we can improve our teaching by looking to psychology—not only to improve argumentation, but also to deepen our understanding of the psychological dimension of reading. For example, psychologists have found that we use systems like confirmation bias, cognitive dissonance, and information avoidance to protect ourselves.

Disciplinary literacy is the last and, I argue, most promising new direction for post-secondary reading research. Several of the chapters in *What is College Reading?* use this new frame. Over the last decade, the shift to the CCSS curriculum expanded disciplinary literacy research in education, as educators sought to better prepare middle school and high school teachers across the curriculum to teach reading and writing in their content areas. Disciplinary literacy researchers study the different "conventions of disciplinary knowledge production and communication" or how scholars in various disciplines read and write in ways that reflect their shared epistemologies (Moje 37). Several chapters in *What is College Reading?* embrace disciplinary literacy—studying reading practices in various disciplines.

In "Utilizing Interdisciplinary Insights to Build Effective Reading Skills," William Abbott and Kathryn Nantz use disciplinary literacy to help honors students connect to reading assignments. They ask students to read texts from economics and history, finding that by combining the two disciplines and creating inspired writing assignments, students are better able to use the readings and explore the different processes of reading based on the discipline. For example, students found that economic arguments and graphical analysis required "considerable time to master" while history texts had to be "skimmed and organized around themes" (149). Laura Davies also uses disciplinary literacy to teach students how reading demands change among genres shared in a discipline. In "Getting to the Root of the Problem," she demonstrates how reading improved when she taught science students to pre-read, read, and post-read as part of a recursive practice. Students read a variety of genres common in the sciences—research article, popular science trade book, magazine article, and textbook. Through detailed descriptions that teachers will appreciate, Davies shows how the reading activities and assignments change for each genre and at each stage of the process. The complexity of reading processes in her classroom support the argument that teaching reading must continue into the disciplines as students continue to refine how they make and share knowledge. These two chapters expand our understanding of post-secondary reading as more than just rhetorical reading in composition courses, and instead demands that as teachers we consider how reading expectations might change in other disciplines as students read like historians, scientists, or economists.

Some chapters illustrate how disciplinary literacy theories can support reading across the curriculum efforts. In "Writing to Read, Revisited," Chris Anson uses a meta-analysis from education researchers Graham and Herbert to help teachers across the curriculum engage students in deeper, more intellectual readings through writing assignments. These assignments must motivate and engage students, have creative pedagogical energy, require cognitive complexity, and position reading in a richer social space. For example, requiring a summary of a text will not engage students. However, creating a scenario and asking students to engage in a debate on the reading will require a deeper engagement.

Like Anson's study, Pam Hollander et al.'s study in "Creating a Reading-Across-the Curriculum Climate on Campus" emerges after a discovery that faculty across the curriculum were dissatisfied with student reading. While Anson offers teachers tools for changing low-stakes writing assignments, Hollander et al. offer a strategy for building a reading-across-the-curriculum climate on campus. They turn to research by literacy and reading education scholar Zhihui Fang to learn about reading like a scientist, then interview science professors and hold discussions with them to reflect on what worked and did not work in the science classrooms. This on-campus dialogue within a discipline is a useful model for Hollander et al. and one that could be repeated on other campuses and in other disciplines. Collectively, these chapters push reading research beyond a focus on composition classrooms to consider how reading practices change in new contexts and epistemologies. Embracing disciplinary literacy theories decidedly moves us beyond the research from the 80s and 90s; moreover, this disciplinary approach brings us back to the connections between education and composition and rhetoric that further strengthen our research methodologies and classroom pedagogies.

During my time as a graduate student of post-secondary reading, the classroom pedagogies that I could imagine were populated by students like the one Hull and Rose taught, students who needed support or better scaffolds for reading difficult texts in the composition classroom. However, these books mark a shift to trends that push those of us who research and teach post-secondary reading to imagine more: the enduring pedagogies I learned in the early 2000s, but also the changing contexts, epistemologies, and genres that will challenge our students when reading in the post-truth culture, in their disciplines, and in their professions. As we continue forward, I hope these trends continue to get more attention. For instance, Carillo makes several claims that could evolve reading instruction, but it would be helpful if researchers could do the empirical research needed to see how an empathic approach to reading changes college students' reading practices. Researchers might ask, for example, How does the annotation activity change student reading? How does empathic reading transfer to reading of public texts? How does empathic reading transfer to various disciplines? Overall, these books demonstrate how much we have to learn by looking at and reflecting on the literate lives of college students, in the composition classroom and, most importantly, beyond.

Moraga, California

Works Cited

Bazerman, Charles. "Physicists Reading Physics: Schema-laden Purposes and Purpose-laden Schema." *Written Communication,* vol. 2, no. 1, Jan. 1985, pp. 3-23.

Bunn, Michael. "Motivation and Connection: Teaching Reading (and Writing) in the Composition Classroom." *College Composition and Communication,* vol. 64, no. 3, 2013, pp. 496–516.

Carillo, Ellen C. *Securing a Place for Reading in Composition: The Importance of Teaching for Transfer.* Utah State UP, 2015.

Downs, Doug. "Teaching First-Year Writers to Use Texts: Scholarly Readings in Writing-About Writing in First-Year Comp." *Reader,* vol. 60, 2010, pp. 19-50.

Goen, Sugie, and Helen Gillotte-Tropp. "Integrating Reading and Writing: A Response to the Basic Writing 'Crisis'." *Journal of Basic Writing,* vol. 22, no. 2, 2003, pp. 90-113.

Haas, Christina. "Learning to Read Biology: One Student's Rhetorical Development in College." *Written Communication,* vol. 11, no. 1, 1994, pp. 43-84.

Haas, Christina, and Linda Flower. "Rhetorical Reading Strategies and the Construction of Meaning." *College Composition and Communication,* vol. 39, no. 2, 1988, pp. 167–183.

Harkin, Patricia. "The Reception of Reader-Response Theory." *College Composition and Communication,* vol. 56, no. 3, 2005, pp. 410–425.

Hull, Glynda, and Mike Rose. "Rethinking Remediation: Toward a Social-Cognitive Understanding of Problematic Reading and Writing." *Written Communication,* vol. 6, no. 2, Apr. 1989, pp. 139–154.

Lindemann, Erika. "Freshman Composition: No Place for Literature." *College English,* vol. 55, no. 3, 1993, pp. 311-16.

Lockhart, Tara, and Mary Soliday. "The Critical Place of Reading in Writing Transfer (and Beyond): A Report of Student Experiences." *Pedagogy,* vol. 16, no. 1, 2016, pp. 23–37.

Moje, Elizabeth Birr. "Chapter 1 Developing Socially Just Subject-Matter Instruction: A Review of the Literature on Disciplinary Literacy Teaching." *Review of Research in Education,* vol. 31, no. 1, 2007, pp. 1–44.

Rosenblatt, Louise M. *The Reader, the Text, the Poem: The Transactional Theory of the Literary Work*. Southern Illinois UP, 1994.

Salvatori, Mariolina Rizzi, and Patricia Donahue. "Stories about Reading: Appearance, Disappearance, Morphing, and Revival." *College English*, vol. 75, no. 2, 2012, pp. 199–217.

Shaughnessy, Mina P. *Errors and Expectations: A Guide for the Teacher of Basic Writing*. Oxford UP, 1977.

Smith, Cheryl Hogue. "Interrogating Texts: From Deferent to Efferent and Aesthetic Reading Practices." *Journal of Basic Writing*, vol. 31, no. 1, 2012, pp. 59–79.

Sweeney, Meghan. "Audience Awareness as a Threshold Concept of Reading: An Examination of Student Learning in Biochemistry." *Research in the Teaching of English*, vol. 53, no. 1, 2018, pp. 58–79.

Sweeney, Meghan, and Maureen McBride. "Difficulty Paper (Dis)Connections: Understanding the Threads Students Weave between Their Reading and Writing." *College Composition and Communication*, vol. 66, no. 4, 2015, pp. 591–614.

Tate, Gary. "A Place for Literature in Freshman Composition." *College English*, vol. 55, no. 3, 1993, pp. 317-21.

Cross-Border Networks in Writing Studies, by Derek Mueller, Andrea Williams, Louise Wetherbee Phelps, and Jennifer Clary-Lemon. Edmonton and Anderson: Inkshed & Parlor Press, 2017. 196 pp.

Reviewed by Christopher Eaton, Western University

Cross-Border Networks in Writing Studies examines writing studies scholars as networked and cross-border, meaning that Canadian and American writing studies scholars are connected through different yet overlapping contexts, histories, and methods. These connections allow scholars to blend a network of methods that can help to understand how disciplines, ideas, and networks have formed across the Canada/US border. The collection encourages researchers to reflect upon disciplinary developments and to see how networks have developed over a half century. By studying these networks, Mueller, Williams, Wetherbee Phelps, and Clary-Lemon argue that the fields of writing studies in Canada and in the United States are more intertwined than previous histories have acknowledged. Their interconnection derives from relationships formed in local contexts that have become larger national and international networks, translating what is localized into wider macro-level conversations that influence the field of writing studies in the United States, Canada, and further abroad. Taken together, these networks help scholars understand disciplinary, conceptual, methodological, and epistemological developments and how they impact writing studies.

The collection's strength is how it balances broad, quantifiable trends in writing studies with focused, qualitative reports on programmatic and personal developments within writing studies communities. The collection is bookended by Mueller (chapter two) and Clary-Lemon (chapter five) who examine broader national/international and programmatic networks. The middle chapters by Williams (chapter three) and Wetherbee Phelps (chapter four) zoom in to examine individual scholars and the various networks they have formed and participated in during their careers. This structure allows the authors to display the multiplicity of networks that have formed and highlight the numerous layers derived from these networks.

By highlighting these complexities, the authors make visible various nodes that have formed within Canadian writing studies and offer new understandings—both micro and macro—that can contribute to an emerging field. Canadian writing studies has struggled to connect research networks across provinces and across the border into the United States, which has hindered writing studies from establishing disciplinary space in Canada (see Clary-Lemon; Paré; Wetherbee Phelps). Understanding how these nodes connect in

Canada and in the United States can bring these networks together for future research collaboration.

Readers may also see these connections and understand how programs on either side of the border are more interconnected than previous histories have acknowledged. Mueller's chapter two highlights border crossings and how scholars form connections between countries. His mapping traces how scholars move between localities and how these moves expand networks over time, whether that is through supervisor-supervisee relationships, institutional affiliations, or shared publication avenues. The maps provide an excellent visual of the fluidity of these networks and how they have expanded over time. The maps are available online, which makes up for the printed screenshots' lack of the color and space necessary to trace the networks thoroughly. The online maps allow readers to go deeper in their exploration and gain a better understanding of the circles in which they float, either consciously or unconsciously. These maps show us that, no matter how disparate and sometimes disconnected writing scholars may seem because of geography and a lack of disciplinary cohesion, few degrees separate us; we could, hypothetically, open networks and connections that were heretofore closed.

This broad view of cross-border networks synthesizes the movement of many individual scholars, each of whom has their own story of how their networks formed. Williams's chapter three delves into these stories to understand how individual scholars saw their intellectual and disciplinary development. The intricacy of these stories, the way that they overlap and complicate each other, creates a tableau of the rich diversity of experiences that shape writing studies. For example, many participants considered the CCCC an integral space for Canadian scholars to develop communities. This was true for scholars like Doug Brent and Anthony Paré in the 1980s, and Daniel Richards had a similar experience twenty-five years later. While their overlapping experiences show how essential CCCC is for forming communities, their stories also identify an ongoing struggle for writing studies communities to form. These stories demonstrate the necessity for cross-border networks to form so that scholars may continue to find innovative ways to connect through research despite having little disciplinary home.

The work of individual scholars and their networked identities is continued in chapter four by Wetherbee Phelps. What stands out the most is how this chapter complicates the relationship between scholars in the United States and Canada. The four scholars that Wetherbee Phelps examines complicate the notion of a "Canadian scholar" because these identities are always shifting. This is evident in the Canadian scholars' desire to have their own publication rather than only meeting at CCCC. Their initiative produced *Inkshed*, a newsletter where Canadian scholars could discuss language acquisition, reading, theory, writing, rhetoric, and discourse analysis. Wetherbee Phelps also highlights the fluidity of writing scholar identities through Catherine Schryer's multidisciplinary collaboration examining communication across professional boundaries, including healthcare and forensics. The chapter highlights the creative paths that scholars take to work across disciplinary borders and to combine expertise. Collaboration allows research and methodological networks to expand and offers writing studies the potential to develop new ways of understanding the work that we do.

Departing from the focus on individual networked identities in chapters three and four, Clary-Lemon's case study on the University of Winnipeg's Department of Rhetoric, Writing, and Communication (chapter five) pushes readers to consider the wider implications of networked identities. By tracing the Department's challenges and accomplishments over time and its recent curriculum consultation and design process, Clary-Lemon demonstrates how networks may draw upon each other to refine programmatic, methodological, pedagogical, and research practice. Seeing this on a programmatic level is insightful because it takes these vast networks and shows how they translate to individual institutions. The way that the department drew upon the CWPA outcomes statement and adapted the University of Rhode Island's (URI) process for forming a writing major made this more than just a Canadian case study. They understood that the contexts differed but that the URI outcomes could help them to refine their degree program outcomes. Rather, Clary-Lemon situates the case study as a complex interrelation of networks formed between the United States and Canada that inform and translate to other geographical locations to suit emerging/evolving programmatic needs. Outcomes from more established American contexts, such as URI and CWPA, can be useful in emergent Canadian contexts where scholars are establishing the foundation for their programming.

Broadly speaking, this collection can prompt writing scholars—whether they are Canadian or American—to go broader and deeper in the quest to define and articulate what we do and how it impacts our institutions. In the short and medium term, it would be useful to extend the questions that they pose to consider the networks that emerging scholars are forming. Chapters two (Mueller), three (Williams), and four (Wetherbee Phelps) highlight how individual scholars became networked through interconnections with each other, through supervisor-supervisee relationships, through conferences, and through research collaborations. A next step for writing scholars could be to trace emerging trends in various writing studies networks to anticipate where the field is going, how these networks may be supported, and where they can be better developed. Examining new scholars' participation in conferences and major publications, new institutional hires, or developing writing studies programs could all provide valuable insight about the field. Granted, this work would be complicated given that it is easier to examine a network that is already formed rather than being formed, but it could be rewarding for disciplinary purposes.

Andrea Lunsford's afterword comments that these essays "will surely inspire other collaborative cross-border efforts to map, explore, and chart out field of study" (181), suggesting that *Cross-Border Networks in Writing Studies* is a collection to which we may return as a benchmark to help define and redefine writing studies as it evolves over the next ten, twenty, or thirty years (on both sides of the border). As these networks evolve and grow into new ones, this collection will offer a map that future scholars may follow and adapt to suit the contexts and challenges that will be associated with this ever-growing discipline we call Writing Studies.

London, Ontario

Works Cited

Clary-Lemon, Jennifer. "Shifting Tradition: Writing Research in Canada." *American Review of Canadian* Studies, vol. 39, no. 2, 2009, pp. 94-111.

Paré, Anthony. "The Once and Future Writing Centre: A Reflection and Critique." *Canadian Journal for Studies in Discourse and Writing/Rédactologie*, vol. 27, 2017, pp. 1-8.

Wetherbee Phelps, Louise. "The Historical Formation of Academic Identities: Rhetoric and Composition, Discourse and Writing." *Canadian Journal for Studies in Discourse and Writing*, vol. 25, no. 1, 2014, pp. 3-25.

The Internationalization of US Writing Programs, edited by Shirley K Rose and Irwin Weiser. Louisville, CO: UP of Colorado, 2018. 277pp.

Reviewed by Megan J. Busch

The Internationalization of US Writing Programs provides a comprehensive analysis of the increasing number of international students on American campuses nationwide and of the impact this exponential growth has for Writing Program Administrators (WPAs) and composition instructors. The collection, edited by Shirley K. Rose and Irwin Weiser, explores "the evolving roles and responsibilities of writing program administrators who are leading efforts to provide all students on their campuses, regardless of nationality or first language, with competencies in writing that will serve them in the academy and beyond" (5). Specifically, the text addresses WPAs seeking to position English as a global language and to transform writing programs into multicultural spaces on campus. Situated within the field's conversation of translingualism (championed by Suresh Canagarajah, among others), superdiversity (from Stephen Vertovec), and the integration of L2 English writers into the first-year writing classroom, the text's debut is timely, as the collection considers the challenges that WPAs and instructors are currently facing as more international students enter the classroom and as English becomes a worldwide language.

I was first drawn to this collection after teaching a semester with a significant number of international L2 students in my first-year composition courses: 17 of 41 total students. I found myself needing new strategies for teaching writing that supported my L2 English writers while engaging and challenging all students in my class. I read *The Internationalization of US Writing Programs* to gain more insight about what administrators and instructors can do to help L2 students succeed in the writing classroom, and the text met my inquiry with passionate, inspiring research and scholarship.

The collection, as a whole, provides a sweeping overview of the challenges of and the practical classroom implications for international student instruction. Four chapters stand out in the collection, each of which offers detailed analysis of programmatic changes implemented specifically to address the rise of global English and the increasing number of L2 learners in US writing programs. "Administrative Structures and Support for International L2 Writers: A Heuristic for WPAs" by Christine M. Tardy and Susan Miller-Cochran provides an important framework of foundational questions that require a response in order for first-year English programs to succeed in supporting L2 writers. Tardy and Cochran also review the current administrative structures for L2 learners entering US institutions. With a focus on practical tools for program assessment, the authors offer a thoughtfully researched heuristic to assist WPAs who are working diligently to welcome international students and their diverse linguistic backgrounds into their first-year writing programs. In a helpful chart, Tardy and Miller-Cochran categorize and detail over twenty questions whose answers are essential to developing writing programs that foreground global English (64-65). "Confronting Superdiversity in US Writing Programs" by Jonathan Benda et. al. outline the in-depth quantitative research completed by a team at Northeastern University from 2014 to 2015 to address the rising number of international students on campus. The researchers surveyed L2 students about writing habits outside the classroom and their perceptions about their own level of proficiency in English. Benda et. al. discovered that *all* students experienced linguistic diversity, and that it was difficult to fit all L2 students in the categories of *international* or *multilingual*. Instead, students are "superdiverse," and Benda et. al. determined that the first-year writing program at Northeastern (and at other institutions) must have a goal of mirroring this superdiversity (80). In "'I Am No Longer Sure This Serves Our Students Well': Redesigning FYW to Prepare Students for Transnational Literacy Realities," David Swiencicki Martins and Stanley Van Horn develop a first-year writing curriculum for native English writers and L2 writers that emphasizes international English use through a "repetition of experience-reflection-response" (152). Martins and Van Horn offer an overview of that curriculum at their institution along with two case studies of students learning within their new program. And finally, offering fascinating insight into what instructors believe to be true about international students, Carolina Peleaz-Morales shares the results of her qualitative research study in "Internationalization from the Bottom Up: Writing Faculty's Response to the Presence of Multilingual Writers." Peleaz-Morales argues most convincingly for ideological change from not merely a WPA's programmatic perspective, but from instructors of first-year English. She provides two pages of useful, bulleted suggestions for instructors and administrators to propel writing programs into an international realm.

Along with these four compelling chapters, which offer researched insight about how US writing programs are evolving to accommodate multilingual, multiliterate students, several others more generally explain new mindsets in writing program administration and steps universities are taking to engage international students in first-year writing programs. These include "Writing Programs and a New Ethos for Globalization" by Margaret K. Willard-Traub, which focuses on "strategic contemplation" in curriculum development (50); "Expanding the Role of the Writing Center at the Global University" by Yu-Kyung Kang, which outlines a foundation for creating an internationalized writing center; and "Building an Infrastructure of L2 Writing Support: The

Case of Arizona State University" by Katherine Daily O'Meara and Paul Kei Matsuda, which details the steps the WPAs at ASU took to reimagine first-year writing with internationalization in mind. Though these chapters contribute significantly to the conversation of L2 learners in the writing classroom and offer first-hand experiential advice, they (along with others in the collection) are more exploratory in nature. Thus, it is harder to determine if the methods adopted are working to bring about an improved learning environment for international writers. Many of the programmatic changes described by these authors are still in the beginning stages of development and implementation; researchers simply need more time to understand the effects of the changes on students and their writing. I am eager to hear from many of these pioneering scholars in the future to learn the results of their efforts to form more internationalized writing programs and curricula.

In the editors' introduction, Rose and Weiser write, "With its emphasis on internationalization of writing programs, we anticipate that this collection will also be a valuable resource for colleagues who teach," and this was indeed the case (15). *The Internationalization of US Writing Programs* not only contextualized the challenges I faced in my writing classroom full of L2 English students, but it also provided a bigger-picture analysis from an administrative level about how to better serve those students as a program. Although the majority of contributors to the collection hold WPA positions and the included chapters are primarily directed toward readers in WPA roles, the collection proved to be immensely helpful for me as both an instructor and a writer. This text is a welcomed addition to our field—for WPAs, instructors, and graduate students—as we seek to make writing programs more inclusive to non-native English speakers and to understand how students learn to compose in English on the global stage.

Columbia, South Carolina

Sustainable WAC: A Whole Systems Approach to Launching and Developing Writing Across the Curriculum Programs, by Michelle Cox, Jeffrey R. Galin, and Dan Melzer. Urbana: National Council of Teachers of English, 2018. 272 pp.

Reviewed by Mandy Olejnik, Miami University of Ohio

As the discipline of composition, rhetoric, and writing studies continues to expand and build more types of writing programs, it is critical for scholars and researchers to look toward approaches for *sustaining* the writing programs that are created. Writing Across the Curriculum (WAC), as Walvrood explains, began as a movement inspired by societal factors: a surge of more students in college after the GI bill and the related "Johnny Can't Write" narrative— borne after the process shift in composition studies—that relied heavily on workshops for faculty across disciplines discussing "writing to learn" pedagogy. The workshop model has proven to be a limited initiative that can easily wane, and much scholarship on WAC is based in anecdote and the sharing of experiences to help others build types of programs. *Sustainable WAC* goes a step further toward emphasizing not only the building of WAC programs from experience but also sustaining them in the complicated system of academia and setting up a solid theoretical framework for doing so.

In *Sustainable WAC: A Whole Systems Approach to Launching and Developing Writing Across the Curriculum Programs,* editors Michelle Cox, Jeffrey R. Galin, and Dan Melzer turn to whole systems theories to develop their theoretical framework for WAC programs, which provide "tools for describing rich and dynamics systems" (like WAC programs) and "tools for creating and assessing change introduced to a system" (25). Cox et al. add to ongoing conversations about WAC as a movement and field. They provide significant contributions by moving beyond strategies used by WAC programs and practitioners to include theorizing a dedicated framework meant to focus on writing program administration, not pedagogy, in order to "better understand WAC program development within the complex and dynamic contexts of higher education" (16). This framework is buoyed by integrated vignettes from experienced WAC directors and concrete strategies throughout the book that connect both the vignettes and theoretical frameworks together into conversation and demonstration, as well as practical questions embedded in chapter sections that WAC professionals would be wise to ask of their programs. As Walvoord notes in her foreword, this book marks an important stride forward for WAC as a much-needed "theoretical framework to guide both our visions and our practical actions" (xi). With such a theory-driven focus, *Sustainable WAC* also aids the ongoing strife for writing program administration work to be taken seriously in academia as meaningful, quality research.

The first third of the book (chapters two, three, and four) focuses on building and describing the theoretical framework of a whole systems approach to WAC, which the authors say they hope will be of value to other WAC scholars in addition to practitioners. They synthesize research on five key theories that build their sustainable WAC framework. Complexity theory (26-31) offers "ways to study interactions among diverse groups of actors" (25); systems theory (31-34) focuses on the macro level and leverage points; social network theory (34-37) operates at the micro level among networked actants; resilience theory (37-41) helps WAC professionals understand system management and stress; and sustainable development theory (41-44) centers on the transformational change in complex systems. Together, these theories build a framework that "[builds] from context and [represents] the complexity of larger-scale reform" (24). WAC programs themselves are not complex systems, the authors make clear, but can be seen as sites to induce change in universities, which are complex systems. Importantly, they note that "no one leader controls all aspects of the system" (49), which reinforces the importance of WAC leaders and practitioners understanding who leads other systems in their university and how their university operates as a whole system.

In chapter two the authors also share ten principles (drawing from Bellagio principles) that they posit as being central to WAC development: wholeness, broad participation, transformational change, resilience, equity, leadership, systematic development, integration, visibility, and feedback (46-47). These principles inform their four-stage methodology (borrowed and adapted from Canada's Sustainable Development Strategy iteration of "plan-do-check-improve" and Bell and Morse's "Imagine" approach) central to their sustainable WAC approach, as outlined in chapter three: understand, plan, develop, lead. These stages focus "on a process for creating change that helps shift the mindset of program assessment" toward one that gauges sustainability that is "holistic, inclusive, concrete, transparent, and practical to implement" (55). Additionally, this methodology represents "theory connected to action" and "principles informing reflective practice" (75). Cox et al. also introduce fifteen strategies in this section (64-75) that they detail and contextualize in later chapters with vignettes, reiterating throughout that the strategies are meant to be flexible and recursive despite their linear representation in print form. These strategies, starting with determining the campus mood and ending with revising WAC programs and creating a plan for sustainable WAC leadership, help WAC administrators understand how to implement a whole systems approach to their work.

In the second section of the book (chapters four-seven), each chapter discusses a stage in the authors' four-stage methodology (understanding, planning, developing, and leading), focusing on strategies and tactics from the fifteen earlier-introduced strategies. The authors also describe the importance of "hubs" as opposed to "nodes" in a network, arguing that WAC programs that operate primarily as nodes (i.e., a program run by one director who runs workshops/does something "extra" and removed from a dedicated program) are not sustainable since they do not connect with the larger network (119). It is in this section where the authors weave together opening vignettes from WAC practitioners and the strategies for WAC programs, demonstrating principle-based strategies (from chapter two) in conversation with the theoretical framework they've set up. For example, in chapter five, Timothy Oleksiak writes about his experience being hired as a WID coordinator at Bloomsburg University where he was able to assemble a WID Advisory Board during the first year of his position. Throughout the book, Cox et al. refer back to Oleksiak's vignette as they outline their fifteen strategies. In chapter five they argue that the existence of his advisory committee with members across the university demonstrates the fourth strategy of "involving multiple stakeholders in the system"; they also refer to his vignette again in chapter six while discussing the fifteenth strategy of "creating a plan for sustainable leadership," noting that Oleksiak's national job search for WID coordinator reflected programs searching for and valuing WAC expertise. The authors weave these strategies, vignettes, and principles together throughout these chapters in a fluid, "networked" manner.

Finally, Cox et al. conclude the volume with chapter eight by looking forward to implications of the whole systems approach for WAC at every scale. They describe two WAC programs that have already begun to implement a whole systems approach, identify limitations of their work (primarily that they have only pieced together part of the five theories which have more aspects to explore), and extend their discussions to the field of WAC itself. They point to the importance of centralizing WAC programs with a central organization, and the creation of the Association for Writing Across the Curriculum (AWAC) and its mission (among other things) to "seek formalized connections among different WAC and other writing-related organizations to reach mutual goals" (232).

Since this is a book that seems primarily written for current WAC administrators and experienced WAC scholars, I see important future implications for graduate students interested in WAC work. For example, I wonder: what is the role of graduate student directors and administrators in WAC work, as more WAC programs grow and more doctoral programs might enable graduate students to serve in WAC administrative assistantships and specialize in WAC? How can programs sustain the work that graduate students spearhead, as they are only in their administrative roles for a few years at most? What might a whole systems approach offer to the training of future writing program administrators, in WAC and out? These are not questions explicitly taken up in this book, but they are important ones that build from the work done here and that can further the implications for WAC as a field of study.

Overall, *Sustainable WAC* is an important, field-defining book for WAC scholars and practitioners alike. The authors move toward a dedicated theoretical framework of approaching WAC supported by relevant theories while also drawing insight from seasoned WAC directors. While the authors acknowledge they have borrowed only certain parts from major theories that might still have more to parse through, this book is a promising step forward and a must-read for experienced and burgeoning WAC scholars and administrators alike. As the authors noted at the beginning of the book, a study by Thaiss and Porter in 2010 found that fifty percent of all WAC programs fail. Hopefully increased attention to WAC as theory and as something that can benefit from rich, theoretical frameworks like the ones described in this book can help decrease that percentage over time across universities.

Oxford, Ohio

Work Cited

Walvrood, Barbara. "The Future of WAC." *College English*, vol. 58, no. 1, 1996, 58-79.

Translanguaging Outside of the Academy: Negotiating Rhetoric and Healthcare in the Spanish Caribbean, by Rachel Bloom-Pojar. Urbana: National Council of Teachers of English, 2018. 157pp.

Reviewed by Rachel Griffo, Community College of Allegheny County

Important questions about effective communication in transcultural medical contexts inspired Rachel Bloom-Pojar to balance her full-time studies as a graduate student of rhetoric and composition (at the time of writing), with her summer volunteer work as a medical interpreter in the Dominican Republic (DR). Her book, *Translanguaging Outside of the Academy: Negotiating Rhetoric and Healthcare in the Spanish Caribbean,* is the result of her close examination of language variance within and outside of the academy and also her experience working on the ground as an advocate, interpreter, and facilitator between United States (US) and DR communities. Working, as she writes, "in the liminal spaces of these transcultural interactions," provides insightful data that challenges the ideologies surrounding spoken Spanish in the DR, further complicating and reframing language practice in medical contexts where acts of translanguaging are useful (5). By moving away from the discussion of translanguaging in academic institutions, specifically, Bloom-Pojar provides insight into how these languaging practices can be used in other critical contexts where clear communication is imperative.

In chapters one and two, "Toward a Rhetoric of Translanguaging" and "Research Design," Bloom-Pojar draws from important interdisciplinary work in the fields of rhetoric and linguistics to promote dispositions that "encourage an intentional approach to privileging the language use and needs of the marginalized speaker in any situation" and also sets the context and methods for her study (9). The rhetorical model used is comprised of three main actions: complicating language ideologies, building relationships, and cultivating translation spaces. While these components may function in this order—language ideologies are complicated by language variance, which leads to relationship building to move past stigmatized repertoires, possibly giving way to different acts of translation to better communicate meaning—as a table provided by Bloom-Pojar illustrates, they all play into each other interactively as needed. Analyzing data from 23 semi structured interviews of DR (10) and US (13) participants, observations, and field notes, she explains that relationship building was a component revisited in her follow-up analysis, drawing on its importance in the development of translanguaging for effective communication.

While standard medical Spanish is privileged in healthcare contexts, at the *El Centro para la Salud Rural* (CSR), it was not the dialect that was best equipped to serve the needs of the local patients. In chapter three, "Complicating Language Ideologies," Bloom-Pojar reveals how local perceptions of the rural Dominican Spanish dialect reflect "language ideologies about correctness and class difference" (46). That said, in order to serve the needs of the patients, doctors from both the US and the DR needed to be open to different varieties of Spanish and other communication practices in order effectively understand the needs of the patients and to likewise communicate important medical information to them.

Chapter four, "Cultivating Translanguaging Spaces," speaks to what happens when individuals try to communicate using different varieties of a language and fail to understand one another—they turn to translation (written speech) or interpretation (verbal speech). In addition, there is need to align to the language practices used by the patient. In her analysis of the Health History form used in the CSR clinic, Bloom-Pojar discusses the way the *ayudantes* (nurses) shorted the formalized questions on the forms in verbal speech to reflect the discursive norms of the patients' Dominican Spanish. Developing the attention and sensitivity to react to marginalized speakers by using their language norms is a translingual disposition that is not only useful in medical environments, but in all discursive contexts where verbal communication is crucial.

Attuning to the rhetoric of translanguaging is made easier through relationship building. In chapters five and six "Contexts and Collective Resources" and "Critical Reinvention between Communal and Institutional Discourses," Bloom-Pojar provides examples of the way the CSR brought local residents and their visitors together for community activities. These engagements were important for establishing real connections with the host families that were also patients at the clinic. Once connections are established, translanguaging only happens as long as interlocutors are open to it. For example, in her interviews with locals, Bloom Pojar illustrates how asking questions about words that come up in conversation, or, to use her words, "acting like a language teacher," creates a space where learning to communicate across language difference is possible.

In addition to learning conjugations within the local dialect, being sensitive to the spiritual needs of the community strengthened the bond between interlocutors and also taught intercultural communication. Bloom-Pojar describes the way that after receiving treatment, locals would thank the practitioners, "but only after thanking God and establishing that the procedure was successful through God" (119). In regular conversation there was also a gesture to God as the deciding source of whether one would see the other tomorrow through the use of the phrase, "*Si Dios quiere*" (if God wants) (127). As Bloom-Pojar illustrates in her data, this phrase was also expected from those outside the local culture.

In part, Bloom-Pojar's book provides a framework for how language and writing teachers might effectively serve in liminal spaces between their institutions and communities. This work has never been more important than it is right now. In the current state of our education system, where funding cuts are being made to programs that could support students in their attunement to institutional discourses, models that help us answer, "what do I do when I encounter language difference?" are crucial.

Translanguaging Outside the Academy is additionally valuable because of Bloom-Pojar's focus on language practice in a transnational healthcare context in general, and within and between local and "standardized" Spanish speaking communities, specifically. Her call for "patient discourses of health" (132) as agentive terminology to use along with more standardized medical terminology is forward-looking. As a language and writing professor at a community college that offers myriad healthcare, STEM, and nursing programs, and that also serves students from diverse linguistic backgrounds, I have anticipated the need for literacy training that prepares students for the speaking and writing they will be asked to demonstrate outside of the humanities, where this training typically occurs. Bloom-Pojar's book compliments the recent work of Suresh Canagarajah, who looks at how "competence is distributed across various material and social networks" ("Materializing Competence" 279) and how "multiple verbal resources can help one in certain professional activities" ("English as a Spatial Resource" 48). Because of this work, community colleges are now better positioned to train students through their workforce development programs. Finally, Bloom-Pojar's book is an excellent resource because of its focus on communities and the grappling itself that occurs in the liminal spaces where we, as educators and speakers, will undoubtedly be asked to attune in order to communicate effectively.

Pittsburgh, Pennsylvania

Works Cited

Canagarajah, Suresh. "English as a Spatial Resource and the Claimed Competence of Chinese STEM Professionals." *World Englishes*, vol. 37, no. 1, 2018, pp. 34–50.

Canagarajah, Suresh. "Materializing 'Competence': Perspectives from International STEM Scholars." *Modern Language Journal*, vol. 102, no. 2, 2018, pp. 268–291.

Thinking Globally, Composing Locally: Re-thinking Online Writing in the Age of the Global Internet, edited by Rich Rice and Kirk St. Amant. Logan: Utah State UP, 2018. pp. 378.

Reviewed by Jeffrey G. Howard, Georgia Institute of Technology

One way of thinking about Rich Rice and Kirk St. Amant's book, *Thinking Globally, Composing Locally*, is as an argument: while today's global citizens are linked to their audiences more closely than ever due to technological progress and development, the relationship between local and global contains an increasing number of complexities that communicators must thoughtfully consider in order to produce rhetorically effective and culturally sensitive communication that leads to positive action. Composing, particularly online, necessitates crossing many boundaries that are racial, ethnic, political, economic, and geographical, among others. Rice and St. Amant structure this collection of essays effectively by identifying three primary categories comprising the process of digital composing between local and global communities and individuals: contacting, conveying, and connecting. The book provides scholars and teachers with new approaches and ideas for implementing a broader understanding of how students can navigate and negotiate their role rhetorically in a growing global network.

Regardless of geographical distance, digital tools and networks produce cultural proximity. Josephine Walwema, in her chapter, "Digital Notebooks: Composing with Open Access," writes, "The global proliferation of online media and Internet access enables individuals from different cultures and nations to interact in different ways" (15). The first section of the collection, contacting, describes means of accessing global audiences whose different cultures imply divergent needs, preferences, and values. There are of course many digital platforms a teacher might use to facilitate contact between students and these "real-world" global audiences. Section one identifies a number of them, including digital notebooks, experience maps, ePortfolios, and online forums and message boards. Of course, the fact of a program's or tool's existence does not obligate an instructor to use it, even if others do, but what this section does well is illustrate how the range of alternatives available provides a number of access points for meaningful communication between cultures.

If a writing or communication instructor wants to help students position themselves as contributors in a global society, there are plenty of tools available that promote critical thinking, reflection, and linguistic control. For example, Cynthia Davidson, in her chapter, "Reconstructing *Ethos* as Dwelling Place: On the Bridge of Twenty-First Century Writing Practices," argues that the networked and fragmented nature of ePortfolios can be one such avenue for augmenting greater rhetorical awareness and cultural situatedness while also promoting articulation of and reflection on individual identity. Davidson writes, "ePortfolios are hybridizations of culture viewed through the lens of an individual's experiences as represented by or her artifacts, the reflections on them, and the connections that she or he makes between them" (82). Such tools can support students as they participate in intercultural collaboration and develop greater awareness of their linguistic resources as a set of choices they can deploy to accomplish tasks and negotiate divides among communities of practice.

Rice and St. Amant's book reminds the reader that, even though these tools or points of intercultural access are as valuable as they are ubiquitous, nothing can substitute for sound principles of communication applied within the restrictions of the affordances those tools make available. They write, "Just because one can contact a given audience does not necessarily mean that audiences will understand the ideas conveyed or the writer's purpose for sharing that information" (8). Ideally, communication, well-planned and -executed, proceeds smoothly from one party to another. Message sent, message received, message understood. On the other hand, Rice and St. Amant, using the analogy of an ice rink that appears flat but actually "is covered by a wide array of dips and pivots and cracks and bumps," argue that intercultural communication—and communication in general—can be fraught with "friction points" that can exert a significant influence on "how smoothly or how quickly or directly information can move from point to point in global cyberspace" (6). For communicators attempting to convey a message to a global audience, the rhetorical situation is complex, comprising factors that can disrupt how a message is understood or determine whether an audience understands it at all. Such friction points are common. They often occur when a composer fails to take into consideration technological, economic, geographical, historical, cultural, or political difference. The composition or communication classroom, at least one organized with a global framework, should provide students with reliable principles of intercultural communication and awareness of potential friction points caused by false assumptions as well as strategies for identifying resolutions when communicative friction inevitably occurs.

The collection culminates in a section about the need for contacting an audience. Rice and St. Amant define contact as an exchange or action on the part of the audience (8). Feedback, too, as Vassiliki Kourbani argues in the chapter "Writing Center Asynchronous/Synchronous Feedback," can be a form of contacting (233). If a communicator has successfully utilized a digital tool and either avoided or navigated potential friction points of an intercultural interaction, the result should be some kind of meaningful action on the part of the audience. In a writing center, this action could take the form of revision, while in other situations or settings it could manifest in the shape of humanitarian campaigns and even political revolution. In her chapter, "Clicks, Tweets, Links, and Other Global Actions: The Nature of Distributed Agency in Digital Environments," Lavinia Hirsu describes digital literacy and intercultural communication in the context of social activism and social media, arguing that "digital environments call for continuous worldwide participation, and model of intercultural communication need to capture dynamic exchanges that reduce the distance between cultural experiences and multiply the site of agency and rhetorical action" (258). If students should question the purpose of learning to communicate cross-culturally and their roles as communicators in a networked, digital world using the multimodal affordances of whatever their program, tool, or app of choice happens to be, the answer may vary in specifics, but should invariably involve contact.

Rice and St. Amant's collection of essays is a valuable resource for composition and technical communication instructors interested in exploring new ways of connecting their students with global audiences and promoting intercultural exchange and understanding. At a time when some argue for a political isolationism that is at odds with social and global realities and well-being, this book aims to facilitate the development of relationships and reduce friction, via effective communication, among local and global partners.

Atlanta, Georgia

Contributors

Sweta Baniya is from Nepal and currently a doctoral candidate at Purdue University. She is working on her dissertation project that studies emergence of transnational assemblages during the Nepal Earthquake in 2015 and Puerto Rico's Hurricane Maria in 2015 by using comparative rhetorics and technical professional communication methodologies. She is one of the founding members and moderator of nextGEN.

Estee Beck works is Assistant Professor of Technical and Professional Writing/Digital Humanities in the Department of English at The University of Texas at Arlington.

Tyler S. Branson is Assistant Professor of English at the University of Toledo. His research and teaching interests include public rhetoric, policy studies, and writing program administration. His book, *Policy Regimes of Writing: An Analysis of College Composition and Public Education Policy in the U.S.*, is under contract with Southern Illinois University Press.

Megan J. Busch is a doctoral candidate pursuing her PhD in English Composition and Rhetoric and Assistant Director of First-Year English at the University of South Carolina. Her primary research interests include digital composition and pedagogy as they intersect with the Englishes of the American South.

Kefaya Diab is the Culbertson Postdoctoral Teaching Fellow in the Department of English at Indiana University (Bloomington). Her monograph in-progress theorizes agency in hybrid (online and on the ground) activist movements with focus on the Arab Spring (2010-2013).

Dr. Sara Doan is Assistant Professor of Technical Communication at Kennesaw State University, where she teaches courses in technical writing, information design, and the rhetoric of health and medicine. Her research examines communication breakdowns across instructor feedback, information design, and home birth in the U.S.

Christopher Eaton is a doctoral candidate at Western University's Faculty of Education. His research focuses on post-secondary writing and explores questions related to teaching and learning in the writing classroom. He is particularly interested in how students can complicate and enhance scholarly conversations about writing.

Jaclyn Fiscus-Cannaday is Assistant Professor of English at Florida State University. Her research and teaching is situated at the intersection of composition studies, linguistics, and feminism, broadly exploring how communication works, how people think it should work, and how we might address those ideologies through pedagogy and policy to better work across difference.

Mara Lee Grayson is Assistant Professor of English at California State University, Dominguez Hills. She is the author of *Teaching Racial Literacy: Reflective Practices for Critical Writing* and articles in *English Education, Teaching English in the Two-Year College*, and *JAEPL*, among other publications. Her second book is forthcoming.

Rachel Griffo is Associate Professor of English at the Community College of Allegheny County where she teaches a variety of English and writing courses. Her research interest include writing studies, literacy, and intercultural rhetoric.

Holly Hassel is Professor of English at North Dakota State University. She previously taught for 16 years at UW-Marathon County, a two-year college in central Wisconsin.

Brian Hendrickson is Assistant Professor of Writing Studies, Rhetoric, and Composition at Roger Williams University. He studies how to design equitable and engaging writing pathways and partnerships across and beyond the curriculum.

Jeffery G Howard is the Marion L. Brittain Postdoctoral Fellow at Georgia Tech, where he teaches first-year composition in the Writing and Communication Program.

Adam Hubrig is a PhD candidate at the University of Nebraska-Lincoln, where he teaches composition and rhetoric as well as co-directs the Nebraska Writing Project. His work has appeared or is forthcoming in *Pedagogy, Journal of Multimodal Rhetorics,* and the *Michigan Journal of Community Service Learning*. His research centers on civic engagement, disability rhetoric, and rhetorical agency.

Gavin P. Johnson is the Edward P. J. Corbett Fellow in Rhetoric, Composition, and Literacy and a PhD candidate in English at The Ohio State University. Using queer-feminist methodologies, his research interrogates the interplay of power, production, and possibility in digital environments within and beyond the university. He is a first generation student.

Dr. Ashanka Kumari is Assistant Professor of English, Composition and Rhetoric at Texas A&M University-Commerce. Her research focuses on first-generation-to-college graduate students and how this population negotiates the professional expectations of graduate study and academia with their lives, identities, and other obligations.

Kyle Larson is a PhD Candidate in Composition & Rhetoric at Miami University (OH). He researches counterpublic and social movement rhetorics. His work is published in the *Journal of Contemporary Rhetoric*, *Peitho*, and (forthcoming) *Rhetoric Society Quarterly*. He is one of the founding members and moderators of nextGEN.

Charles Lesh is Assistant Professor of English at Auburn University. His research and teaching interests include public and community writing, critical spatial theory, genre, and ethnography. He is at work on a book that ethnographically explores the ways that graffiti writers in Boston make and unmake rhetorical spaces.

Stephen McElroy is Assistant Professor of Arts and Humanities at Babson College, whose professional interests include digital production.

Regina McManigell Grijalva is Associate Professor of English, Director of Composition, and Eleanor Lou Carrithers Endowed Chair of Writing at Oklahoma City University. Her recent works focus on minority faculty and students in the academy, indigenous and Latinx/borderlands studies, and a second anthology of new indigenous plays, which is in process.

Cara Marta Messina is a PhD candidate at Northeastern University in the English Department and current Assistant Director of the Digital Teaching Integration. She received the 2019 *Kairos Journal* Graduate Student Teaching Award. Her research is in fan studies, new media, digital pedagogy, and digital humanities/writing analytics.

Oksana Moroz is a PhD candidate and graduate assistant in Composition and Applied Linguistics at Indiana University of Pennsylvania. Her research interests include gender and teacher identity, digital identities of students, issues of accents and language ideologies, and teaching with Wikipedia.

Kelly Myers teaches undergraduate and graduate level writing and rhetoric courses at Boise State University. As the project director for Boise State's Storyboard initiative, she works to integrate reflection and narrative practices across campus, helping undergraduate students synthesize, complicate, and share the stories of their college experience.

Mandy Olejnik is a doctoral candidate in Composition and Rhetoric at Miami University (OH). She teaches professional writing courses and works as the Graduate Assistant Director of Writing across the Curriculum at the Howe Center for Writing Excellence. Her research interests include graduate student writing, transfer, and threshold concepts.

Ryan Roderick is Assistant Professor at Husson University, where he is currently working on an interactive e-textbook for professional communication and studying how social contexts factor into the self-regulation processes of undergraduate student writers.

Andrea Francioni Rooney is Director of Undergraduate Programs for the Department of Civil and Environmental Engineering at Carnegie Mellon University. She also teaches professional writing courses for undergraduate and graduate students in the department.

Dr. Iris Ruiz completed her PhD at the University of California at San Diego in literature and is currently a lecturer in Ethnic Studies at CSU Stanislaus. In addition, she has been lecturer for the Merritt Writing Program at UC Merced since 2010. Her teaching background includes Chicanx studies, advanced composition, and journal editing.

Virginia M. Schwarz is a PhD candidate in English at the University of Wisconson-Madison. During her studies, she also earned a Master's degree in Education Leadership and Policy Analysis and became interested in contextualizing writing classrooms in theories of higher education and society. Her primary areas of research are assessment and the social construction of difference and merit.

Amanda Sladek is Assistant Professor of English and Composition Coordinator at the University of Nebraska at Kearney. She holds her PhD in English Rhetoric and Composition from the University of Kansas. Her research and teaching interests include multiliteracies, composition and basic writing pedagogy, and English language studies.

Meghan A. Sweeney is Assistant Professor of Composition and Rhetoric at Saint Mary's College of California. She studies postsecondary academic literacies and her most recent research can be found in *Research in the Teaching of English* and *College Composition and Communication*.

Matthew A. Vetter is Assistant Professor of English at Indiana University of Pennsylvania and an affiliated faculty member in the Composition and Applied Linguistics PhD program. Vetter's work has appeared in journals such as *College English, Composition Studies, Computers and Composition, Technoculture, Pedagogy*, and publications sponsored by the Wiki Education Foundation.

Sophia Watson is a recent graduate of the University of Washington where she majored in both English and Law, Societies and Justice. There, she developed a background in justice advocacy, mainly concerning women, girls, and persons with disabilities, and an interest in feminist studies.

Grace Wetzel is Associate Professor of English at Saint Joseph's University, where she serves as First-Year Course Coordinator. Her research and teaching interests include feminisms and rhetorics, nineteenth-century women's journalism, first-year writing, and contemplative pedagogy.

Amy Williams is Assistant Professor of English at Brigham Young University where she teaches writing and researches how students write in and outside of classrooms.

Joanna Wolfe is Director of the Global Communication Center at Carnegie Mellon University. She is the author of *Team Writing: A Guide to Working in Groups* and is currently working on a new series in technical and professional communication to be published by Bedford St. Martin's/Macmillan.

PARLOR PRESS
EQUIPMENT FOR LIVING

NEW, IN LIVING COLOR!

Exquisite Corpse: Studio Art-Based Writing Practices in the Academy ed. by Kate Hanzalik and Nathalie Virgintino

The Afterlife of Discarded Objects: Memory and Forgetting in a Culture of Waste by Andrei Guruianu and Natalia Andrievskikh

Type Matters: The Rhetoricity of Letterforms ed. Christopher Scott Wyatt and Dànielle Nicole DeVoss (**BEST DESIGN AWARD-Ingram**)

NEW RELEASES

Creole Composition: Academic Writing and Rhetoric in the Anglophone Caribbean edited by Vivette Milson-Whyte, Raymond Oenbring, and Brianne Jaquette

Retellings: Opportunities for Feminist Research in Rhetoric and Composition Studies edited by Jessica Enoch and Jordynn Jack

Tracing Invisible Lines: An Experiment in Mystoriography by David Prescott-Steed

KONSULT: Theopraxesis by Gregory L. Ulmer

Best of the Journals in Rhetoric and Composition 2018

Other People's English: Code-Meshing, Code-Switching, and African American Literacy by Vershawn Ashanti Young, et al.

CONGRATULATIONS, AWARD WINNERS!

Strategies for Writing Center Research by Jackie Grutsch McKinnie. **Best Book Award, International Writing Centers Association (2017)**

Antiracist Writing Assessment Ecologies: Teaching and Assessing Writing for a Socially Just Future by Asao Inoue, **BEST BOOK AWARD, CCCC, BEST BOOK, COUNCIL OF WRITING PROGRAM ADMINISTRATORS (2017)**

The WPA Outcomes Statement—A Decade Later edited by Nicholas N. Behm, Gregory R. Glau, Deborah H. Holdstein, Duane Roen, & Edward M. White, **Best Book Award, Council of Writing Program Adminstrators (2015)**

www.parlorpress.com

www.ingramcontent.com/pod-product-compliance
Lightning Source LLC
Chambersburg PA
CBHW031316160426
43196CB00007B/557